Building a Love That Lasts

THE SEVEN SURPRISING SECRETS OF SUCCESSFUL MARRIAGE

Dr. Charles D. Schmitz

and

Dr. Elizabeth A. Schmitz

JOSSEY-BASS
A Wiley Imprint
www.josseybass.com

Published by Jossey-Bass

A Wiley Imprint

989 Market Street, San Francisco, CA 94103-1741—www.josseybass.com

Jossey-Bass books and products are available through most bookstores. To contact Jossey-Bass directly call our Customer Care Department within the U.S. at 800-956-7739, outside the U.S. at 317-572-3986, or fax 317-572-4002.

Jossey-Bass also publishes its books in a variety of electronic formats. Some content that appears in print may not be available in electronic books.

Previously published by the Authors as *Golden Anniversaries.*

Library of Congress Cataloging-in-Publication Data

Schmitz, Charles D., 1946-
    Building a love that lasts : the seven surprising secrets of successful marriage /
by Dr. Charles D. Schmitz and Dr. Elizabeth A. Schmitz, foreword by Scott M. Stanley
        p. cm.
    Includes index.
      ISBN 978-0-470-57154-5 (pbk.)
      1. Marriage. 2. Love. 3. Man-woman relationships. I. Schmitz, Elizabeth A., 1948- II. Title.
  HQ519.S34 2010
    646.7'8—dc22   2009035141

Printed in the United States of America
FIRST EDITION
PB Printing   10 9 8 7 6 5 4 3 2 1

Contents

*W*E DEDICATE THIS BOOK

to the thousands of successfully married couples we have

interviewed over these past 25 years and to our own enduring

love for each other.

Foreword

THIS IS A WARM BOOK. I don't mean that it's warm because you are holding it or because it may have been lying in the sun. It's warm because the authors are warm, candid, and friendly people. The warmth of Charles and Elizabeth jumps off every page as you digest their practical, direct, and very doable ideas for success in marriage. As is fitting with their decades of work, they want to be your companions in your journey to build and sustain a marriage of lasting love.

I've been conducting and publishing research on marriage for three decades. I know what the vast literature on marriages can teach us but I also know its limitations. One of those limitations is that researchers can too easily focus more on what goes wrong and how to fix it than on what is going right and how to sustain it. Both are valuable and both can teach you a lot. This is a book focused on the latter, based on the authors' study of very happy, long-term married couples. What are those happy couples doing right? That's what you are about to learn here. Best of all, these are things you can do and things that, in the doing, can make a difference in your marriage.

I want to highlight two of the things that Charles and Elizabeth accomplish in this book that seem to me most important of all. First, through their stories, insights, and advice, they are teaching realistic and healthy expectations for marriage. In a day and age where so many people have learned to expect levels of unending bliss that are simply not the essence of what really great marriages are like, this is a direct and helpful look at how it really happens.

Second, Charles and Elizabeth have a particular focus that I think is one of the hallmarks of making a difference. They want you to focus on the smaller, daily things you can do—the things that combine over the years to make a life together. This is crucial because you can do the small, meaningful things every day. From my research on sacrifice and commitment, I believe that the small, regular acts of compassion and care between partners trump the big events. To do something big you need a big opportunity. To do something small that matters, you only need today. You have many "todays" ahead, and here's a great book full of encouragement for how to live them.

Scott M. Stanley
University of Denver
Author of *The Power of Commitment*
www.slidingvsdeciding.com
Coauthor of *Fighting For Your Marriage*
and *A Lasting Promise*

Special Thanks

WHEN YOU ENGAGE IN a research project for more than 25 years there are a lot of people to thank, especially when your work culminates in a finished book like **Building a Love That Lasts: The Seven Surprising Secrets of Successful Marriage**. We have worked with many wonderful people along the way, but several stand out.

First and foremost, we would like to thank all of those marvelous and wonderful couples we have interviewed over the years. We have learned so much from them about love, successful marriage, and relationships. They were and continue to be an inspiration for us, and a model for successful marriage in the United States and around the world.

Our colleague David Riklan, at www.selfgrowth.com, provided us with the opportunity to greatly expand our work via the Internet. His offer for us to become the **Official Guides to Marriage** on SelfGrowth.com has changed our lives. David gave us an unbelievable "platform" for our work. Our writings about love and marriage are now read around the world. Thank you, David. Your support means more to us than you will ever know.

Our heartfelt thanks to our literary agent, Peter Rubie, of FinePrint Literary Agency in New York City. Peter has always been steadfast in his faith in us and our "marriage project." His confidence has lead to things we could never have imagined. We thank Peter from the bottom of our collective hearts. Because of him, we persevered and success has come our way. When others doubted us, Peter believed in us! We will be forever indebted to him.

A special thanks to Alan Rinzler, executive editor of Jossey-Bass, for his enthusiasm about our project. We absolutely love people who are action-oriented like Alan. Our relationship will prove to be a "marriage made in heaven." From our first lunch together in Florida, we knew Alan was our soulmate!

We cannot say enough about June Clark and Robin Blakely of *Get There Media*. They are wonderful to work with and have opened our eyes to new possibilities. We appreciate their marvelously creative ideas and their undying support for us.

We are especially indebted to our friend and colleague Pat Kloepfer (PK, as many friends call her). Her final editing work on our manuscript is yet another example of her "eagle eye" when it comes to accuracy. Working with her over these past 14 years has been a joy. PK is one of a kind and we love her for it.

And finally, to our daughter, Kristina, and our two beautiful grandchildren, Hudson and Hope. Their love has inspired us to greater heights to share our message of love, hope, and success. When you are surrounded by family and love, all things are possible. We love you guys!

Introduction

"TILL DEATH DO US PART" are the words couples use in committing their lives to each other. It is the promise we made to each other 43 years ago, and to this day we have a lasting love that burns even brighter now than when we first said, "I do." Why has our love lasted when so many of our friends have long since ended their marriages in divorce? This is the question we began researching more than 25 years ago.

We continually remind others that the divorce rate in America is all too high—some estimate it as high as 50%. And the news gets worse—nearly two-thirds of those who get remarried following a divorce get divorced again, and those who get married a third time have a failure rate of nearly 75%! The simple truth is, almost all of this suffering and unhappiness could be avoided. Yes, avoided! How, you say? Well, successfully married couples can tell you. They know!

That is why we are committed to reducing the divorce rate and increasing the success rate of marriage by sharing what we have learned from decades of research and our own 43 years of marriage—*most marriages are worth saving and can be saved!*

Hundreds of marriage and relationship books have been written in the past 30 years telling people how to have a successful marriage. So why would anyone want or need another? Well, to begin with, the practical advice outlined in these other books is almost exclusively derived from experts who have studied relationships that *have failed* in order to predict what will work.

On the other hand, we have taken a *completely different approach*—we decided that the best way to understand how to make a marriage a success is to study *successful marriages.*

Our criteria for determining a successful marriage are stringent:

… First, the couple had to be married to each other for at least 30 years.

… Second, in response to the question, "How would you rate the overall happiness of your marriage on a scale of 1 to 10 (with 10 the highest)?" the couple being interviewed had to agree that it was a 9 or 10.

We gathered more than 15,000 years of collective wisdom from happily and successfully married couples in the United States—people of different faiths, ages, and ethnicities, including Caucasians, African Americans, Latinos, and Asian Americans married in the Judeo-Christian tradition. In addition, we interviewed successfully married couples in over 40 countries on five continents of the world. After 25 years and thousands of interviews with successfully married couples (as well as our own successful 43 years of marriage) we discovered *seven pervasive characteristics* present in all successful marriages.

While successful marriage isn't difficult to understand, many couples fail to do the simple things required to make their marriage work. They either forget to do them or they haven't learned them in the first place.

Successful couples talked about their marriages going through cycles similar to the stages of life. Many of the couples described experiencing difficulties and turmoil with the transition into a different stage, such as the addition of children, the increased pressures of striving for success in their careers, or the empty nest syndrome. While each change brought its own rewards, it also brought with it stress on each individual and on the relationship within the marriage itself. Their stories shed light on ways to use the Seven Surprising Secrets to effectively handle the stress of these anticipated transitions.

Johnny Cash and June Carter said it best in their famous duet, "We got married in a fever hotter than a pepper's sprout. We've been talkin' 'bout Jackson ever since the fire went out." So, how do successful, happily married couples keep the fire from going out? How do they stoke their fire until it warms everything around them? Marriages change over the years, and in enduring marriages the partners find ways to grow closer together and improve the relationship that once began with the fiery passion of young love and then matured into a lasting love. Their stories are here, within these pages for you to enjoy.

These poignant, real life stories were garnered from thousands of interviews conducted over decades with happily married couples so the secrets for success could be uncovered and explained. Obviously, rather than divulge the true identity of the people we are describing who have been happily married for at least 30 years, we changed their names and the places to protect their identities, unless they granted us permission to identify them by name. However, their stories had to be told, because no writer could create such perfect examples of how to build lasting relationships. Only the real life experiences of long-time happily married couples could be filled with such intrigue, humor, sadness, and joy. We know you will find their stories fascinating and helpful.

The important point is that successful love and relationships are an accumulation of the little things. The little things matter! It isn't enough to just think about the little things or just talk about the little things. You have to just DO the little things every day. That's what makes love and relationships last! If you understand and implement the simple ideas presented in the pages to follow, we are convinced that your marriage will be well on its way to becoming a very successful and wonderful experience.

THE MARRIAGE QUIZ

> What are the chances of you and your spouse—or
> spouse-to-be—being happily married in 50 years?
> Think you'll make it? Take "The Marriage Quiz" and see
> if your relationship measures up with those who have
> been happily and successfully married for 30 to 77 years.

CIRCLE TRUE OR FALSE

COUPLES WITH SUCCESSFUL MARRIAGES ...

TRUE OR FALSE 1. Report that marriage is simple to
understand and simple to make work.

TRUE OR FALSE 2. Give up their individual identities to
form a perfect union with their spouses.

TRUE OR FALSE 3. Have private issues that they do not
share with each other.

TRUE OR FALSE 4. Consider their spouses to be their most
trusted friends.

TRUE OR FALSE 5. Help their spouses overcome weaknesses by
pointing out things that need improvement.

TRUE OR FALSE 6. Give their spouses privacy and time alone.

TRUE OR FALSE 7. Would ignore their spouses' large weight
gain because they understand that personal
appearance is not an important part of
their relationship.

TRUE OR FALSE 8. Focus on cooking healthy meals together
as a sensual and fun activity.

TRUE OR FALSE 9. Would make a major purchase only after joint
agreement with their spouses.

TRUE OR FALSE 10. Explain that it is critical to maintain financial
independence from each other.

TRUE OR FALSE 11. Report that sexual intimacy is at the heart of
their marriage and it forms the foundation for
their successful relationship.

TRUE OR FALSE 12. Playfully tease about their spouses' faults
with others.

TRUE OR FALSE 13. Are careful to keep their lives together routine
and predictable so their relationship remains
stable and sane.

TRUE OR FALSE 14. Find ways of adding surprise, excitement,
and adventure to their marriage.

TRUE OR FALSE 15. Report that cheating on their spouses would
cause irreparable damage to their marriage.

TRUE OR FALSE 16. Have experienced very few stressful situations
in their 30 or more years of marriage.

TRUE OR FALSE 17. Grew closer together following tragic events
in their lives.

TRUE OR FALSE 18. Find that children only add to the enjoyment
of their marriage.

TRUE OR FALSE 19. Enjoy learning about the interests of each other,
even though their interests are not always the same.

TRUE OR FALSE 20. Cannot imagine life without their spouses.

You will find the answers to the quiz on the next page. Have fun seeing how you rate compared to couples who have been happily and successfully married for 30 to 77 years.

ANSWERS: The answers to the Marriage Quiz are based upon more than 25 years of research on successful marriage.

1. F	11. F
2. F	12. F
3. F	13. F
4. T	14. T
5. F	15. T
6. T	16. F
7. F	17. T
8. T	18. F
9. T	19. T
10. F	20. T

If you answered all 20 questions the same as the thousands of couples we interviewed who had successful marriages, **congratulations.** You have a very good chance of being happily married and celebrating your Golden Anniversary together. You will want to read *Building a Love That Lasts: The Seven Surprising Secrets of Successful Marriage* to hear the poignant, real life stories of other successfully married couples.

If you scored a 16 or less on this marriage quiz, you will want to read the book today! You and your spouse (or spouse-to-be) can learn the important secrets from thousands of successfully married couples.

CHAPTER 1

How Will I Know I Am in Love?

You suddenly and out of nowhere are inspired to say
I LOVE YOU! I LOVE YOU! I LOVE YOU!
You shout it to the stars. You are in love!

*I*N OUR MANY INTERVIEWS with people "in love" we ask them, perhaps, the most revealing question of the interview—"How did you know you were in love?" We have heard very consistent answers. And conversely, many people involved in a new loving relationship, particularly young people, often ask us, "How do I know if I am in love?" We think we know the answer.

While we have heard a number of answers to our "How did you know you were in love" question, we can place them in **seven** categories. And, perhaps surprisingly, they have stayed the same over our 25 years of research on couples in love. Here they are, in a nutshell.

The first category is *physical*. People who say they are in love report getting "goosebumps," "a palpitating heart," "sweaty palms," "a lump in my throat," "teary-eyed when I say goodbye," "a tingling sensation all over my body," and the like. People in love have a positive physical reaction when they think about or see the one they love in person.

The second category is *emotional*. When they think about or see the person they love, most lovers report similar feelings—"I laugh more often when I am with the person I love," "an uncontrollable smile comes over my face whenever I see her," and "I miss him when he leaves the room." People in love feel emotions for the person they love that they do not routinely feel for others.

The third category is *positive worry*. Over the years, we continue to be amazed about the consistency with which people in love report to us that they "worry about their lover" when they are not around. Little thoughts of what we have come to call "positive worry" about the one they love begins to creep into their mind—things like car accidents, falling down, getting hurt at work, and getting sick. The folks we interview for the most part do not worry compulsively or negatively. These thoughts are normal and natural when you are "in love."

The fourth category is what we call the *I-cannot-imagine-life-without-her* category. This is the point in love when you begin to think about the future—your future with the one you love. When you cannot imagine your life without him, you are in love!

The fifth category focuses on the *oneness of your relationship*. You begin to realize that you truly want this other person in your life. You want to be with her. You want to share with her. You want to live with her, share a bed with her, hold her, and hug her. In our book, we refer to the notion of "turning two into one." You actually begin to think about the one you love and not just about yourself or your needs. You think about his—his wants, his needs, and his desires. When the feeling of oneness consumes your body, you are in love!

The sixth category is about *preoccupied love*. Simply stated, you think about the one you love most of the time. You can't get her out of your mind. You pull her photo out of your wallet and you smile. You are preoccupied with him. When you are preoccupied with him, you are in love with him!

The seventh and final category is *love itself and your ability to express that love*. You finally have the courage to tell her you love her! You miss him when he is not around. You worry about her. You care about his safety and welfare. You feel about her in ways you have never felt about another human being before. You suddenly and out of nowhere are inspired to say I LOVE YOU! I LOVE YOU! I LOVE YOU! You shout it to the stars. You are in love!

CHAPTER 2

Learning to Dance

Whether the beat of your marriage is a tango, salsa, swing, or waltz, when each of these seven characteristics threads throughout your marriage and describes your dance together, you will have achieved a successful marriage.

WHAT SEPARATES the couples we interviewed in marriages that achieved lasting love from those that failed? In our research we discovered pervasive characteristics threaded throughout the relationships of all successful marriages … but not the unsuccessful ones. It is uncanny the way the successful couples talk about their lives together. The characteristics are a pervasive part of who they are *together*, as if describing the steps of a well-choreographed dance.

Successful couples have learned and practiced these characteristics, and committed them to memory. It is like watching a pair of ice dancers gliding through a perfectly executed triple jump—they are beautiful skaters individually, but magnificent when together.

On the other hand, failed marriages are like dancing in the dark without knowing the steps. The steps appear to be easy at first, but tragically, divorce statistics tell us that half of all married couples never learn the dance. Instead, they stumble and fall until they eventually give up and quit dancing altogether. If they had learned to make the seven characteristics part of the fabric of their marriages, they could have learned the dance of lasting love.

If you want to achieve a successful marriage with lasting love, first learn and understand the seven characteristics present in the relationships of all successful marriages. Then accept the commitment to practice each of the characteristics. While the seven characteristics would seem to be so simple, successful couples described the hard work it took to make each of the characteristics become a habit in their relationships. As one of our favorite couples said when we asked them what advice they would give newly married couples, "Never give up. It takes real work to be happily married, but it is so worth it."

As we probed deeper into these characteristics, we found that once successful couples learned and mastered the characteristics, they made them such a major part of their relationships that the seven characteristics actually became the definition of who they were together as couples. Whether the characteristics were naturally occurring early in their marriages or they learned the characteristics in the course of time throughout their marriages, the successful couples all talked about the hard work it took to fully develop them. It is no different than learning to dance the two-step or learning to ride a bicycle. Once you learn, you never forget how to do it. But the learning can be challenging and filled with obstacles, and requires constant practice.

If you didn't start early in your marriage to learn and develop the seven characteristics, it definitely will be more difficult to learn and effectively develop them into habits. However, it is possible at any time in your marriage to learn new characteristics and incorporate them into the fabric of your marriage. It is no different than easily learning to tap dance as a small child rather than waiting until you are an adult to try to become a successful tap dancer. You can still do it at any age—it just takes greater concentration and harder work.

Whether the beat of your marriage is a tango, salsa, swing, or waltz, when each of these seven characteristics threads throughout your marriage and describes your dance together, you will have achieved a successful marriage. You will then be well on your way to achieving a long lasting love like the successful couples we have interviewed who celebrated their Golden Anniversaries together.

C H A P T E R 3

Character in Love and Marriage

In our interviews over the past 25 years with couples
that have had successful marriages we are always struck
by their undying trust in each other. They literally trust
each other with their lives, their fortune,
and their sacred honor.

*I*N CASE YOU DIDN'T KNOW IT, there is a
character element in love and loving relationships. People who say
they love each other and then cheat on their spouse or lover, or lie to
spouses on a regular basis, aren't really in love. Oh, many think they
are, but they really are not. People who love each other have character
when it comes to their marriage or relationship.

In our interviews over the past 25 years with couples that have had
successful marriages, we are always struck by their undying trust in
each other. They literally trust each other with their lives, their
fortune, and their sacred honor. The words they use to describe the

one they love more often than not include words and expressions like trust, honesty, loyalty, respects me, admires me, always there for me, never lets me down, truthful, and never lies to me. Their trust for each other is about as complete as you can get. And when we ask each couple in love during our interviews to place, in an overall sense, where their relationship is on a 10-point scale, with 10 being "Absolute Trust," without exception, they say "10!" Isn't that wonderful? Remarkable? These are the couples that will celebrate their Golden Anniversaries together!

Trust is not something all loving relationships start with. For some couples the trust becomes complete in a few years. For others, it takes awhile. But one thing is for sure: happy and successful marriages and relationships survive and thrive on the basis of this trust. Trust is so pervasive in their relationship that they never give it a second thought. They expect it. It's always there. It is part of the fabric of their marriage.

There is one thing you can take to the bank—all people in love have faced temptations in their relationships. The pretty girl in the restaurant captures your fancy. The handsome man walking down the street draws your attention. The flirt at work is tempting at times. And, we will dare say, sometimes in every relationship you think about slipping in the sack with some of the beautiful people you meet. But here's where it stops—these are only fleeting moments of passing fancy. These are the moments of momentary lust for another human being that are not acted on. Why? People in love who are happy in their relationship control their urges because they know that while a moment of sexual fantasy is healthy and normal, following through and enjoying sexual satisfaction with someone other than their mate, cheating on their mate, is destructive to the loving and trusting relationship between them. It's okay to have sexual urges and fantasies regarding another person, but to act on them ruins all that trust. It destroys the tie that binds.

People who are truly in love in their relationship know that a few moments of sexual satisfaction can NEVER replace the loving, trusting, and caring relationship they have developed with their mate. As someone once said to us, "I have a marriage license but I didn't give up my looking license!" Admiring others in intimate ways is normal and healthy. But acting on those urges has ruined many a marriage and many a loving relationship.

Those wonderful couples we have interviewed resist these normal urges and temptations of life because they know their relationships are so much more important to them. Destroying the trust between them causes the foundations of their marriages to crumble.

Character in a successful marriage or relationship does matter, and character is about trust. Being honest and trustworthy is at the heart of all the best loving relationships we have studied. It really is a 10 on a 10-point scale. In our estimation, character is the foundation of true love!

CHAPTER 4

It's the Little Things That Matter

Being IN love is easy. But why do so many people
"IN love" not do the simple things required to help
their relationships stand the test of time?
Why do so many couples fail to make it long
enough to celebrate Golden Anniversaries?

E HAVE BEEN SAYING IT
for years, and our 25 years of marriage research proves it—having a
successful loving relationship is simple to understand! Yes, simple!
Yet, so many couples are incapable of doing or unwilling to do the
simple things required to make their relationships work. And we
continue to be amazed at how the pundits, the mainstream media, the
book publishers, and the psychologists strive so hard to make love and
relationships complicated. Sometimes, they even scoff at the simple
ideas—the simple notions that expose the truth about what makes
loving relationships work. It seems that they believe relationships and

marriage must be complicated—must be difficult to understand. Hard to believe, isn't it?

Being IN love is easy. But why do so many people "IN love" not do the simple things required to help their relationships stand the test of time? Why do so many couples fail to make it long enough to celebrate Golden Anniversaries?

Frankly, we think some folks get a little snobby about successful relationships. They want these relationships to be complicated. Maybe they think that if loving relationships are made complicated and difficult to understand, we will have to call upon them to sort it all out—to understand it all. Don't believe it! Truth is, if you do the simple things in your loving relationship, your chances of making it work, of making it last, will be much better. You don't need complicated explanations from the so-called experts. Trust us on that.

Here is your assignment—do the simple things and your relationship will stand the test of time. Ignore the simple things and your loving relationship will fail.

So, what are the simple things? Here are just a few examples:

… Remember birthdays and anniversaries.

… Say "thank you" and "please."

… Tell your lover "I Love You" each morning and before you go to bed each evening.

… Help clean the table after dinner.

… Guys, put the toilet seat down after going!

… Gals, keep your make-up in a case, you don't need the entire bathroom countertop.

… Go through the rituals of telling each other to "Watch for people running stop lights," "Watch for ice on the road," "Be safe."

… Call if you are going to be late.

… Help carry in the groceries and packages.

**… Send your lover an email or call at least once
a day to say you are thinking about him.**

… Be more unselfish, it isn't just about you.

… Give your lover at least a dozen hugs a day.

And the list goes on.

The important point is that successful love and relationships are an accumulation of the little things. The little things matter! It isn't enough to just think about the little things or just talk about the little things. You have to just DO the little things every day. That's what makes love and relationships last!

CHAPTER 5

Nicknames: The Private Code for Love

You see, love has a private code.
People in love understand!

OVER OUR **43** YEARS OF
MARRIAGE we have met thousands of couples that deeply loved each
other. We have interviewed many, many of them for our book on
successful marriage. In nearly every case, they had an affectionate
"secret" nickname for each other—a sort of private code for saying, "I
love you."

Some of the nicknames are ones you have probably heard many
times before—"lovey-dovey," "sweetie-pie," "sugar," "snookie-poo,"
"honey," "darling," "sweetness," "sweetpea," "baby girl," "lover boy,"
"sunshine," "sugarplum," "baby-doll," "hey, handsome," "hey, beautiful," and so forth.

Some of the nicknames are unusual and funny. Names like
"butch" in reference to a very petite wife seem unusual, but to her

husband, it is an endearing term. "Snookems," in reference to a very manly man, does not compute with most people, but to his wife, the term is an expression of love and affection. And the list goes on.

Over the years, the funniest "affectionate" nickname we ever heard was from the wife who lovingly referred to her husband as "turkey-fart!" It is not important to understand the origin of "turkey-fart." What is important is that the name has special meaning to the husband and wife team that coined it. You see, love has a private code. People in love understand! Nicknames are a private code for saying, "I Love You."

CHAPTER 6

And Then ... Along Came Kids

You thought your marriage was nearly perfect—
And Then ... Along Came Kids.
To quote Nora Ephron in Heartburn: *"Having a first child*
is like throwing a hand grenade into a marriage."

KIDS! WE LOVE THEM. We cherish them. They bring joy to our lives. When we have children in a marriage, we understand finally, and once and for all, what eternity means. While we are not immortal, we learn the meaning of everlasting life when we are blessed with children. They make us feel like we will live through time. We carry on through them. We know that through them our lives will have meaning beyond our time on this earth.

But our children are also a pain in the butt! They challenge us. They taunt us. They demand much from us. They argue with us. They divide us. They unite us. They run up one heck of a childcare bill!

On the other hand, most who are successfully married with children wouldn't want it any other way. They know that without a doubt, their children enrich their lives in innumerable ways. They value their children immensely. But be clear regarding this—successfully married couples with children understand the challenges children pose to a blissful and romantic marital relationship.

You thought your marriage was nearly perfect—*And Then … Along Came Kids*. To quote Nora Ephron in *Heartburn*: "Having a first child is like throwing a hand grenade into a marriage."

While a marvelous blessing, adding kids to a marriage brings a whole different set of issues, stressors, and dynamics for couples to deal with. Successfully married couples report that the addition of children to their relationships changed their family lives; and in many ways caused periodic stress in their relationships. Childrearing responsibilities are even considered by some experts to be the main cause for the "U" shaped curve in the level of satisfaction for couples over the lifetime of their marriages—dipping dramatically after the first few years of each marriage (with the addition of children) and then increasing steadily in the last half of the marriage (after the "nest" is empty).

In the last several months a great deal has been reported about the purpose of marriage, lamenting the fact that Americans no longer consider children among the most important purposes of marriage. While most experts are concluding that this is a negative change, we would like to offer a different perspective based on our two and a half decades of research on successful marriage.

In fact, as you have discovered, we have found seven pervasive characteristics present in all successful marriages. And guess what— *the quality of the relationship between husband and wife trumps everything else in a marriage!* And you know why—it's simple, really—without a positive, loving, and thriving relationship between mom and dad, children often don't prosper; they are not well adjusted;

they don't do well in school; and they are **not** as healthy, both physically and mentally. In all of our interviews over the years with those couples who have had long and successful marriages, not one of them ever mentioned that the purpose of their marriage was to have children. Oh, to be sure, they loved their children very much. They were delighted they brought children into this world and were very proud of them for the most part. But they also reported to us time and time again that it was the strength of their relationships with each other that made their marriages happy and allowed them to attend to myriad responsibilities and issues present in their marriages.

Marriages thrive and survive more than anything else because of the quality of the relationship between mom and dad. It's no more complicated than that.

Let's look at the facts—73% of women 30 years old and older are currently married or widowed. Most important, 94% of all women will have been married at least once by the age of 50.

The truth is, Americans love marriage! We just need to learn how to get it right the first time around instead of having nearly one out of every two of our marriages end in divorce. And the simple truth is, 65% of those that re-marry after divorce get divorced again. So you see, the relationship between mom and dad does trump everything else. Get it right and good things follow. Get it wrong and lots of bad things often happen!

A women quoted in the *Washington Post* got it right when she said, "When I think of marriage I don't think of children at all. I have them. But with marriage, I think of a husband and a wife, and I don't think it's the children that make it work."

The purpose of marriage within the historical and social context is strengthened when the focus is on the development of a strong, positive, and blissful relationship between husband and wife. That relationship trumps everything else. Make this relationship work and everything else follows.

So, how do successfully married couples survive and even thrive through the childrearing years? They explained that they had to work especially hard to keep the Seven Surprising Secrets characteristics alive in their relationships during these years. Their first-hand stories about the stresses of children and the associated challenges of dealing with them within the context of their marriages are enlightening. Each couple tells their stories fondly and often hilariously about how they effectively dealt with such issues as loving both their spouse and their child but loving each differently, the competition for their atten-tion, the demands of dual careers and parenting, the miscues involved in getting children to activities, the difficulties of finding a trusted child-care provider, the guilt of leaving their children in childcare, the pressure from not enough time, the stress for the primary caregiver, the skill of their children in taking advantage of situations, and the curse of raising teenagers when "all bets are off."

Many couples shared with us the difficulty of finding intimate time for each other after their children were born. The case of Steve and Jane illustrates just how difficult it can be to find quality time for each other. It all started when they decided that they couldn't resist each other any longer while on a weekend trip with their son. Six-year-old Christopher was fast asleep in the other room—or so they thought—and they had done without sex for more than two weeks. No phone, no chores, and no interruptions—the stage was set for a wonderful and intimate evening. At the peak of sexual delirium a little voice at the side of their hotel bed said, "Daddy why are you hurting mommy?" Needless to say, the mood suddenly changed. They were overwhelmingly embarrassed about being caught in the act!

Just getting through that moment put everything in perspective for Steve and Jane. They were in great need of a real plan for how they were going to get quality time for each other.

When Christopher was born, Steve and Jane made a promise that they wouldn't use childcare or a babysitter for their child. They would just re-arrange their schedules or do whatever was necessary to work it out. What they didn't realize was that they needed quality time together—alone without their son. The stark truth of that fact hit them hard that night in the hotel room.

After they got Christopher settled and off to sleep, Steve said, the conversation they had over the next several hours changed their lives forever. They recognized for the first time in their marriage that unless they had time for each other to nurture their own relationship, they would never become the great parents they always talked about being. They came to the realization that while raising a child is wonderful and rewarding, it can also be an unbelievable pain and mighty inconvenient at times. That was a difficult admission, since both Steve and Jane loved kids and had wanted to be parents from their first year together. They believed that children would only add enjoyment and excitement to their lives.

Since both of their families lived too far away to help them with Christopher and they had very little money at that stage in their marriage, Steve and Jane had to be creative. They talked about options such as swapping childcare time with their friends, church-provided childcare, and Mother's Day Out services. Jane said that the first time Christopher went to childcare was terribly stressful because they couldn't stop worrying about him. However, as you might have guessed, everything went beautifully and their son seemed to genuinely enjoy the childcare time with playmates.

During the rest of Christopher's early years, Steve and Jane arranged for childcare or swapped time at least once a month to give them the quality time they needed with each other. The rest of the time Christopher went everywhere with Steve and Jane. He seemed to be permanently attached to Steve's shoulders for trips to the zoo, park, ball games, and science center. Those wonderful memories are etched in their minds forever. Now, almost 33 years later, Steve and Jane still laugh about their child's untimely question that night in the hotel. They said that it always strikes them as funny that this was an important turning point in their marriage, because it forced them to work hard to find time to keep their passion and romance alive, even with a child!

Many successfully married couples told us similar stories about their difficulties finding time for fun and ways of keeping their relationships strong during the childrearing years. Each stage in the lives of their children seemed to bring with it entirely new challenges. Jim and Iris said raising their three children reminded them of the voyage of the Endurance trying to cross Antarctica. Every time they thought they had the conditions figured out and a working solution, the conditions changed and the solution was no longer workable. A new solution was needed! Just like the expedition force stranded on the ice fields of Antarctica, when the ice moved and conditions changed, they found new ways to survive. Jim and Iris told us that maybe it was the fact that they had three boys that made their situation so challenging. Finding unity and balance in their lives while raising three rambunctious boys was not easy, but they rolled up their sleeves and did it together.

Their biggest relationship issues always seemed to center around the innate ability of their boys to divide and conquer. It seemed that even the slightest disagreement between Iris and Jim always blew up into a major situation with the boys, until they got smart and agreed to always back the other one up in front of the boys. They then settled their own disagreements out of earshot of the children. In that way, they presented a unified front. While it sounds so simple, Iris and Jim said that their boys had such a talent for dividing and conquering that they had to work hard not to give themselves away by their facial expressions or body language.

The first time Iris and Jim knew they were in trouble was over the issue of riding tricycles in the driveway. Iris had totally forbidden the boys from riding their tricycles in the driveway because of the danger of people using their driveway to turn around in. Soon after Iris had "laid down the law" and Jim was alone with the boys, one of them politely asked him for permission to ride their tricycles in the driveway. Jim was so taken with his oldest son's newly found manners that he immediately said yes. The first thing he did upon greeting Iris was to brag about how his work on manners was paying off with the boys. Unfortunately, when Jim got to the part about how he told the boys they could ride their tricycles in the driveway, Iris hit the ceiling. How could he have been so buffaloed by the boys? Didn't he have suspicions that the boys were up to no good since they were "too polite for words"? What was he thinking? After Iris calmed down, she explained that the boys had put her through argument after argument about the tricycles and she had finally set them straight about the fact that it was simply too dangerous and there was to be no further discussion of the topic. The answer to riding their tricycles in the driveway was "absolutely not!" At that point Jim said he felt like crawling under the table, except he wouldn't fit. There he sat feeling like a fool. What seemed like such a little issue to him was indeed a major issue of safety. After much discussion, Iris and Jim decided that whenever the boys found innovative ways to secure different answers from them, they would work together to maintain a unified front. When their three sons were going through their challenging teenage years, Jim said that their unified approach and support for each other kept them from losing their sanity.

Even in the best marital relationships, there are times when situations arise with their children that pull hard at dividing them. One such story sounded all too familiar, as the craziness of managing dual careers with young children presents some of the most unusual challenges even to the most organized of individuals. Mindy and Fred thought they had things going beautifully with the care of their two children in spite of their hectic schedules. On Mondays, Tuesdays, and Fridays, Mindy would pick the children up right after school to shuttle them off to their lessons, games, or home. On Wednesdays and

Thursdays, Fred would pick the children up from the after-school care center before 6:00 pm. As with everything in their lives it was all subject to change depending upon work schedules, meetings, appointments, etc.

Since they didn't have cell phones back when their children were young, Mindy and Fred had to organize their plans each day and then stick with them. Somehow on that fateful Tuesday, Mindy and Fred both thought the other one was responsible for picking up the children. To this day, neither one can remember who was really at fault for the situation, but both take equal blame. It seems they arrived home at around 6:30 pm, exhausted from a difficult day at work. After greeting each other, it dawned on Mindy that the house was too quiet. Where were the children? It took only an instant for pure panic to hit both Mindy and Fred. What had they done? Where were the children? Tuesday—oh my God—they were supposed to be picked up right after school and taken to their swimming lessons. Both of them were too much in shock to even begin trying to figure out what went wrong. They immediately hopped into the car and headed off to school. Everything was closed up and dark. Now what? Where were the children? In a moment of calm, Mindy thought to head back home to check the telephone messages. Why hadn't they checked them before heading off to school? Too much panic … too much guilt … too much embarrassment and too much confusion due to their hectic lives. In fact, when they got back into the house there were six messages.

As they started to listen, they took a long breath. First, both of the children's teachers had tried everything to reach Fred and Mindy at work. Both were not in their offices all day and were totally out of reach in the late afternoon. Both of the children's teachers and the principal had made attempts to contact them at home. The principal had even driven to their house to find them, because one of their children had broken his arm and needed to go to the hospital. That message was left around 1:30 pm—more than five hours ago. By the time they listened to the final message from the principal, both Mindy and Fred were shaking. The children were now okay. Sam's arm was in a cast and he was resting quietly at the principal's house. Their daughter was fine and eating dinner at her teacher's house. They headed toward the principal's house first, as they worked hard to fight back the tears and talked about how lucky they were to have such a terrific principal and teachers for their children. They spent the next several days developing contingency plans for all types of emergencies so this would never happen again. Oh yes, they made sure the principal and teachers of their children understood just how grateful they were for taking care of their children on that terrible day. While today's communications are a great deal easier with cell phones and pagers, contingency plans are still required in case of traffic jams, accidents, emergencies, and weather situations.

It seems that successfully married couples do whatever it takes to work through the difficult issues with their children while continuing to strengthen their relationships. The trials and tribulations of child-rearing brought them closer together and made them appreciate each other even more when they finally made it to "empty nesthood."

There is one more recurring theme we heard over and over during our interviews with successfully married couples—the "empty nest syndrome" is grossly over-rated! All of the couples we interviewed who have been successfully married over 30 years and now are "empty nesters" reported to us how much they loved their children, that they missed hearing their sounds throughout the house, that they cherished the times when they visited with their grown children and grandchildren, and that they did really miss having their children around. On the other hand, because their relationships with each other had stayed so strong over the childrearing years, the impact of the empty nest was substantially lessened for them as they quickly adjusted to the change. In fact, if the truth be known, they reported that their sex life was better, they had more time for fun, they traveled more frequently, they took more long walks and bike rides, they ate out more often, they took more vacation time, and they really enjoyed a clean house. You see, happily married couples love each other and practice the Seven Surprising Secrets throughout their marriage, even when the children are living at home. When the children are gone, they are not left with those empty and aimless feelings. Like the commercial says, many empty nesters really do want to go to Disney World by themselves!

While your obligation to your children is critical, the relationship with your spouse is the foundation for making it all work. You only set yourself up for failure if you do not continue to work even harder on your relationship during the often difficult childrearing years. Remember, when the nest is empty and the children are gone, the strength of your relationship during those childrearing years will determine to a large extent how you will spend the rest of your lives together.

— *Advice* —

While we could write an entire book about what successfully married couples had to say about how they kept their sanity and their marital relationships strong during those childrearing years, we have tried to capture only the most important pieces of advice for you from their 15,000 years of collective wisdom.

1. **Don't pretend that kids will bring only love and joy to your marriage.** Most successfully married couples with children wouldn't want it any other way. But, successfully married couples with children understand the challenges that children pose to a blissful and romantic marital relationship. You have to acknowledge and accept that as fact before you can work on keeping the Seven Surprising Secrets alive and well during the childrearing years.

2. **Find ways to keep the passion and romance alive with your spouse.** Lack of time is the greatest obstacle to romance for married couples with children. Successful couples said that once they realized just how important it was to keep the romance alive, they changed their priorities to make time for each other. Ways they used to gain time alone were to find a trusted childcare provider; swap childcare times with their friends; use the free services of their churches, synagogues, or women's organizations; or creatively meet at home for an extended lunch time when the children were in school. It didn't seem to matter how they worked it out. What was consistent was that all successfully married couples reported that they did make their passion and romance a priority and found ways to keep the fires burning even during their childrearing years.

3. **Recognize exhaustion from childrearing when it hits you and learn to take care of the resultant needs.**

This is just another fact of life when raising children. You can never have enough strength to match the boundless energy of children. Successfully married couples talk about putting their relationships first and about how they learned to recognize when exhaustion was interfering with their relationships. They talked about taking the steps necessary to get a break by enlisting the help of relatives, friends, and childcare providers to make it through their most difficult times.

4. **Don't whine about your plight; instead, deal with it—make adjustments.** Learn coping techniques so you can focus on the best part of raising children. While it is natural to sink into a world of negativism and self-pity because you are overwhelmed, overworked, and underappreciated, to do so will not result in a stronger relationship with your spouse. Know that you will get through this stage by maintaining the philosophy that "This too shall pass."

5. **Keep a unified front.** There will most certainly be times when your children use their uncanny ability to drive a wedge between you and your spouse. Don't let your children divide and conquer. Be consistent in front of the children with all decisions and then settle any disagreements behind closed doors. Demonstrating your support for each other in front of the children not only provides a unified approach but also provides you with the courage to stick with the hard decisions required to raise your children.

6. **Remember to enjoy the precious moments of each stage in the lives of your children—those moments never come again.** With all of the challenges and frantic

craziness of raising your children, don't forget to take time to enjoy the beauty of what the two of you have created. In your care is your future. You will live through time as they carry on. Your children give meaning beyond your time on this earth, so cherish the moments.

7. **Focus on keeping the Seven Surprising Secrets characteristics of successfully married couples strong in your marriage.** What successfully married couples discovered early in their childrearing years is that the strength of their relationships provided the solid foundations they needed to get through the difficult times and to address the challenges posed by their children. Focusing on the Seven Surprising Secrets characteristics will carry you and your spouse through almost anything. Raising children is an awesome responsibility, but doing it well requires the two of you to keep your relationship strong, happy, and successful.

CHAPTER 7

Seven Surprising Secrets #1:
It Takes Two to Tango

And then, suddenly, it dawns on you—it takes two to tango!
You can't tango alone. This simple notion describes the best
marriages we have studied over the years—a marriage,
like the tango, works best if the partners
move with great synergy and togetherness.

A COUPLE OF YEARS AGO, we
traveled to Buenos Aires, Argentina, for our annual vacation. What a
beautiful city. It is full of excitement, romance, energy, memories of
Evita, color, charm, and most important, the tango. If you have
ever been to Señor Tango for an evening of dinner with lomo (beef
tenderloin), one of their remarkable Malbec wines, and a tango show,
you know that Buenos Aires and the tango are inseparable. One goes
with the other—a lot like two people dancing the tango.

Tango dancing is romantic, sensual, athletic, and full of energy.
The two dancers depend on each other totally. They dip, they spin,

they pirouette, they embrace, and they mirror each other's moves in so many ways. When you see the tango for the first time you are overwhelmed by the beauty and grace of what you see. And then, suddenly, it dawns on you—it takes two to tango! You can't tango alone. This simple notion describes the best marriages we have studied over the years—a marriage, like the tango, works best if the partners move with great synergy and togetherness, learning to be a unit of one.

Successfully married couples learn the synergy and togetherness of turning two into one early in their marriages and don't want life to be any other way. The best qualities of both individuals come together to form a unit of one that is greater than either of the two individuals alone. One couple summed it up by saying, "We are one. We are a team. We support and need each other."

Happily married couples cannot imagine life without each other. It is so inconceivable to successfully married couples that when you ask them if they could, their eyes fill with tears while they contemplate the question.

In successful marriages neither the husband nor the wife dominates the relationship. They have achieved the art of dancing the tango, without losing their individual identities. So how did they do it? There are three aspects of turning two into one for successful couples. First, sharing interests, feelings, ideas, and memories gives your marriage a uniqueness all its own. Second, compromising to form mutually agreeable decisions that both of you can support is critically important. And third, the best marriages we have observed thrive on mutual helpfulness and support for each other. In this chapter we will talk about each of these aspects of the characteristic *It Takes Two to Tango,* so you can understand the important role each plays in achieving a successful marriage.

Virtually all of the successful couples started forming two into one with the practice of sharing. Whether it was hiking, biking, tennis, traveling, dancing, skiing, baseball, television, movies, exercise, poker, music, or antiques, these couples talked to us about how they worked hard to develop shared interests with their spouses. Over time, they each learned about the interests of their mates, then built upon those interests they had in common. Some of the couples described having similar interests from the beginning of their marriages, while other couples had to work hard to discover interests they could learn to share. What successful couples had in common was that they developed the enjoyment of mutual interests until it became a part of who they were together as couples.

The only way for the marriage to become "WE" instead of "YOU" and "ME" is to make sharing the first and foremost part of your marriage. One of the best examples of how sharing each other's interests can enhance a marriage came to us from a couple in their middle 50s whom we met at a psychological association conference. Everything about them seemed to radiate joy and excitement. They appeared to be so natural with their enjoyment of each other that we just had to ask them if they had always had this kind of relationship even at the beginning of their marriage. To our surprise, they said that their first several years of marriage were the pits.

It seems that Jesse and Mary were very much in love when they first got married; however, they didn't have any interests in common. What Jesse liked, Mary knew nothing about or openly despised. What Mary liked, Jesse didn't understand or totally disliked. Mary had begun to ask herself how she could have fallen so madly in love with Jesse when they seemed to now have nothing in common. They soon discovered that even vacations were impossible with this kind of situation. Either they had to start sharing, or their love would be stifled or worse!

Jesse loved the outdoors and everything about it. He would go camping in the wilds every weekend if Mary would only go along. Mary, on the other hand, thought that a poolside room at the Holiday

Inn was roughing it. She never took the time to learn why Jesse loved the outdoors so much, and he never took the time to appreciate the advantages of hotel service.

What brought the whole problem to the boiling point was a two-week summer vacation coming up, with no agreement on where or how to go. Obviously, Mary wanted to travel via Holiday Inns, and Jesse wanted to pitch a tent in the backwoods. They had to find a solution or scrap the vacation. After hours of discussion, they finally agreed to a compromise. The first week would be spent in the wilds and the second week in Holiday Inns. Almost a month of preparation and discussion occurred about what to bring and how to survive in both environments before Mary and Jesse were finally ready to embark.

Mary was scared to death of anything that crawled, flew, or moved in the woods. She really meant it when she had jokingly referred to a Holiday Inn as "roughing it." To her the outdoors was to be viewed and enjoyed from the safety of a comfortable car or truck seat. But, she had agreed to try this with Jesse and she wasn't about to back out now.

When they turned into their campsite, the beauty of the tall pine trees and the mountain brook running through the edge of the campsite were overwhelming. For a fleeting moment, Mary thought this might just be okay. Maybe it wouldn't be as bad as she had conjured up in her mind? Maybe she could overcome her fears? Mary arrived with the very best of intentions.

But, when they snuggled into their sleeping bags for the night, all of Mary's fears proved greater than she could handle. Mary recalled with a laugh that the first night was absolutely horrendous. She didn't get a wink of sleep, since even the slightest noise terrified her and just added to her growing sense of panic. She tried to visualize being in her grandmother's kitchen, safely warming her hands at the wood stove. But nothing seemed to quiet her fears. To her amazement, Jesse slept like a baby all night long. How was she going to survive a whole week of this?

In the morning over breakfast, Mary confided in Jesse that she couldn't sleep at all after the sounds of howling pierced the quiet of the evening. For the first time, Jesse began to understand the depth of her fear and dislike for the wilderness. Jesse wanted Mary to know everything about the wilderness so she could overcome even her greatest fears. He just knew that if Mary was willing to try this hard, it just had to work out all right. Jesse immediately began sharing the information and appreciation he had gained from the many years of outdoor experiences. Jesse told Mary that the howl of a single timber wolf was what started her fears escalating. He explained that there had never been a reported attack by timber wolves on humans at this camping area. As Mary listened, she learned about the howling and why the timber wolf was probably not the kind of animal that would enter their campsite, since the campsite was well lit and offered nothing the wolves wanted to eat. The more Mary understood about the sounds, sights, and smells of the wilderness, the more she learned to deal with her fears.

Jesse offered to zip the two sleeping bags together, not for romantic reasons, but to guard Mary so she could sleep. He promised to stay awake all night if that would help her feel safe. Mary instantly agreed to the new sleeping arrangements, since she felt it might be the only way she was going to be able to close her eyes, let alone sleep. Even the cramped space created with the two sleeping bags zipped tightly together didn't matter to Mary. The new arrangement gave her such a feeling of safety that she found enough courage to tell Jesse he could sleep a bit if he wanted to. He only had to promise to wake up if she got scared. Mary loved the wilderness during the day and with Jesse's help learned to survive her fears at night. Jesse shared something so special with Mary that it changed their entire relationship. It was then that she realized there was a hidden part of Jesse she had totally been missing because her fears had stopped them from sharing and learning about each other.

The next week was heaven to Mary. They were traveling via Holiday Inns. That meant no dishes, no making the beds, and a swim or sauna any time she wanted. Jesse appreciated Mary's efforts at outdoor living so much that he too made the same kind of effort to enjoy the hotel living. Much to his surprise, he grew quite comfortable with breakfast in bed, maid service, saunas, and swimming pools. It turned out to be a wonderfully relaxing part of their vacation. While Jesse adapted quite easily to the hotel part of their vacations, it took several wilderness camping trips together over the next couple of years before Mary began to overcome her fears and actually enjoy the wilderness with Jesse.

Needless to say, each of them learned a fundamental lesson about sharing. They had taken the time to share their interests and knowledge with each other, and in so doing they both grew closer to each other. No wonder when we first met them these two looked like they were enjoying every second of each other's company... they were!!!

The kind of sharing Mary and Jesse experienced is simple to explain but often difficult to do. Sharing within this context is really a program for developing ongoing communication in a marriage. The sharing of interests, feelings, and ideas on a continuous basis is absolutely essential in establishing, maintaining and, enhancing the fundamental relationship between partners. Periodic sharing with your spouse allows you to take time out from everyday living to look at yourself and your relationship with your spouse, and to examine where your relationship is and where it is going. It forms the foundation for achieving two into one.

Since achieving two into one requires that sharing become a habit, we've developed a little inventory of sharing to help you. It is included in the Appendix of this book (p. 282). Why don't you turn to it right now? As you can see, it contains 84 statements we developed based upon our examination of successful marriages. We arranged all of the statements into groups, making it easy for you to take just a few minutes each week to focus on a single group of statements.

in accordance with the applicable warranty.

Returns or exchanges will not be permitted (i) after 14 days or without receipt or (ii) for product not carried by Barnes & Noble or Barnes & Noble.com.

Policy on receipt may appear in two sections.

Return Policy

<u>With a sales receipt or Barnes & Noble.com packing slip</u>, a full refund in the original form of payment will be issued from any Barnes & Noble Booksellers store for returns of undamaged NOOKs, new and unread books, and unopened and undamaged music CDs, DVDs, and audio books made within 14 days of purchase from a Barnes & Noble Booksellers store or Barnes & Noble.com with the below exceptions:

A store credit for the purchase price will be issued (i) for purchases

YOU MAY ALSO LIKE...

His Needs, Her Needs: Building an...
by Willard F. Harley

Before Saying "I Do": The Essential...
by Michael Batshaw

How to Improve Your Marriage Without...
by Patricia Love

Take Back Your Marriage: Sticking...
by William J. Doherty

101 Things I Wish I Knew When I Got...
by Linda Bloom

Now that you've looked through the inventory, answer these two questions: Could you answer each of the questions to your satisfaction? Do you know how your spouse would answer them? If you are not absolutely sure how your spouse would answer, why not just find out? As you begin discovering the similarities and differences in the answers you and your spouse give to the same questions, the two of you can engage in even deeper conversations that will lead to a habit of sharing in your marriage.

Only when you are willing to share your innermost feelings within your most cherished relationship are you able to say, "We are truly married." Marriage is after all, by definition, a shared relationship. That includes sharing your innermost feelings that can be really hard to express. Have you ever said this: "Why do I have to tell my wife I love her? She knows it." The question is, does she? Does she really know? Or, "My husband knows why I love him." How do you know he knows why you love him? When was the last time you told him why? Sharing in a marriage is a learned sort of thing. We learn how to share much like we learned how not to share … by practice. Why don't you and your mate set aside at least 30 minutes per week for the next seven weeks in order to afford each of you the opportunity to share your responses to each group of the statements in greater depth. We bet by the end of seven weeks you won't need our little inventory anymore. What you will learn is that the sharing of information about you and your spouse's interests, perceptions, fears, hopes, dreams, and loves will add to the richness and fullness of your relationship with your mate. It builds the foundation for achieving two into one.

The more experiences you share together, the stronger your marriage bonds become. Every shared experience, whether good or bad, adds to the uniqueness of your marriage. You can laugh or cry or talk about those experiences with others, but only the two of you can really feel the richness of those moments or memories you have had together. Each of those moments and memories are unique to the two of you and bring you closer to truly becoming one.

Perhaps the best-shared experiences occur for a lot of us on those "restful" vacations. Have we had a few of those! One of our most memorable moments came on a muggy August day in Washington, D.C. Before that afternoon was to end, we had shared every imaginable emotion together.

It was about 3:00 pm on a Friday, when Washington, D.C., finally came into sight. One year of diligent planning and waiting was just about to pay off. We made the journey from Missouri to our nation's capital by car. Charley suggested a quick jaunt around the main sights by car, since we couldn't check into our hotel until 4:00 pm Liz instantly and wholeheartedly agreed. So, off we went.

Oh, there it was … the Capitol! Just as we passed it, with a sigh, our famous map reader Liz said, "We better make a quick right." However, to Charley's chagrin, he was in four lanes of one-way traffic cruising along in the far-left lane. The other vehicles did not seem to even slightly consider yielding to our unsuccessful attempts to merge right. No way was a right-hand turn possible, unless we took out ten other cars in demolition derby style.

So … over the bridge we went, right into the most "UN-tourist" part of town. You know the place—old broken-down cars, four-letter words spray painted on the buildings, busted-out windows, drunks laying in the doorways, and definitely NO street signs matching our tourist map. After 15 minutes of aimless wandering, we developed two pressing problems requiring our immediate attention. First, we were just about out of gas; but more importantly, Charley had to go to the bathroom. And, when Charley has to go, things can get critical almost instantaneously. He hops around in the seat, gets very impatient, and shows a kind of newly found irritation with everything. This just wasn't the kind of place to fill either of our needs.

As we drove even deeper into the area, our conversation included statements like … "Can't you find any of those streets on the map?"

"Just tell me if I should go right or left." "Where are we?" "Just look straight ahead and don't stare!" "Maybe we will look like we belong here." Right!!! Our Missouri license plates and the stuffed-full vacation car just wouldn't give anyone a clue that we were totally lost!

Then it happened, the car started to sputter. We knew it was only a matter of time until we were on foot … a couple of Missouri folks with their teenage daughter, just out for a leisurely stroll through the streets of town. THIS was the kind of relaxation we were both hoping for???

If only we could find a gas station. Finally, there it was—only about three blocks ahead. From both of us came a simultaneous sigh of relief. Little did we know what was to happen next.

Into the self-serve gas station we pulled. Charley managed to fling over a 20-dollar bill just before he bounded out of the car toward the men's room. It was about that moment in time when we became keenly aware of our surroundings. The gas station just happened to be the local gathering place. There were several groups of three or four tough looking "gentlemen" discussing whatever it is that is discussed by men in their 20s and 30s who have too much idle time on their hands. Immediately, Liz gave Kristina orders to duck down, lock the doors, and honk the horn non-stop if anything happened to them. While Liz was putting gas in the tank, she could feel the dozen or so pairs of eyes staring at this jerk from Missouri standing in a dilapidated gas station pumping gas. Worst of all, Liz had on only a pair of skimpy shorts, a "cool" T-shirt and sandals. This was hardly the proper attire for this particular gas station.

After ten dollars of gas was in the car, Liz decided she had endured enough, and calmly put the pump handle up in its holder. In she walked to the cash register to pay. Then came the situation that put everything into perspective. On the counter sat three men, each over six feet tall, cleaning their fingernails with very large knives. The biggest one said, "That will be ten dollars." Liz politely handed him the

20-dollar bill. After waiting for what seemed to be an eternity, the tallest one mockingly said, "Whatcha waiting for?" Liz replied emphatically, "The change." All at once the three of them roared with laughter. It was then that the old school teacher in Liz came out. To her astonishment, she heard herself boldly stating, "Fork over the change." In an instant, the biggest one obeyed the command, and handed Liz the ten dollars change. About that time, Liz came to her senses and made an immediate escape to the safety of the car. Not running, just walking firmly and quickly.

Meanwhile, Charley had arrived at the door of the men's room in pain, with no patience of any kind left. To add insult to injury, a coin box blocked the entrance. Digging into his pocket, he located the necessary dime. To his total disgust, the dime did not open the box or the door. There he stood, so close and yet so far away. At that precise moment in time, the hair on the back of his neck began to bristle. He heard the unmistakable popping sound of a switchblade knife as it flashed open. Charley saw his whole life pass before him. Oh, if only he could have gone right instead of left at the Capitol. Then he heard a gruff voice saying, "It always sticks, man, just let me show you how it works." In a wink of an eye, the man had the lock picked, and the door opened. Even the stench of the room did not alter Charley's feeling of relief.

We met each other at the car doors, both moving at a quickened pace, and totally silent. Nothing had to be said to communicate what we had just been through. As we got into the car and rolled out of the gas station, both of us started talking at once, sharing each detail and emotion that was bound up inside of us. To our amazement, all three of us were still alive and safe. In the two hours that it took us to find our way back to the hotel, we exchanged stories, emotions, laughter, and relief. What could have been a horrible tale turned out to be one of those priceless experiences that married couples share, as they travel on their road of life together.

After experiences such as these, you can laugh or cry together for years to come, recounting each of those precious moments you have shared. Think of all the things you have experienced together and those you will share together in the years to come. These shared experiences add to the richness, fullness, and uniqueness of your marriage. Capitalize on this uniqueness, remembering that no two couples share the same set of experiences.

The second aspect of achieving two into one is compromising to form mutually agreeable decisions that both of you can support. One couple married for 43 years said it best, "Marriage is a compromise. Sometimes it is 50/50, sometimes it is 90/10 and sometimes it is 70/30. Sometimes it goes your way and sometimes it doesn't. That's just how it works." Developing in a marriage the threat-free environment needed to negotiate compromise is what makes it work over the years for successful couples.

Compromising and negotiating agreements are part of daily living in a marriage. We share the bed, the toothpaste, the car, the house, the kids and the bills. While this sounds so simple, it can cause some unusual challenges as the two individuals in a marriage have to discuss and work out mutually agreeable arrangements for such minor issues as who uses the shower first, which way the toilet paper goes on the holder, and what temperature the heat is set on, as well as for such major issues as where to live, when and if children will be a part of the family, and what car to purchase.

One of the funniest stories we have heard about learning to compromise came from a couple happily married for 38 years. It seems that Bradley and Cheryl both liked long showers in the morning. During the first few years of their marriage, Cheryl always got to the shower first in the morning and stayed there long enough to use most of the hot water. Bradley just figured he needed to adapt and put up with the last couple of minutes in lukewarm water to start his day. Things just progressed along in this fashion until one day Bradley had a terrific idea. He set his alarm clock five minutes early so he would beat Cheryl to the shower. It worked. He had a wonderful, long hot shower with no lukewarm water to start his day. He was in heaven. Cheryl, however, experienced lukewarm water for the first time. So, that night Cheryl set her alarm clock ten minutes early and made a quick dash into the bathroom as soon as she popped out of bed. Her long, hot shower was delightful and started her day out right. Bradley now was thinking about the issue. Should he continue to quietly accept Cheryl going first and using the hot water, should he just sit down and talk to her about it, or was there another solution? He decided to try setting his alarm a bit earlier one more day, but this time he wouldn't turn on any lights. That way, maybe he could get in and out of the shower before Cheryl even got out of bed. With his plan intact, he fell blissfully asleep.

As soon as the alarm rang, Bradley jumped quietly out of bed and headed straight for the shower. No sooner then he turned on the water in the dark, he felt Cheryl approaching from behind. There she stood, stark naked ready to hop into the shower. This stuck both of them as so funny that they could not stop laughing, even when Bradley pulled Cheryl into the shower with him. The laughing only stopped when they engaged in another type of "activity" together. Needless to say, Bradley left the sentence hanging without further description of the activity in which they engaged. We can tell you that Cheryl was blushing brightly from Bradley's glance while he was telling us this part of their story. Watching them, our imaginations had no trouble figuring out the activity.

Bradley and Cheryl said that evening they talked at length about their stubbornness and inability to sit down and talk about finding a compromise with the shower issue. They laughed long and hard as they told us that for the life of them they still can't figure out why they didn't just sit down and talk about it the way they do now. Cheryl said it was a lesson they just needed to learn. Neither one of them had good role models for marriage in their own families, so they had to learn a lot of things the hard way—by making mistakes and together learning from them. They have learned the hard way to trust each other and talk about any issues bothering them until they come to a compromise they both can live with.

Compromising and sharing require trust. To trust we must share. Sharing is a critical part of turning two into one for successful couples.

The third aspect of learning to turn two into one so you can dance the tango with great synergy and togetherness is achieved through mutual helpfulness and support for each other. Those in the best marriages we have observed over the years have made mutual helpfulness and support for each other so much a natural part of who they are that the beauty and grace of their tango can be seen by all.

Our hero, Dr. Leo Buscaglia, in commenting on the importance of loving relationships, once said, "When I take you into my life, I have four legs, four arms, four hands, two wonderful bodies, and two heads. I also double my chances for joy, love, and wonderment." Leo really defined, in our estimation, the concept of helpfulness in a marriage. Helpfulness in a marriage means essentially this … being there by your spouse's side as often as you can, to share her burden.

Just think, if you share your partner's burden, neither of you will have to work as hard. In a marriage, both the burdens and joys of living should be carried on four shoulders. When you help someone, you are making it easier for him to survive. You are sharing his labor.

Successful marriages embrace this team effort approach to life. The marriage partners have developed a kind of helping relationship that remains constant throughout everything they do. It has been nurtured and developed over the years they have spent together, until they truly act with one hand and one heart.

We found that these successful marriage partners do not lose their own individual identities by forming these close bonds of helpfulness, but rather their own identities seem to grow stronger and fuller. Both partners work to bring out the best in their spouse, by enhancing their feelings of confidence and self-worth. They become each other's strongest supporter. Where would a team be without fans? Without support, a team has no reason to continue to play. So it is with marriage. Without the support that a loving spouse can provide to her partner, there would be no reason to continue on with the relationship.

In a marital relationship, helping and supporting your spouse is, perhaps, the ultimate form of love. In the 43 years we have been married, perhaps no story best illustrates the art of helping better than a story from a very tragic period of time in our lives together.

Back in 1968, we discovered the meaning of the word "helpfulness." At the time, we were living in a mobile home that we bought by selling our motorcycle to make the down payment. Liz was a junior cost analyst for the University of Missouri system and Charley was a high school history teacher. Needless to say, like everyone else we were experiencing the typical difficulties with having enough money to pay all of our bills each month. However, we didn't care because we had each other and the thrill of knowing that we would soon be parents, since Liz was pregnant.

Over a period of the next several weeks our world started to fall apart. Charley was drafted by Uncle Sam to serve in Vietnam. Because of the uncertainty of his military status, Charley had to resign his teaching position effective at the end of the academic year. Charley losing his job and getting drafted at the height of the Vietnam War was hard enough on our marriage, but the most devastating situation occurred just two days after Charley received his draft notice. What started out as a routine delivery turned into our worst nightmare. The baby contracted a serious viral infection she just didn't have the strength to fight. Instead of celebrating parenthood, we had to find a way to deal with the loss of our baby girl. All of this happened over a one-week period. God Almighty, why were these bad things happening to such good people? What had we done so wrong to deserve this kind of punishment?

We had a choice to make. Either we could let events shape our lives or we could endeavor to shape our own lives. We choose the latter. But before we could get a handle on our lives another unfortunate negative circumstance raised its ugly head. When Charley took his physical for the Army, the doctors discovered he had a heart murmur of sufficient magnitude to endanger his life. As you might guess, Charley failed his physical exam. Now he did not have a job, was concerned about his health problems, and was stricken with grief over the death of his baby girl.

What in the world does a couple do when their seemingly wonderful life together is beginning to resemble the sinking of the Lusitania? You begin by helping and supporting each other. We discovered at that point of our young marriage, the only way we were going to survive was to count on each other. We shared responsibility for each other's lives to a degree that we did not think possible. There was hardly a thing we did not help each other with. When one of us broke down the other one was there standing strong to lean on for support. Throughout the next year we cannot remember who broke down the most or who provided the most support. What we can remember is that we just passed the roles back and forth as the moments of challenge came and went. Little by little we were able to move forward with our lives.

Liz returned to school to finish her bachelor's degree while she continued to work full time. Since there were no teaching jobs available by the time Charley was free to apply for a job, he returned to school to continue his graduate program full time and worked as a graduate assistant at the university. Studying became a team effort as we learned and grew together. Even the sharing of household duties took on a team approach. Everything was viewed in terms of "we," as together we regained our health, both physically and emotionally. We learned the true meaning of the word "helpfulness." The lessons we learned in 1968 shall guide our lives today as we look forward to reaching and celebrating our Golden Anniversary together.

In a successful marriage, you literally assist and support each other with everything, from healing emotional trauma to cleaning the house. The helpfulness we displayed then will always be a part of our relationship with each other. Perhaps the Paul Williams song says it best: "It's you and me against the world. Sometimes it seems like you and me against the world."

Your marriage is not complete unless you and your spouse help each other by sharing together the burdens and challenges the world puts before you. Sometimes, just sometimes, this is the only way couples can survive. With the understanding of how important it is to share life's burdens with your partner comes the foundation for a life-long team effort that makes for a successful marriage.

Sometimes helpfulness can also turn into some of the most humorous moments in a marriage. Sally and Rusty said that right after they built their first home they decided to finish the basement themselves. Did you ever try to put drywall on the ceiling by yourself? Frankly, it is not easy. As a matter of fact, it is darn near impossible. As you might have guessed, they needed to help each other. Rusty is 6 foot 3. Standing on tiptoes, he could raise one end of the drywall to the ceiling … but what about the other end? Well, Sally is also tall, but 5 foot 9 is not tall enough to be too helpful when you have to reach an 8-foot ceiling.

The discovery of this dilemma was quick in coming. How could they hold the drywall up high enough to nail it to the ceiling? They would build a "T" out of 2 by 4s. The engineering feat was simple and spectacular. Rusty would stand on a chair and pick up one end of the drywall. Sally would raise the other end with the "T." Up went Rusty's end … up went Sally's end. The first piece of drywall went up smooth as silk. This helping stuff was great! Then it happened, as Sally looked around to see how Rusty was doing with the second piece of drywall, she spun the "T" around, striking Rusty smack in the head. Instantly, he fell to the floor, drywall and all. Dazed and shaken, he just lay there staring up at Sally. For several moments he wasn't sure where he was or what exactly happened. However, the look of fear and concern on Sally's face was enough to tell him it wasn't good. Sally just kept asking him if he was all right, in between her apologies. Luckily for Rusty, he said he had a hard head. Within a couple of minutes he was sitting up. As Sally kept apologizing and worrying about his head, the humor in the situation suddenly struck him. Rusty burst into laughter imagining just how silly he must have looked getting hit in the head by his wife with a 2 by 4 "T" they built to hold up the drywall. As he sat there laughing, Sally just kept apologizing. The more she apologized, the funnier Rusty thought it was. They told us that they spent the next ten minutes replaying the situation and couldn't stop laughing. In fact, to this day, they still chuckle when they think about Sally's drywalling helpfulness. Even though helping has its risks, successful couples would still prefer to help each other with most of the things they do than not to have helped at all.

Just like Sally and Rusty, we have gotten so much in the habit of helping each other that it is now second nature. Thank goodness it is. If we did not have this type of relationship, a man would be dead today.

Several years ago, we had our little speedboat out on the Lake of the Ozarks. It was one of those beautiful days when the sun sets over the water in such a way that you would swear that you must have died and gone to heaven. Wow, was it beautiful that day. Quite honestly, there could not be anything prettier than the sun setting over the Lake of the Ozarks on a lovely Missouri summer day!

We felt so good we decided to stop by some friends' house to say hello. After a couple good, cold glasses of iced tea, we decided to hop in our boat and head back to our cabin. Just as we got in the boat, one of the ladies yelled for us to come up to their cottage immediately. There was enough panic in her voice to suggest that something was seriously wrong. Running up the catwalk as fast as we could, we heard more screaming and yelling coming from the cottage. Up the stairs we bolted. When we arrived in the kitchen we saw the whole group staring at the floor with a look of horror in their eyes. One of the guests was lying on the kitchen floor. He was as blue as the lake water on a clear day. Obviously, he was dying or perhaps already dead.

As Mighty Mouse used to say, here we come to save the day. They had already called 911, but we knew the rescue team would never arrive in time to save him. So, we rolled him over to get a good grasp and picked him up. He weighted well over 250 pounds, so it was a struggle even for the two of us. Charley gave him the Heimlich hug, thinking that he had a piece of food stuck in his throat. One, two, three, four, five, thrusts upwards from under his rib cage made no difference. We laid him on the floor face down. Liz stuck her fingers down his throat and swept the mouth for obstructions. Nothing seemed to be lodged or in any way blocking his airway. We turned him over on his back … still no pulse. Liz tilted his head back and listened for breathing—nothing. Liz quickly pounded on his chest for any type of reaction. She hit him so hard his wife started screaming, "Please don't hit him anymore. He's dead. Don't hurt him anymore." Liz, of course, ignored her.

In the meantime, Charley was shaking his legs and, in general, doing everything possible to get his blood circulating. The ambulance was still at least ten minutes away, so we began C.P.R. in earnest. Charley started the chest compressions to Liz's counting rhythm, 1, 2, 3, 4, 5, … 30. Then Liz tilted his head back, covered his nose and gave two quick breaths into his mouth. Together we shared the duties and

C.P.R. cadence for each motion. We worked on him for what seemed like an eternity. Both of us were showing signs of fatigue and were just about to switch positions when finally, it happened. He started coughing, choking, vomiting, and then breathing on his own. Five minutes later, the deep blue skin color was fading into a pale pink hue and he was sitting up. Five minutes after that he was standing. Lord Almighty, we had just saved a man's life. What a wonderful feeling. We had gotten so used to helping each other we just did what came naturally to us. On the boat ride home, we held hands, satisfied that our actions had saved a man's life. We did it together by helping each other, as usual. When you help your spouse, you make it easier for her to exist … you make it easier for you to exist … you make it easier for others to exist.

This kind of helping relationship between two people does not just happen. It has to be nurtured and developed. The more each partner helps the other, the better each of you become at helping. When you both have mastered the art of helping to its fullest, you will find that you have a team effort in most of the things that you do. This team effort forms one of the foundational pillars for a strong marriage, in which life can become easier and more enjoyable for both of you.

Another aspect of helping is the assignment and acceptance of roles in a marriage. Is your marriage characterized by stereotypical roles? Does she clean the house, make the beds, cook the meals, take care of the children, clear the dishes after a meal, and do the shopping? Does he cut the grass, wash the car, carry in the wood for the fireplace, read the paper after a meal, and make the big decisions? If your answer to these questions is generally yes, you need to examine this critical aspect of your marriage. Roles assigned in a marriage according to gender alone generally have not proven successful in enduring marriages. Of course, only mother can breast feed the baby. However, if the baby is fed from a bottle, why can't dad also do the feeding? If dad works outside the home and mom stays home, or vice versa, then certain roles need to be assigned out of necessity. Unfortunately, however, roles in a marriage are often assigned on the basis of gender stereotypes alone without analyzing what works best for both partners. What's wrong with that, you say! We're glad you asked.

We've discovered that your real strength lies in what you are and not what others want you to be. When you stereotype in a marriage, you are assigning roles that, in effect, take away from the strength of each individual. There is an old proverb that says, "Carrying life's burdens on four shoulders is easier than carrying them on two." Hence, the burdens of a marriage are lighter if you both carry them equally. You double your opportunity for joy when you can share the joy of your partner as well as your own.

While much has been made in the media over the last 20 years about women's rights and equality in the work place, unfortunately very little has changed on the home front in many marriages. All too often we hear horror stories from dual career marriages when the husband is so wrapped up in his career that he doesn't even realize that his wife is somehow trying to manage both a career and all of the household chores by herself.

On the other hand, a common characteristic ran through all of the successful dual career marriages we studied. They learned to rely on each other's talents to share and accomplish all of the household chores needed to maintain their daily lives and succeed in their careers. While sharing and becoming a team sounds so simple and easy to work out between the two of you, it has proven difficult even for some of the long-time happily married couples we interviewed.

Sammy and Pam are a perfect example. They spoke with us earnestly about their struggles early in their marriage with managing dual careers and still finding a way to get all of the tasks accomplished, such as paying the bills, cleaning the house, doing the wash, etc.

As they tell it, this was the one issue that had them thinking seriously that they were not going to make it together.

When Sammy and Pam first got married in 1964, women were just beginning to demand equality in the work place and the cultural expectations were still strong for women to focus on the home and child rearing. Pam was an exception to every stereotypic rule, and fiercely independent. She was fascinated with architecture in high school and was the only girl in her mechanical drawing classes as well as in most of her higher-level mathematics classes. Pam assumed when she entered college in Boston, there would surely be many more girls with her same burning desire to pursue a career in architecture. What she found was the same situation in college as she faced in high school. Again, Pam was the only girl in almost every class related to her chosen field of architecture.

Pam battled her way through the program in spite of the odds and into the world of designing structures magnificent enough to have a lasting impact and for future generations to use and enjoy. This was very important to her, since she grew up in Boston admiring the architectural boldness and beauty of the historic Trinity Church in Copley Square. Its breathtaking interior, with the arches, curves, and LaFarge stained glass windows, was fascinating to her even as a child. Every time she was discouraged by the challenges of her chosen career, she would think about the genius who created such a magnif-icent structure as the Trinity Church, and it inspired her to continue. In fact, it pushed her to seek her first job at a major architectural com-pany rather than settling for a small company that wouldn't provide her with the opportunities she desired to create a lasting impact on the cityscape of her beloved Boston with her beautiful and gracefully designed buildings.

When she met Sammy, she had been a successful architect for more than three years. Pam was making it in a male-dominated field because of her talents and total love for her work. She had little interest in any type of romantic entanglement. However, that suddenly changed after her first candlelight dinner with Sammy.

While Pam continued to love her work, she also fell madly in love with Sammy. He was a department manager for a large downtown department store and seemed to be on the fast track to running the company. Yet, he took her career ambitions seriously and encouraged her to excel. The two of them were instantly good for each other. Their courtship lasted only six months before they were setting a wedding date. It was a complete whirlwind affair. They explained that throughout their romance everything just seemed to be torn right out of the pages of a best-selling romance novel. Their family and friends all decided that theirs was truly a match made in heaven.

Pam and Sammy moved into their beautiful home just two weeks after the honeymoon. They seemed to be just bubbling with excitement all of the time. Pam was influential in finding an older home that had undergone recent renovations to modernize the appliances and electrical and mechanical systems without altering the lovely architectural features of its historical period. Both Sammy and Pam truly loved the old home and the neighborhood around it. They considered themselves the luckiest couple in the world.

However, even before they could celebrate their first wedding anniversary, the stress began to mount. Sammy and Pam were not only pushing hard to excel at work, they now had to figure out how to find time for each other and all the tasks that had to be done to maintain their new home life. Pam was trying diligently to be a superwoman at work and at home. She had always felt that she had to work twice as hard as anyone else because she competed daily with the other 14 architects in the firm, all of whom were male. Pam could not let go of the feeling that she had something to prove. So, this new added pressure of an expectation to maintain the household was just naturally something she took on without even thinking about it. Isn't that what her mother had done so beautifully when she was growing up? Funny thing though, Pam forgot that her mother never worked outside of the home. She never had to balance the responsibilities of two completely separate roles.

Day after day, Pam would rush home from work to fix dinner, clean the home, do the shopping, do the wash, pay the bills, etc. Then, she would finish the architectural drawings she needed to meet with her clients before the next day. Sleep was a thing of the past. The harder she tried, the more Sammy kept telling her how wonderful she was and how lucky he was to find her. Pam couldn't stand to disappoint him, so she worked even harder to make everything perfect while trying to hide her growing stress level. Her boiling point was simmering just below the surface.

As anyone might have guessed, they didn't even make it a full year before Pam collapsed. She caught a nasty virus and missed almost two weeks of work. The doctor gave her a lecture about getting enough sleep, eating right, and taking some time for herself. Pam almost laughed in his face. That was just not possible with her commitments. By the end of the first week of Pam's virus, Sammy had begun doing the wash, fixing the meals, cleaning the house, etc. Pam realized that everything was getting done on the home front and she didn't have a thing to do with it. It made her feel immediately guilty. She was failing as a wife. What would Sammy think? What would her family think? She couldn't even manage the house and her job?

Without discussion or even much thought, when Pam was well enough to return to work she attempted to pick up right where she left off with managing the household. Unfortunately, Pam found herself completely overwhelmed by the work she had missed while she was sick. It was all she could do to get caught up. Clients were depending upon her for their drawings before they could begin their construction projects. She could not let them down, so the house began to slip miserably. Sammy and Pam began arguing and blaming each other on a daily basis. Even though everyone who knew Pam considered her to be an unbelievably strong person, Pam found herself close to tears most of the time. The tension between Sammy and Pam began to escalate until the inevitable explosion came. Incredibly, both Sammy and Pam could recall the episode and all of the details leading up to it as if it were yesterday, in spite of the fact that it had occurred nearly 44 years ago.

They received several overdue bill notices on the same Friday that the vacuum cleaner gave out, the roof sprang a leak, and their best friends were coming to dinner. Nothing in the house had been done during the week, since the household work was Pam's domain and she had been working with an exceptionally demanding client. She had completely redone the building drawings for the client three times.

Sammy knew better than to try to offer to clean the house or help with dinner because that inevitably caused Pam to feel defensive, which always resulted in an immediate argument with no winners. That evening you could cut the tension between them with a knife. Somehow, Pam and Sammy managed to survive the dinner without making complete fools out of themselves. But, the very second the door closed behind their guests, they both exploded into yelling and screaming insults about the situation and each other. Pam could not hide her frustration and stress any longer. All of the pressure over the last year erupted suddenly to the surface. Sammy explained how he was completely disappointed with her and how embarrassed he was about the bills and the condition of the house. When Pam broke into tears sobbing uncontrollably, Sammy suggested that she take a few days off work and get things in order. Little did he know what he had just stepped into. Instead of taking the suggestion as help, Pam let him have it about the importance of her work as an architect and how she could not just take off to attend to the house. Then the inevitable question came from Pam, why didn't he just take a few days off? It hit him hard, since he was on his way up in the company and could not even consider taking a few days off. What was she thinking?

Finally, after an hour or so of getting all of the yelling, screaming, and crying out of their systems, they grabbed a bottle of wine and began to talk in earnest. Long into the early dawn hours on that cold, misty night they continued to talk about what had happened to their perfect marriage; about their expectations before getting married; about the grind of trying to manage life; and of course, about Pam's need to do everything by herself and to do it perfectly. Sammy explained how he was afraid to tread on her territory by doing any of the household chores and admitted for the first time that he really kind of enjoyed doing some of the chores. He also said that he would love to help her, but knew that it wasn't something a man should do. Pam didn't know what to say. For the rest of the weekend, they talked non-stop about potential solutions. They came up with a solution that was pretty radical for couples in the 1960s—they would share the load. Each would take a part of the responsibilities and make sure that they offered to help the other during especially difficult times at work. To this day, they continue to share the responsibilities and never forget to ask for help when they are struggling at work. Sammy and Pam agreed that this had been the most challenging obstacle in their long marriage. Even now, nearly 44 years later after the explosion, both of them still feel the pain they experienced during the first year of their marriage—a pain that would have led to the end of their beautiful relationship if they had not worked out a lasting solution.

Remember, you have to put their story into perspective—this was 1965. Expectations for women were quite different in the 1960s. The household management and care was a woman's responsibility and it was almost impossible to secure outside help unless you were rich. If a man ever discussed in public taking on those roles, he was referred to instantly as a sissy or worse. So, their solution was shockingly different for couples in that era. Today, it is just a natural solution if dual career marriages have any chance of success.

We communicate positive messages to our spouses when we offer to share their burdens. However, we take away from their strengths by stereotyping and placing limitations on them. We are communicating to them this message: "You are only capable of performing the roles you have been assigned." When we share roles we have more time to communicate ... to be with each other. We have more time for each other.

Helpfulness has a way of communicating love all by itself. The very nature of being helpful expresses the caring and love you feel for your spouse. What better way to express your love than by making life easier for the one you love the most? As the team approach becomes a habit in your marriage, you and your spouse will learn to dance your own tango. The beauty and grace of the tango danced by the successful couples we studied over the years is to be admired. They turned two into one elegantly through their sharing, compromising, and mutual support for each other.

— *Advice* —

The more we learn about successful couples achieving two into one, the more we are convinced that a great marriage ceases to form if the husband and wife do not attain that feeling of "WE" as a unit of "ONE." It is imperative that marriage partners learn how to share and practice it on a routine basis. Equally as important is learning the art of compromise and negotiation to form mutually agreeable decisions that both partners can support. We hope that the following advice will help you and your spouse learn how to develop an excellent sharing and supportive relationship that achieves two into one, so you can dance the tango with great synergy and togetherness as if you are one.

1. **Use the seven-week program for developing ongoing sharing in your marriage that we have placed in the Appendix (p. 282).** If you will follow the plan laid out in this sharing program, it will only take you about 30 minutes a week to establish a pattern of sharing with your spouse. Maybe the two of you will get so excited about the ideas that you will find you both want to spend a lot more than 30 minutes a week on sharing. Soon you won't even need the inventory to start sharing. All you two will need is the time to share with each other about yourselves, your perceptions, your fears, your hopes, your dreams, and your loves. This is one area where practice does make perfect. Learning to share is simply a matter of regular practice.

2. **Share your own personal expertise and interests with your spouse and learn about the special expertise and interests of your spouse.** Help your mate to feel the love you feel for your special talents or interests. That does not mean that he has to know everything that you know. It only means that you need to take the time to share your knowledge and enthusiasm for your special interests with your spouse. It also follows that you need to

learn about the special talents or interests of your spouse. Find out as much as you can as quickly as you can.

Find the common interests you already have or develop new interests with your spouse. If you started your marriage with common interests, that's terrific. Talk about them. Grow the common bonds. On the other hand, if you started out in your marriage without much in common, then put in the hard work needed to develop those common interests. The investment of time early in your marriage to find and develop common interests will pay great dividends and help carry you through those inevitable rough times.

Think about your unique moments and memories together. Laugh often and much with each other as you think about these unique experiences that only the two of you can fully appreciate. These are the things that bind you together and make your marriage so special.

3. **Sharing is trust.** To trust we must share. To share we must trust. Communicate trust to your partner, for only then can either of you truly experience the sharing relationship needed to achieve two into one. When you make a promise, keeping that promise builds trust and allows for continued sharing. Trust can take a long time to build and very little time to lose. When sharing occurs on a daily basis, the opportunity is greater to build lasting trust.

   Sharing can make your marriage a rich, exciting, and rewarding experience. Life holds so many treasures and burdens that can only be truly enjoyed with a partner whom you totally trust. Take the time to stop and look back over those wonderful times you have shared together and continue with each experience to add more joy to your marriage. There is no other person in the world that knows better than you what you two have shared over your years together. Make those memories special, whether they are good or bad. All of your experiences are to be valued and learned from as a part of building trust in each other. When you do, you are building a trust that forms the foundation for achieving the two into one found in successful marriages.

4. **Compromise is a part of daily living in a marriage.** Discuss how the two of you make decisions. Establish a plan to work through important issues until the two of you can find a mutually agreeable solution. Each partner has to give a little to have a smooth and balanced relationship. No one can have it all his way. When you share a marriage, you must learn the art of compromise—giving a little to gain a lot. Build trust with your spouse once the mutually agreed upon decision has been reached through your full support of that decision.

5. **Carry the burdens of your marriage on four shoulders, not just two.** It is better to have tried to help than not to have helped at all. Helpfulness should become such a matter of habit that you will feel and act like a winning team. Both of you individually are good, but the two of you together working well make for a dynamite team. You will truly experience first hand the notion of one hand, one heart. By sharing, each of you will carry a lighter load—that is for sure.

Learn to help solve your problems together. The old saying that two heads are better than one is very true in a marriage. Ideas that the two of you generate can be better than most ideas generated alone. Just as with the teamwork you use to accomplish all of the routine responsibilities for the household, use the same approach to problem solving. Provide a sounding board for your spouse to try out ideas and solutions in a non-judgmental atmosphere.

Learn to sense when your spouse needs help, even when she does not ask for it. Those are the moments your spouse needs you the most. Learn about the outside stress your spouse is dealing with and when your help can make a difference in his attitude by relieving some part of the stress for him. Learn to recognize the verbal and non-verbal warning signs of stress until you feel like you have a "sixth sense" to know when your spouse is in need. Then be on the alert to watch for her signals.

It is especially important to watch for signals of stress in your spouse during particularly difficult times. That's the time to provide that positive support and encouragement. It is a wonderful feeling to know that you can count on your spouse when life's road gets rough. Successfully married couples talk about the importance of always being able to count on their spouses for moral support when they are down in the dumps.

6. **Decide the roles each of you will fill in your marriage.** Roles should be determined by your strengths, not by using the stereotypic "proper roles" society considers are for the wife or for the husband. Make a list of each of the routine responsibilities that need to be accomplished and then talk about each of your strengths and desires as well as your time commitments. Work out responsibilities that each of you can accomplish well, so that no one is overloaded with work. In long-time marriages, successful couples report that the load balance changes and shifts with the outside burdens from work, relatives, illness, or other circumstances pertaining to one spouse or the other. From time to time one spouse can carry a greater share of the burden until such a time when things can come back into

balance. The point is, every couple has to find equilibrium, where neither partner is carrying a heavier load of responsibilities. Periodically sit down together and talk about the ways the two of you could help each other. Confide in your spouse what things you really could use help with. The more that each of you knows about the other's burdens, the better chance you both will have to successfully help each other.

7. **Be the number one cheerleader for your spouse.** Support your spouse in every way that you can. Let your partner know just how important she is to you and to the rest of the world. Give her encouragement in everything that she does. It will help enhance her feelings of success. And as you know, nothing builds success like success. Perhaps the best help that you can give your spouse is to give him the confidence he needs to become all that he can be in everything that he endeavors to do. Be your spouse's strongest supporter. Become her cheerleader. Help her reach heights she never thought imaginable. Remember that when your spouse reaches the top of the mountain, you will be standing there with her.

In a sense, the concept of *It Takes Two to Tango* is the essence of successful marriages. A marriage is the joining of two people who work together as a team, sharing everything, and always supporting each other. It is the main reason why successfully married couples cannot imagine life without their spouses. Successfully married couples have grown to rely on each other for friendship, encouragement, help, and support. They have truly mastered in their relationships the beauty and grace of the tango dancers we watched in Buenos Aires, Argentina.

C H A P T E R   8

Seven Surprising Secrets #2: No Sacred Cows

*Successful couples cherish the fact that they have the freedom
and security to talk about anything without fear of reprisal
in their relationships. They report that they don't
know how they would survive the stresses of life
if they couldn't talk about everything
with their spouses.*

*I*N SUCCESSFUL MARRIAGES there are
No Sacred Cows. Simply speaking, happily married couples talk about
everything. All subjects are fair game. They trust each other. They rely
on each other's good judgment. They depend upon each other for
truth and straight talk. They share insights about everything—the
good, the bad, and the ugly. They are each other's best friends.

Talking is one of the favorite pastimes in healthy and happy
marriages. But when it comes to talking about those sacred cows, such

as their fears, things they dislike, what makes them angry with their spouses, or differences in child rearing practices, the natural instinct is to clam up. However, this approach will not work if you want your marriage to survive and thrive. Successful couples are willing to risk arguing about the things that matter and even hurting each other's feelings by telling the truth, because they know it is worth it. They have developed the trust needed to make sure there are no sacred cows in their marriages.

As we listened to each couple's description of their relationship, it seemed as if they were describing a life-long friendship built upon trust and support rather than any particular focus on the romantic part of their marriage. How did the relationship develop into a supportive friendship? Was it always that way or did it develop over time? These were questions we sought answers to as we listened intently to their stories. All of the couples explained that their friendships deepened over time as they worked to listen effectively and understand what their spouses were saying and truly meaning. Very carefully each couple explained to us that the romance in their marriage was a beautiful part of it, but their friendship and support for each other made all things possible.

So how do those relationships of life-long friendship develop for happily married couples? Throughout the thousands of interviews, successful couples reported a powerful constellation of notions that worked together to form the characteristic of *No Sacred Cows*— talking, listening, understanding, observing, and remembering. Each is critically important before a successful marriage can have *No Sacred Cows*.

First of all, it follows that marriage partners must learn to effectively talk with each other. Talking, like any other skill, doesn't necessarily come naturally, but once you've learned the basic rules of talking you have to practice, practice, practice. You can't talk today and not talk tomorrow. You can't talk about this but not talk about that.

Great conversations occur in an environment that is non-threatening, non-judgmental, and empathic. In the proper environment, constant practice will lead you and your spouse to a point where there are *No Sacred Cows* in your marriage because you have met a prerequisite for discussing those *sacred cows*—effective listening to the spoken words and non-verbal cues with true understanding. When this happens in your relationship, you will find the companionship that long-time happily married couples have found with each other. Successful couples cherish the fact that they have the freedom and security to talk about anything without fear of reprisal in their relationships. They report that they don't know how they would survive the stresses of life if they couldn't talk about everything with their spouses.

Finding the right conditions and setting the stage for good conversation is also important. We have our best talks walking hand in hand around our neighborhood. We often head off to Starbucks or one of the nearby cafés with our Wonder Dog, Jake. All of the problems of the world seem solvable when we sit at a small outdoor table with a cappuccino or a glass of wine and engage in meaningful conversation. These are the times when we don't bring a cell phone, don't let anyone else know where we are, and don't let anything interfere with our conversations. And our dog, Jake, is always the consummate gentleman. He never interjects a negative word about even our wildest ideas. He just wags his tail, showing appreciation for everything we've said.

One of our other special places to talk is on our backyard patio on those crisp fall evenings or cold winter nights in Missouri. Sitting there, gazing at the stars on a crystal clear night, just inspires great conversation. This is where some of our best thinking and our most helpful discussions have occurred over the years. Wherever you find a special place that inspires deep and honest conversation, gravitate to it again and again until those conversations are part of the very fabric of everyday existence for you and your spouse.

One of the successful couples we interviewed learned the hard lessons about attentive listening and talking early in their marriage. During their first ten years of marriage, Carlos had talked with Irene many times about visiting his native country of Argentina. He dreamed of walking down Calle Florida to the Casa Rosada where Eva Peron once stood on the balcony waving to her adoring public. Among the crowds back then were his own parents, with Carlos cradled in his mother's arms. His childhood was filled with tales of Eva Peron and her generosity to the poor. Carlos yearned to see all of the places he had been to as an infant with his parents. All he knew about those places came from his family's oral history.

While Irene listened intently to all of Carlos' ramblings about Argentina, she lacked the real desire to travel to Buenos Aires, Argentina, because of the instability of their government back then. However, Irene was content to let Carlos talk, never thinking he might seriously be considering that type of trip. The Falklands/Malvinas war had recently been lost by Argentina to Great Britain and President Alfonsin did not have the military establishment under control. In Irene's mind, all she had to do was hear Carlos out without protesting or starting into an argument over his idealistic vision of his homeland. What Irene didn't realize was that Carlos interpreted her quiet listening as her approval of the trip. And sure enough, with what he thought was confirmation, Carlos began planning the trip of his dreams. He and Irene would actually stand in the Plaza de Mayo where his mother listened to Eva Peron. He realized that he had wanted to be there his whole life.

Over the next several weeks, he gathered every bit of travel information he could about Buenos Aires. He found airline time schedules, hotel locations, city transportation information, immunization requirements, and costs for everything. Carlos knew the costs would be tough, but they could manage.

With the excitement of a child presenting his first report to the class, Carlos shared all of his new knowledge with Irene. It was only then that Irene began to actively listen. Carlos was serious about going to Buenos Aires. What she thought was just more of his ramblings turned out to be honest conversation about his true yearning to visit his birthplace. Irene didn't want to anger Carlos, so she never told him what she was thinking—that he was absolutely out of his mind to consider traveling to a country in such terrible political turmoil just to see where he was born. She never expressed to Carlos that every time he talked about Argentina and Eva Peron it sounded more like a fairy tale than any story about Argentina that she had read. The *sacred cow*—her real feelings about the instability of Argentina—now had to be unearthed and put out in the open in a potentially cruel and brutally honest way. What could have been easily discussed years ago was now going to come as a total shock to Carlos.

Irene didn't know how to start so she just blurted out, "Wait, this is crazy, let's talk about this." Not the best approach to exposing a *sacred cow*! The shocked look on Carlos's face told the entire story. Because Irene had remained silent all those years, Carlos was totally dumbfounded when she began protesting the trip of his dreams.

After hours of arguments, tears, blaming, and apologies, Carlos and Irene agreed not to take the trip to Buenos Aires until the political situation settled down. That day, Irene and Carlos had learned the hard lessons about *No Sacred Cows*. They said from then on they talked about anything and everything and were always honest with each other about their feelings, even if it was potentially an emotional or difficult subject for them.

By the way, Carlos and Irene finally made that trip to Buenos Aires a couple of years ago. They told us it was one of the highlights of their 31 years together. They stayed at the Plaza Hotel at the entrance to Calle Florida for an entire week. The first thing they did was stroll down Calle Florida all the way to Plaza de Mayo. They stood staring at the actual balcony where Eva Peron once stood. The rest of the week Carlos and Irene visited all of the places Carlos had heard about from his parents. Even though he had lost most of his ability to speak his native language, the people of Argentina were gracious and welcoming to these two Americans. When Carlos explained that he was born in Buenos Aires and left as a small boy, they were instantly accepted as family. With the description they gave about their trip and the people of Buenos Aires, it was little wonder Carlos and Irene experienced such wonderful satisfaction with having learned the lessons over 20 years ago about keeping *No Sacred Cows* in their marriage.

Taking into consideration all of the non-verbal signals you are giving off, as well as those of your spouse, is just as important as listening to the words being spoken before you can talk about those *sacred cows*. Did you ever listen to someone talk to you, but what he or she said didn't match her body language? For example, did you ever ask your spouse if he wanted to go out to a movie, and he said yes even though his facial expression told you he would really rather stay home? Or what about this one—you ask your spouse a series of questions and she responds with head nods. So, you ask her some off-the-wall question. "I traded the new car in for a bicycle today. Is that okay with you?" The head still continues to nod approval. It's clear she is not listening because you know her answer should have been an emphatic No!

So many terrific stories over the years have been told to us that beautifully illustrate the importance of listening to the words being spoken as well as the non-verbal cues. After much deliberation, we finally settled on two of our favorites to share with you. The first one came to our attention recently at a party. Since we've been writing this book, a lot of successfully married couples have wanted to share their personal stories with us. The story that follows is one of our favorites because both of us have known many individuals like Darla and understood why Bob finally reacted the way he did.

In the seventh year of their marriage, Bob and Darla had an experience that changed their relationship forever. In a general sense, they had a good marriage. However, one of the problems they had in the early years of their marriage centered around communication. Bob is a quiet sort of fellow, rarely speaks except when spoken to and then only occasionally. On the other hand, Darla talks all the time. If you didn't talk to her, she would talk to herself. She would carry on for hours whether someone was listening or not. As you might guess, Bob rarely found a way to get a word in edgewise. Early in their marriage he tried to participate in conversations with Darla but to no avail. Darla didn't listen anyway. So, Bob became increasingly silent. It didn't seem to bother Darla, but it sure was beginning to bother Bob.

To illustrate his frustration, Bob told us the following story. Every week for seven years, Darla would fix Bob tuna casserole. It was Bob's favorite, thought Darla. She never really asked him or watched his body language when she served the casserole; she just decided to make that decision for him. Only one problem, Bob absolutely hated tuna casserole. He always had and always would! He never communicated his dislike to Darla because he thought she probably wouldn't hear him anyway. He just slumped his shoulders and ate bite after bite just to satisfy his hunger. Well, on one Friday evening, Bob had decided that enough was enough! No more tuna casserole would pass through his lips!

After eating a bite or two, Bob turned his plate over on the table, leaped from his chair, and shouted, "I hate tuna casserole!" Darla heard him, make no mistake about that. She was shocked. "Why didn't you tell me you didn't like tuna casserole?" she asked. To which Bob replied, "Would you have listened when you didn't even notice that I hated each bite?" You see, the tuna casserole was a symbol of Bob's frustration with Darla's habit of doing all of the talking and none of the listening or observing the non-verbal cues. For the next hour, Bob let Darla have it with both barrels. He was sick and tired of all of their communication being one-way. If she wouldn't listen to him, he would find someone who would.

Isn't it a real shame that Bob allowed his frustration level to wear on for those first seven years? You bet. Bob should have confronted his concerns long before his frustration built up to such an explosive level. At any rate, Bob and Darla have had two-way communication with each other for the past 25 years. It was a hard lesson for them to learn, but they learned it together. Bob and Darla told us they started talking about everything—and they listened and understood each other. Bob admitted to being just as responsible as Darla for the results of the first seven frustrating years of their marriage. If he'd had a heart to heart conversation with Darla sooner, the patterns of behavior could certainly have been altered for the better.

Speaking of the need for heart to heart conversations, we have a dandy little story to tell you that we could hardly believe when Ted told us. It seems Ted and Diane decided they would build a new house. Or, we should say, Ted decided to build a new house! He picked out a pretty little piece of land only 500 yards from the house where he and Diane currently lived. The view was spectacular. Everywhere Ted looked, there were tall oak trees. In the morning, the dew would sparkle on the leaves of the trees in such a way that they looked like thousands of diamonds dancing across the valley. You could see horses grazing on the luscious green grass. All around, the sweet smell of clean air. Oh, what a sight to behold. This is where we'll build the new house, thought Ted. When he brought his idea to his wife of 28 years, she agreed.

Since Ted decided to design, build, and decorate the house without a contractor, he spent almost every evening in his study perusing magazines, sample house plans, and decorating ideas. This house was going to be just perfect for them. After all of their planning, the project was finally underway. Ted and Diane watched daily with anxious anticipation. With the completion day close at hand Ted could hardly contain his excitement about moving into their new house. Unfortunately, there was one major problem—Diane just couldn't bring herself to leave their home of the last 26 years! Ted couldn't believe it. They had built the house of their dreams and it turned out as perfect as they had planned it. Apparently, it was not the house of Diane's dreams, or at least that is what Ted thought when she refused to move. He was crushed! All he could think about was how obstinate Diane was being about the move.

The problem was simple. Diane thought the idea of building a new house sounded terrific until the actual time came to leave the house they had raised their three children in, the house they loved each other in, and the house they one day would have their grand-children visit. It was full of wonderful memories everywhere. She was fearful of abandoning a place that had meant so much to her. Unfortunately, she never communicated her deep feelings and fears to Ted. As a matter of fact, they never discussed the issue at all because Diane thought she would just be able to get past it on her own.

When moving day came, Diane informed Ted that she wasn't moving! Period! After as much pleading with Diane as he could do, all that was left for Ted was to pack up his belongings and move into the new house alone. So, he lived in the new house and Diane lived in the old house. Can you believe it? Since they were still married but living in two houses only 500 yards apart, Ted decided to cut a path between them. They would alternate meals, holidays, and the like between the two houses. Even though they had a strong relationship, like many couples they hit a wall that had the potential of destroying their 28 years together.

After almost three months of this stalemate, the situation changed suddenly at Thanksgiving dinner. Diane looked around the table at their three children with their families and began to openly weep. Everyone knew the cause was that *sacred cow* no one would dare talk about. Ted took the first step when he instinctively went to Diane to console her. With that simple act of kindness began the healing process. Ted and Diane talked about the wonderful family they raised together; how much they really loved each other; and yes, how stubborn they both had become over this issue. They agreed to work through these issues openly and honestly. By Christmas, Ted and Diane moved back together. Liz just had to ask Ted the obvious question—which house did they move into? Ted grinned from ear to ear. It seems Diane really did like the design, setting, and feel of the new house, but because of her fear and stubbornness she had backed herself into a corner she didn't know how to get out of. Once Ted agreed to move back into the old house rather than live separately, Diane found her opening to tell Ted just how she felt. Now, almost ten years later, they swear they talk about everything. The strength of their 28-year relationship brought them through a very challenging period in their marriage. And while admittedly this is an extreme case, it does demonstrate the critical need to talk about everything openly and honestly in a marriage, because the potentially devastating consequences are real.

To most people, talking is an obvious form of couple communication. However, you would be surprised at the number of marriages beset by the problems illustrated in the stories we have just shared. Frankly, we find it almost impossible to believe that so many couples do such an inadequate job of talking and listening. In some marriages, the partners don't even talk beyond the normal "What do you want for supper?" "What time do you want to get up?" "Are we going to the store tomorrow?" So why would anyone think these same couples would engage in meaningful discussions about those *sacred cow* issues?

Charley has been reminded of this several times during his past 14 years as a dean after he has offered a position to a prospective new faculty member. More than one professor has accepted the position, only to back out at the last minute. A frequent reason given has been that her spouse would not agree to move. What in heaven's name were they thinking? How could you go through an entire interview and hiring process without having had a discussion about a potential relocation? This is one of those major decisions that can never be made without a great deal of open conversation.

Making major decisions jointly can cause the same extensive conversation and debate as working through other difficult issues that occur from time to time in all marriages. One of our favorite couples have been happily married for 42 years and gave the perfect example of why it is so critical to continue these discussions and debates until a resolution is found. They said the toughest issue they faced within the first few years of their marriage was about how to raise one of their sons. Their difference of opinion had gotten so severe that they were arguing constantly. At one time the tension between them was so great that Sheila said, "I think I need to go away from you for a while." Nathan kept pushing the issue. He wouldn't back off. Sheila had had enough. Just as she got ready to leave to go to her mother's house, Nathan said, "Sheila, this won't solve the problem. You will just go away and still be mad. You will just be mad in a different place. The only way we are going to solve this is to talk it through or argue it through until we come up with a solution." What incredible wisdom, and so early in their marriage!

Sheila decided Nathan was right. They talked for many hours until finally Sheila told Nathan that what she was most angry about was Nathan's behavior and that it was unacceptable to her. To her surprise, Nathan agreed that he had been totally obnoxious and would work on it. After that ordeal, Sheila felt comfortable telling Nathan whenever he was pushing an issue to the point that it was about to send her over the edge. They agreed on an arrangement to work together to address the difficult challenges they were having with raising one of their sons.

Being tuned in is another important aspect of *No Sacred Cows*. "You say you are listening, but you don't understand what I said. Are you really listening?" Have you ever made these statements to your spouse? If you are like most couples, there have been times when you probably have felt or said these things.

One of the most unforgettable experiences we have had in our marriage is a perfect example of not really listening. A number of years ago we woke up on a splendid Saturday morning to a most unusual smell. So here we go, around and around the house with our sniffers working full blast. Surely, we thought, something must have died. Being unable to find the origin of the smell upstairs, we went down to the basement. Nothing was found in the family room. Nothing was found in the bathroom. Nothing was found in the laundry room. Boy, did we find something wrong in the storage room! We opened the door and were knocked over by an overwhelmingly pungent smell. Instantly we gagged and covered our noses. The whole storage room was full of raw sewage. Raw sewage! Can you believe it? The sewer drain in the floor had backed up all over the place! You guessed it; we found the source of that most unimaginable smell that had permeated our house!

To make matters worse, we had guests who stayed overnight. A sewage-flooded basement, overnight guests, and the day of the big football game, Missouri versus Nebraska! Needless to say, it appeared that this Saturday was not going to be one of our most stellar days. When you live in Columbia, Missouri, and it's a football Saturday, and you're playing Nebraska … well, the sewer problem would just have to wait until after the big game.

We arrived home about 4:30 in the afternoon and guess what? We won! That is, we won on the football field but we lost at home! When we opened the door to the house, it smelled to high heaven. The sewage had backed up into the rest of the basement. Apologizing to our friends, we sent them on their way home to Kansas City. Then, it was time for us to get down to the ugly business of figuring out what to do with the sewage issue. You have to understand that back then we didn't have the money to go out and hire a plumber at weekend rates, so we tried to do everything by ourselves to avoid what surely would have been an ungodly plumber's bill. Sometimes, we must admit, we fixed problems with just plain old dumb luck. Truth is, on this day we should have just called the plumber in from the very beginning.

However, being the optimistic type, Liz brought Charley the plunger. No surprise to either of us when it turned out to be of no use at all. At least we could say we tried the plunger. By now you are probably asking yourself, why didn't they just call a plumber, they must have rocks in their heads! Well, we really are pretty self-sufficient folks. And besides, it was a pretty day and relatively warm for Missouri in October. So, what the heck, we grabbed shovels and off we went into the backyard.

We both instinctively knew there would be only one solution. It made sense that we had to go into the backyard to dig up the sewer line. We had a suspicion that the problem was a clog (how's that for understatement?). Where would a clog first appear? Easy. A clog would most likely appear at a bend or elbow in the line. Brilliant, huh? Since we visited the house every day it was being built, we knew exactly where the bend in the sewer line was. The plumber could have gone straight, but we suspected his drinking problem was especially acute the day he installed the sewer line, and that's why it had almost a 90-degree bend near the bottom of the hill. The plumber was a nice guy that the builder had befriended, so we had just kept our fingers crossed and hoped that all of the plumbing was installed correctly. At least in this case we did know where to start digging.

Since the ground was soft from the last rain, in a little over an hour we had the sewer line exposed at the bend in the pipe. Down into the hole Charley went to clear away the remaining mud and rock off the elbow. Charley made one thing absolutely clear to Liz, "Whatever you do, don't pull the elbow out of the line while I'm down here in the hole." It seems Liz wasn't really listening. The next thing he knew, Liz had wiggled the elbow just slightly. At least, that is what she still swears to this day. Now, please note, the sewer line went downhill from the house and the bend in the line was nearly 85 feet away. A whole lot of pressure can build up in an 85-foot sewer line running down a steep slope. Well, you guessed it. When Liz "slightly wiggled" the elbow, the raw sewage exploded out of the exposed pipe like Niagara Falls. Poor old Charley! The force of the sewage spray knocked him down and literally covered him with that sweet smelling stuff. Oh GREAT! Can you imagine? This, friends, is a perfect example of NOT really listening. To this day, almost 30 years later, we can still "smell" the raw sewage spewing out of the end of that pipe.

When we attempt to be tuned in we are making a conscious effort to hear. In order to truly listen, we must attend closely to the one sending the message. To be effective listeners we must pay particular attention to the verbal and non-verbal messages the other person is emitting. A psychologist friend of ours says that in a normal conversation you can listen best when you square your body toward the one sending the message, lean forward approximately 10 degrees, and make direct eye contact. In this way, listening becomes a very conscious effort.

There are a few things listening isn't. When your spouse is talking to you and you are hiding behind the morning newspaper, you are not tuned in—you are not really listening! When your spouse is talking and you walk away, you are not listening. Even if you think you are, your spouse's perception is that you aren't listening and therefore don't really care about what she is saying. That perception alone can be most damaging to your communicative relationship. When you fail to make eye contact with your spouse you give her the impression you are not listening.

Not being tuned in so you are really listening can also have tragic effects on a marriage. One of the saddest stories we have ever heard came from a dear college friend. We had been very close to Bill and Jan throughout our college days. Together, the four of us studied, worked, and played. Long into those midnight hours we would share our dreams of the great future we all had in front of us.

Bill was seeking a degree in marketing management and Jan in elementary education. From the time they graduated from high school and got married, Bill and Jan knew exactly what they were going to do with their lives. Their goals were set and they did everything right to successfully accomplish them. They were two of the most exciting and wonderful people we have ever been around. They made us feel like all of our dreams were possible.

In the spring of their senior year, Bill landed a fantastic job on the East Coast, heading up a marketing team in a young, rapidly developing company. Jan was delighted when she secured a teaching position in the company's home city. The two of them quickly embarked on the next phase of life's journey. As is often the case, we had lost touch with Bill and Jan soon after college, since each of us departed in different directions to pursue our dreams.

It was at least six years later when we spotted him in a crowded airport terminal. You just couldn't miss Bill, even at Chicago's busiest airport. He stood six foot six, had blond hair and an athletic build, and always had a radiant smile. However, we should have been more observant and noticed the absence of Bill's characteristically glowing smile.

We waved and exchanged greetings; then all three of us embraced in a long-overdue hug. When we found out that Bill also had a two-hour layover, we quickly suggested the coffee shop to catch up on our six lost years. We noticed that Bill seemed uncomfortable, but he agreed. It took us about two seconds to turn a pleasant experience into one of the hardest emotional ordeals we have experienced with friendships. Charley's first question was of course,

How is Jan? At that question, Bill's face turned ashen gray and his expression was one of abject sorrow. He stammered out, "She … she … Jan is dead."

Charley quickly responded, "Oh, Bill we are so sorry. How did it happen?" At that point, the tears began to roll down Bill's face, and he remained silent. It took well over five minutes before Bill could look at both of us and attempt a response.

Liz carefully said, "Bill, if it is still too painful, let's talk about what you are doing." Bill responded quickly, "No. You both need to know. I've picked up the phone to talk to you all so many times in the last seven months, but I just didn't know how to start. You see, all I could find myself saying was, 'If only.'" Charley and Liz just sat there in complete silence, listening and trying to provide the warm comfort Bill needed to relate his painful story.

When he finally began again, he did not stop talking for over an hour. All of the pent-up guilt and sorrow just exploded out. It seems that both Jan and Bill embarked on their careers in earnest right out of college. Their fun-loving college days turned into high-pressure job responsibilities and career ladder moves that proved to be overpowering. For the past three or four years, Bill was consumed by his daily work needs and had very little time for his home life. Jan on the other hand was teaching a third grade class, maintaining the entire household, and waiting up late each night for Bill to arrive. This same pattern took on a permanent kind of arrangement with no end in sight, since Bill continued to receive promotions with additional responsibilities. Bill kept saying, "Things will settle down as soon as I get a handle on these new job responsibilities. Then we will take that vacation and I'll be able to spend my evenings at home. Our time is just around the corner." Bill's story was momentarily interrupted by a long sigh and his muttering, "If only I had seen the signs … if only I had really listened … it's all my fault…. Oh, God, how I loved her … and now it's too late."

As he continued his story the pieces began to make sense. For months Jan had been begging Bill to slow down, come home, and just spend some time with her. She said that she wasn't feeling very well and she really needed his help at home. Bill described how he thought that since Jan had experienced some slight depression early in their marriage, it was just more of the same. He dismissed her pleas and continued his chase after career success. He would get back to Jan later.

As Bill sat there looking back at things, he explained that all of the warning signs and pleas for help that Jan had made were so obvious to him now, but he just didn't take the time to really pay attention to what she was saying and how she was behaving. Bill was on the fast track and excelled at everything he touched at work. His supervisor had nothing but praise for his ability to lead his marketing team from start to finish on each major campaign. So, taking time to attend to his home life had the potential of derailing the upward mobility of his career.

Bill explained that it had been seven months since Jan committed suicide. In the note that she had left for Bill, she told him of her undying love for him and her guilt for not being able to be a better wife. There was nothing we could say to really help Bill. All we could do was comfort him and help him look toward the future.

Taking the time to listen and really understand what your husband or wife is saying is so immensely valuable to your relationship. While the consequences of not listening may not be as devastating as they were for Bill, they can still do major damage.

Let's look a little further at why listening and understanding are such critical aspects of the characteristic of *No Sacred Cows* in successful marriages. When we understand something, we grasp or perceive it clearly. When we really understand, we comprehend the meaning of the message we received. Try this next time you and your spouse are communicating with each other. When your mate says something to you, pause, then respond as follows: "Honey, is what you are really saying . . . ?" In other words, paraphrasing gives your spouse an excellent opportunity to restate what she said for clarity and understanding if it doesn't match what you thought she meant. Or, if your spouse says one thing but his eyes tell you something else, try this: "Sweetheart, you seem to be saying ... but you didn't look like you really meant that, or did I misunderstand?"

Some of the most interesting tips about listening and understanding have come from couples we interviewed that had already celebrated their Golden Anniversaries. What immediately caught our attention was that each of these couples referred to their spouses as their best friends, whom they could talk to about anything, and who always took the time to listen and understand how they were feeling.

Erma and Donald said their 58-year marriage began as a high school romance. Erma blushed and giggled just a bit as she told us how they were passionately involved even before their official wedding day. Back in those days not only was it forbidden to have sex before marriage, it was certainly not a proper topic of conversation. Erma said they must have just been ahead of their time. We suspect that from what we learned from other long-time successful couples, Erma and Donald were not as unusual as they thought they were, it's that pre-marital sexual relationships were rarely talked about 60 years ago.

Donald explained that as he focused more of his attention on his work and Erma focused more of her attention on the three children, it became harder to keep the passion at the same level as it had been during the first five or six years of their marriage. They experienced the usual difficulties and challenges with raising their three children, making a living, and taking care of everyday routine matters. He said there never seemed to be enough time to get everything done, let alone engage in a passionate love affair. As Donald explained, when their children were still young their friendship began to blossom.

He said, "To put it bluntly, we needed each other's friendship and support if we were going to make it. Each day seemed to bring another challenging situation, putting stress on us as individuals and stress on our relationship."

Erma and Donald decided to spend the first 20 minutes after all of the children were in bed talking and listening to each other. "We didn't do it because someone told us to or because we were great relationship experts, we decided to do it because we needed the time together without the children," Erma explained. It was hard at first because the major topic of each of their first conversations included griping about problems both of them were experiencing at work or with the children. However, that changed when Erma and Donald came up with a great solution to the morning chaos of getting the children ready for school. Both could remember the discussion and how good they felt afterwards. The old adage—success breeds success—was certainly true for Erma and Donald. They were both committed to finding quiet time together for talking, listening, and understanding, when the children could not distract them from being fully tuned in to each other. They became so accomplished at talking, listening, understanding, supporting, and helping each other when they were raising their three children, they continued the practice even after all of their children were grown and left home. Donald and Erma also told us that their friendship and support for each other is still the most important part of their 58-year love affair.

We have an excellent contemporary example of talking, listening, and understanding that should hit home. When the iPod came on the market several years ago, we were two of the first "kids" on the block to own one. Since we have been Mac users since the 1980s, buying one of these babies was a natural thing for us to do. And since both of us love music and both have very eclectic music tastes, the thought of downloading a billion songs gave us chills up and down our respective spines! To date, we have about 9,000 songs on our iPods. Not quite a billion but we are working on it!

Now, you are asking yourself, what does the iPod have to do with love and marriage? Well, it goes like this. Remember our constant refrain regarding successful loving relationships—"Love is simple to understand. The problem is people won't do the simple things required to make love work." The iPod is a good example.

We walk a lot and we always take our Wonder Dog, Jake, with us. The many miles we spend walking around our lovely hometown of St. Louis has allowed us to solve most of the problems in the universe! If we could walk more there would be world peace, everybody would have a job, there would be no empty stomachs, and everybody would love each other. Talking and walking is fun and probably has as much to do with our own successful 43-year marriage as anything we do. And our creativity begins to explode on those walks. Everything seems possible. Every problem seems solvable.

Here is where the iPod comes in.

When we first got our iPods we started listening to them as we walked. Oh, sure, the exercise was still good and the music was beautiful. The fresh air still smelled the same. But guess what happened—we stopped talking when we walked. It didn't take long for us to realize how much we were missing on our walks. Our creativity began to wane, and for the first time in many years, we begin to feel a little tension in our relationship.

Since both of us have worked for a combined 90+ years, we needed those walks together to problem solve and to do the creative thinking required for our book, our research, and our other writings. Those walks were important quality time together. They were so important to our mental health as well. Now, we were messing up all the good things because we were listening to our iPods when we were together instead of to each other.

We also began to notice other couples (lovers, friends) wearing their iPods as they walked with each other. And they weren't talking, just like we weren't! Something had to be done and we did it—no more walking with each other while listening to our iPods. No more sitting together in the family room listening to our iPods. No more listening to our iPods when we were together except when we were on a plane flying somewhere. Since the normal noise on a plane makes it hard to talk anyway, the iPod shuts out the bad noise and replaces it with beautiful music.

Don't get us wrong—we love our iPods. We can't imagine being without them. But like most things in life, there is a time and place for everything. The time you spend together is precious. Walking and talking is one of the best things couples can do for their relationships. Leave the iPod at home when you spend those moments. Save the iPod for the times you are alone or on a noisy plane. Your relationship and your love will thank you for it.

So, if couples have mastered the aspects of talking, listening, and understanding, why do you suppose some married couples can't answer simple questions about each other? We believe it is because they haven't taken the time to observe their spouses or remember significant events in their lives together. Life is often so hectic and fast paced they barely have enough time to take care of the essentials, much less each other. For many couples, taking the extra moments necessary to observe and remember is too often lost in the fast-paced grind of daily living. Successfully married couples on the other hand don't allow this to happen. They always seem to find the time to observe and remember. They understand the importance of these two aspects to the characteristic of *No Sacred Cows*.

In our interviews with successfully married couples many of them talked about the importance of taking a few minutes each day to observe and recall important events about their spouses and their lives together. In other words, when you observe and remember things about your mate, you are really telling him that you find him interesting, worth studying, and most certainly worth remembering.

Try this tonight. Both of you sit down at the kitchen table with a pencil and paper. Each write down all the important dates about yourself, your spouse, and your lives together. For example, your list might include birthdays, anniversaries, and when the kids were born, when you had your first date, and when you bought your first house or rented your first apartment. We're sure you can think of many others. When the two of you are finished, compare notes. When your spouse has a date that doesn't ring a bell, talk about it. What is the date and why is it significant to your partner? Why should it be significant to you? Merge your lists together. Add to the list from time to time. Post the list in a good location. Check it over periodically to always remember why each date is important to you and your spouse.

One of the sweetest stories we have heard about observing and remembering important events in a marriage was told to us by a couple married happily for 44 years. Robert and Gina had their usual wonderful plans made weeks in advance of their 30th wedding anniversary. They were going to their favorite restaurant in the world, Giovanni's on the Hill in St. Louis. Robert would get into a verbal argument with anyone who questioned the fact that Giovanni's was simply the very best Italian cuisine anywhere in the United States. Robert had eaten at most of the four- and five-star Italian restaurants during his many business dinners out of town. So he felt with some level of certainty that he would qualify as an expert connoisseur of Italian cuisine at the best restaurants in the country. While Gina did not frequent many Italian eateries on her business trips, she knew Robert had to be right because Giovanni's was her favorite place to eat no matter what type of cuisine. It was such an automatic decision that Gina just made the reservations for their 30th anniversary before they even had a chance to discuss it. Of course, Robert could think of nothing he would rather do to celebrate.

Since their 30th anniversary was so special to them, Gina and Robert even talked about what they wanted each other to wear that evening. Gina decided she loved seeing Robert in his black pin striped suit with the light pink shirt and tie. Robert told Gina he wanted her to wear the emerald green dress because it made her eyes look even greener. They just couldn't wait.

Unfortunately, three days before their anniversary Gina's boss told her that she had to make an emergency trip to San Diego to solve a major problem with one of their biggest clients. He explained carefully that Gina was the only person he could trust to mend fences over a misunderstanding with one of his department heads and their biggest client. In fact, he explained that this department head ticked off every one of the top executives as well as the president of the company. Gina tried to explain the importance of her 30th wedding anniversary to no avail. He already had her flight booked with all of the arrangements made. It was obvious that she would have to tell Robert and work on mending her own fences after she returned from solving the company's problem.

Gina gave Robert a call right away. Not only did he understand but he also took her to lunch before dropping her off at the airport. Gina spent the entire flight trying to get off her mind the let-down she knew Robert was feeling. While he said and did the perfect things, Robert's expression could not have been more telling when Gina explained the details to him about why she had to fly out to California. He looked as if someone had just unexpectedly punched him in the nose.

When Gina got to the hotel, the first thing she did was check on return flights to St. Louis on their anniversary. There was a flight that would get her into St. Louis before 7:30 pm. She could still get to Giovanni's in time for their 8:00 pm dinner reservation. Her boss had booked her on a flight the day after her anniversary with non-refundable tickets; so changing tickets would not be easy. However, if she could find a way to solve the problems with the client, maybe she could pull this miracle off. Gina spent the rest of the evening planning her fence-mending strategy for her meetings the next day with each of the top executives in the firm. If she could do a terrific job that first day, she would be ready to meet with the president of the company the morning of her anniversary and wrap things up by mid-morning. Even though Gina was by nature an optimist, everything had to go perfectly to pull this off. One catch— she also had to convince Robert to go to Giovanni's alone without giving any clues as to what she was planning, for fear that if she failed to get there it would make the disappointment even worse for Robert.

Gina had her plan and was all set before she called Robert. After much coaxing, Gina got Robert to agree to keep the reservation and celebrate anyway, with the promise that she would fix a special romantic candlelight dinner at home as soon as she returned from California.

Robert couldn't help feeling sorry for himself over the situation. But he had faced similar situations with work and totally understood. Gina was right. He loved Giovanni's and would make a nice evening of it. How often do you get an excuse to take yourself out to your favorite restaurant alone—just you and your thoughts? At least, that is what he kept trying to tell himself so he would keep his promise to Gina and actually go to dinner rather than staying home and heating up a frozen pizza.

Gina's plan worked splendidly with all of the top executives. The only thing left was to do the final fence mending with the president of the company and be finished by mid-morning so she could try to switch tickets to fly home in time for dinner. By late morning everything was taken care of. She was elated with the timing until the president let her know that he had arranged for lunch with her and his top executives to work on some new ideas. Taking a big risk, Gina explained her situation with Robert and their 30th anniversary celebration at Giovanni's. Not only did the company president understand, he also arranged for his driver to take Gina to the airport and had his assistant take care of making the ticket exchange. To her surprise, the non-refundable coach ticket had been exchanged for a seat in first class. She found out later that the president, who had been happily married for 25 years himself, was quite touched by Gina's concern for her husband on their 30th wedding anniversary.

Meanwhile, Robert reluctantly headed off to Giovanni's around 7:30 pm to keep his promise to Gina. However, he was less than enthusiastic about going without her. This was not how their 30th anniversary should be spent—half a country apart.

His arrival at Giovanni's brought his spirits up with the usual warm welcome and handshake. Robert explained that Gina was in California on business, so unfortunately he would be dining alone. Luigi took him back to their favorite table off in the corner. It was nicely separated from the other tables—just enough for privacy and romance. The warm cappuccino and mocha hue of the room, with the soft lighting and paintings by the great Italian masters, always gave him the feeling of entering a private Italian villa. Tonight was no different.

Even with the magnificent ambiance, Robert sat there for several minutes feeling totally depressed. Why did he agree to come there by himself? It was their place—his and Gina's—not his alone. Just as he was mentally processing the possibility of getting up and going home, there in the far doorway of the restaurant was a tall woman, about the same height as Gina, wearing an emerald green dress just like Gina was going to wear for him. She was facing away from him toward the entrance, so Robert could only see her tall silhouette as the light from the street shown behind her. As Luigi appeared at his table with the wine list, Robert was embarrassed that he was staring intently at the woman in the doorway. He quickly moved his gaze to the wine list, ordering the Ruffino Chianti Classico Reserva from Tuscany. As he did, he heard Gina say, "Happy anniversary darling."

What on earth could have made their anniversary more special and unforgettable than that? Yes, Gina had studied Robert so intently that she knew everything about his feelings and reactions. Nothing could have made Robert happier than Gina's efforts to remember their 30th anniversary.

Like we said in the introduction, the reason we use the stories from the successful couples we interviewed is that no writer could create any better examples to illustrate the important keys to a successful marriage. The obstacles Gina overcame to remember the importance of their anniversary spoke volumes about her love for Robert. While their story demonstrates observing and remembering those special times together, another way of observing and remembering is quite simply to observe when your mate looks especially nice and then tell him how and why he looks so nice. If you like her hairstyle, tell her. If you like his tie and how it looks with his suit, tell him. What are you communicating by doing this? That's simple. You've told her that you are paying attention to her and that you find her interesting. That you care about the way she looks. But more important, you are acknowledging her importance to you.

So friends, take special notice of your partners … pay attention to them and remember those wonderful events in your lives together. While it has been our goal for a long time to carefully remember each of the important events in our 43 years together, there is one event in our lives together we shall never forget.

Back in the early 1960s, Charley, a small-town Missouri boy, went off to college at the University of Missouri-Columbia. Being somewhat short of financial resources, he got a job as a busboy at an all girls' school. The job didn't pay money but he did get three square meals a day and a chance to walk through a dining hall full of lovely ladies from all over the United States! For a young man who grew up along the Missouri River and lived a Tom Sawyer existence for the first

18 years of his life, this job was pure ecstasy. As Charley's grandpa used to say, with that many choices you could have "the pick of the litter." He was referring to pigs of course. But be assured these girls were anything but pigs! There was one young lady in particular who caught his eye. Her name was Liz. Liz was from sunny southern California. As the Beach Boys used to say, "I wish they all could be California girls."

Charley sat on the park bench in front of the dining hall each evening to watch the girls go by. Every night, Liz would pass by the bench on her way to the chapel, or the library, or wherever. Charley would be cool and pretend not to notice her. But he always did. Finally, one night, he got up enough courage to call her and ask for a date. She refused. Charley was crushed. However, being possessed with a lot of that famous Missouri stubbornness, Charley kept asking. Then it happened, one night she accepted.

When Charley arrived at Liz's residence hall and she came walking up, it was love at first sight. That first evening together was wonderful. We felt like we had known each other for years. Believe it or not, we were talking marriage on our second date. For the next several months we were virtually inseparable. Then the fateful day came, the end of the school year. Liz had to return to California and Charley accepted a summer job with the Missouri Pacific Railroad. The first week of separation was pure hell. The phone bills were staggering. Remember, 40 years ago there were no such things as nationwide calling and cell phones. Every minute was billed separately and added up quickly at the high rates of calling between Missouri and California.

What the heck, Charley would fly off to California for a short visit. The feelings were stronger than ever when Charley arrived in California. Seeing each other at the Los Angeles airport made us both realize that our lives would be miserable unless we spent them together. So we decided we would get married. The date was set, August 27.

We would get married in Los Angeles. Charley flew back to Little Rock, Arkansas, where he was working for the railroad and Liz would continue her summer job at May Company as a model. A week before the wedding Liz would fly to meet Charley in Little Rock and then both would fly back to Los Angeles together for the wedding. Only problem, when Liz did arrive we discovered that our plane tickets had depleted our respective cash reserves. It seems that when you are in love, you forget important things like how you're going to get to your wedding!

Fortunately, working for the railroad had its fringe benefits. Charley was able to secure half-price tickets for the round trip to Los Angeles and back. On August 23 we got on the train and headed for Los Angeles. Little did we know when we boarded that train the type of adventure we had embarked upon.

As you know, Texas is a BIG state! Well, somewhere in southwest Texas the train stopped dead on the tracks. After nearly an hour of no movement at all we started to get antsy and asked the conductor what the problem was. He responded by telling us that 17 miles of railroad track were under water. When it rains in southwest Texas, it pours! The rainwater apparently rolled across the flat plains of west Texas like a river, with nothing to stop it. We asked him how long it would be before the tracks were passable. Wrong question! "Two to three days" was his response. We had a wedding to go to … ours! And we were a long way from Los Angeles.

Can you imagine, being late for your own wedding? So, we grabbed our suitcases, left the train, and walked to the nearest highway. We walked until we came across a little restaurant and gas station. As we ate a hamburger and drank a cup of coffee we prepared ourselves to hitchhike, something neither of us had ever done before. We walked for about a mile dragging four awkward pieces of luggage without wheels, when an 80-year-old gentleman in a dirty pickup truck asked us if we needed a lift. He was probably thinking that these two kids had to be just plain stupid or in terrible straits to be out in the middle of west Texas in the heat of summer hauling suitcases around on foot. We were so happy to see him that we accepted his offer immediately without even giving it a second thought. We quickly piled into the back end of his truck and off we went. It seems that we were in a tiny little town somewhere close to Pecos, Texas. He was going only as far as the town of Pecos. "Does Pecos have a bus station?" Charley asked the old gentleman. All Charley and Liz thought was thank God when his answer was, "Yes, only bus station around these parts is in Pecos."

When we arrived at the busy little station, Charley went straight to the counter and asked when the next bus for Los Angeles was leaving. "Four minutes" was the clerk's response. Since we wanted to take time to call our folks, Charley asked, "When is the next one going to leave." "Three days. The roads have water running over them already," the clerk loudly replied. Then he yelled for all to hear, "Bus has to leave NOW! All Aboard."

We quickly bought our tickets and made it to our bus seats just as the doors were closing. We breathed a long sigh of relief. That was, until the words of the clerk began to sink in. What did he say about the roads having water running over them already? We saw what the water did to the Missouri Pacific Railroad tracks. What would it do to the road on which we would be traveling?

Everywhere we looked was water. Liz turned to Charley and asked, "How can the driver even see where the road is, let alone drive on it?" It was then that the reflection of the flashing red lights following behind the bus caught our attention. What was happening? Astonishingly, the Texas Rangers were closing the highway behind the bus as we continued to drive ahead. So there we were—inside a bus making its way slowly down a highway with water running over it to the point that the road was no longer visible and was being closed behind us. For the first time it dawned on us that we might never make it to our wedding, or any place else for that matter, ever again. We might just be washed into the miles and miles of floodwaters. But our guardian angel had other plans for us. Miraculously we managed to avoid being turned back or washed off the road into the raging flood waters.

Late in the afternoon three days later, we arrived in Los Angeles. The date was August 26th. We were relieved to be there but we had two major problems. We were required to take our blood tests and apply for a California marriage license before the Los Angeles County Courthouse closed at 5:00 pm. As soon as we arrived, we called Liz's father. Anxiously awaiting our call, he immediately drove to pick us up and head for UCLA Medical Center so we could take our blood tests. From there he drove like a California madman to the Los Angeles County Courthouse to secure the necessary application for a marriage license. We made it in the doors of the Courthouse at 15 minutes to 5:00 on the Friday evening before our wedding!

License in hand, we were married the next day, August 27. Now you know why our wedding anniversary is so deeply etched in our memories. It was a miracle we made it to our wedding at all, let alone making it there on time.

Even if the events leading up to your wedding day were not as hair-raising as ours were, or your events together have not been ones that have been etched into your collective memory, they are your special moments together that should be observed and remembered always.

Do you pay attention to your spouse? Or better yet, do you pay special attention to your spouse? Okay, if you answered yes, we have got some questions for you. What color shoes did your mate put on first thing this morning? Describe the color of your lover's eyes. What was the color of the shirt or blouse your spouse had on last night? Describe in detail the way your spouse was dressed the last time she left the house for work or shopping or whatever. If you answered all of the above correctly, congratulations! However, if you are like many married couples, you probably missed two or more. Be honest, how many did you answer incorrectly?

We've got some more of those challenging questions for you. When is your anniversary? When was the last time you gave your sweetheart a real hug and told him why you love him? What is your spouse's favorite meal? When was the last time you cooked your spouse her favorite meal? Had enough?!?

When we do our workshops, one of our exercises is to have the couples in attendance sit back to back with their partners. We then instruct them not to peek or converse. Then the crusher ... we give them both a little 12-item instrument we've developed entitled *Observing and Remembering*. The instrument has 12 questions similar to those mentioned above. We give them five minutes to write down their answers. And guess what, rarely does either of them get more than four right! Remember, they have been sitting side by side for at least an hour and have probably been together for the good part of a day. It's also a good bet they have been married for somewhere between one to ten years. What we found in those successful marriages of more than 30 years was that they did pass this test every time.

Unfortunately, we have heard all too many stories illustrating the hard lessons couples have learned before they fully understood the important role remembering plays in a marriage. For five consecutive years, Patsy forgot Derrick's birthday. Derrick would give Patsy a gift and a mushy card on her birthday each year. He never forgot. Patsy would not give Derrick anything on his birthday because, as usual, she had forgotten his birthday again. She would make up some lame excuse about how she had ordered his gift but that it hadn't arrived yet. The next morning, she would hop in the car and head for the local shopping mall to purchase Derrick's gift. At dinner that night, she would say something like, "Derrick guess what, your gift arrived today. Better a day late than not at all." Derrick would graciously accept the gift but in the back of his mind, he was feeling hurt that Patsy had really forgotten his birthday.

Derrick was beginning to have all sorts of doubts about his marriage to Patsy. Was she cheating on him? Did she not love him? Was his birthday not a time of joy for Patsy? Patsy's forgetting his birthday was certainly affecting their communication with each other.

Derrick had a plan. He would test Patsy and hopefully teach her a lesson. When February 27th rolled around, Derrick would pretend it was his birthday. It really wasn't of course. His birthday was March 27th! On the evening of February 27th, Derrick showed Patsy what the guys at the office had given him and talked about his surprise party. Patsy played her usual game again. You know the one … she ordered his gift but it didn't arrive, etc., etc. The next day when Derrick got home, Patsy gave him his birthday present. This time, Derrick reacted differently. He confronted Patsy with her one-month error. Patsy was embarrassed! Derrick had taught her a lesson. You see, Patsy was just plain forgetful. She didn't mean to hurt Derrick. She was not cheating on him and did love him very much. To Derrick, however, her continuing to forget his birthday troubled him deeply. Since his birthday was terribly important to him, why wasn't it to her? Patsy's failure to remember this important event in his life almost cost her the man she loved more than anyone in the world.

Patsy now has every important date written down in her notebook. She consults it regularly. Since she learned the significant role remembering plays in marital communication Patsy hasn't forgotten an important event in her marriage to Derrick. Ah, observing and remembering … so central to successful marriages.

Before the characteristic of *No Sacred Cows* becomes a natural part of your marriage, the aspects of talking, listening, understanding, observing, and remembering must be fully developed. When all of these aspects work together, you will have the relationship needed to talk about anything and everything. Like other successfully married couples, you will find a life-long friendship with your spouse that is built on mutual trust and support. There will be *No Sacred Cows*!

— *Advice* —

In your marriage, talk, talk, talk and listen, listen, listen until you are capable of dealing with even the most difficult and delicate issues. There must be *No Sacred Cows* in your relationship. It takes talking, listening, understanding, observing, and remembering to build the foundation necessary for celebrating your Golden Anniversary.

The ideas we provide for you are only the basics for improving the aspects of the characteristic of *No Sacred Cows* in your marriage. They are like the other secrets of success—simple to understand, but often hard to practice consistently in our daily lives.

The art of talking, listening, understanding, observing, and remembering constantly needs revitalization and practice in all successful marriages. Mastering the prerequisites of successful communication in your relationship is essential. Practice makes perfect.

1. **Never go to bed mad—talk it over first.** One promise that we made to each other when we said our marriage vows was that we would never go to bed mad. Well, we have had some very late nights because of that promise, but it really has eliminated the age-old problem of letting little molehills grow into real mountains overnight. It has also enhanced the restfulness of our sleep, however long (or short) it turns out to be.

   Ever been at a friend's house when one partner is pouting or sulking about some terrible thing the other one did? When you ask him what's wrong, he never seems to be too sure. In some marriages this can go on for days. Talk about making a mountain out of a molehill! If they had worked on the premise of never going to bed mad, they might have one very long night without sleep, but they would have resolved the problem.

2. **Talk openly about anything and everything.** The more you know and understand about your spouse, the more you will be able to effectively communicate on all levels. What does your spouse think about the current economic trends? What about the car, how is it working? How is the president doing his or her job? Do you both agree on the discipline strategies you use with the children? How satisfied is your spouse with her job? Are you living where both of you want to live? Remember to talk often. Talking openly also requires honesty. You cannot say one thing and really feel another. This is true in all facets of any relationship; however, it is especially true with talking. A marriage built on truth and honesty is one that will last forever. If you have something unflattering that needs to be said to your husband or wife, find a tactful way to say it, but say it. That same adage holds true for a compliment. Everybody wants their positive qualities to be noticed and appreciated. So say something.

One of the best ways to work on your listening skills is to set aside a special time just to talk and listen to your spouse. Make it on a private walk or over a cup of coffee. Let your spouse know that it is a time when you are there just to listen to him. So much pressure can be taken off a person if he knows there is someone to whom he can turn—someone who will really listen and understand. You need to establish a calm and quiet environment sometime during each day to help promote the listening process. Chaotic surroundings do not enhance listening or understanding. Sometimes in a busy household, this calm and quiet atmosphere is one of the hardest things to provide for your spouse. Work at it. The more often you accomplish this, the better your chances will become for successful listening.

3. **Discuss and make all major decisions jointly.** Any important decisions regarding jobs, moving, vacations, purchases of large items, child rearing practices, etc. must involve both of you. This means that the discussion as well as the actual decision must involve both husband and wife. It is important to note that you cannot say the decision will be made jointly about a major issue and in reality feel the opposite. Research shows that the highest divorce rates are among couples that do not talk over decisions. It is critically important to openly discuss all major decisions until a consensus can be reached that both of you can support.

   We have a family rule for all major decisions—we discuss, tentatively decide, and then sleep on it before the final decision is made. You can't imagine how many dream vacations to exotic places we walked away from the next day after sleeping on it. Believe us, if you both still want to go ahead with the decision on a major issue after you have slept on it, it is a decision you will both appreciate and be able to live with. At the very least, you won't end up blaming each other if it turns out to be a bad decision.

4. **Keep your emotions in check when discussing *sacred cows*.** Some *sacred cow* discussions can be contentious and often heat up quickly. Don't let your emotions interfere with the importance of talking openly about everything. You do not want it to turn into an argument that gets to the point where you will regret what is said. A verbal disagreement about one of those *sacred cows* is one thing; out and out warfare with personal attacks is

another. There should be ground rules established for discussions and debates that exclude personally hurtful statements. The first step in all this is the realization that problems occur when we let arguments get out of control. A difference of opinion is normal and healthy. Sometimes, heated arguments ensue. However, the sooner the ground rules are established, the better. A whole lot of hurt feelings and unhappy moments can be avoided by just taking a breather for a minute or two and then getting the discussion back on the issues in a rational and caring way.

5. **Make a conscious effort to hear what your spouse is really saying with an attitude of acceptance.** Work at becoming an effective listener whenever your spouse is talking. Listen for the real meaning behind the words. Help your spouse feel comfortable enough to tell you how she is really feeling and what she really means. Part of the art of good listening is to be accepting rather than judgmental, critical, or argumentative. It is okay to disagree, but not to be disagreeable. Avoid reacting to the superficial words, rather than to the real meaning behind those words. This takes time and practice, but it is truly worth the effort.

If your spouse is upset about a problem or mad at something, give him the right to unload those feelings in a safe environment, rather than to immediately start a fight just because he yelled about something else. Many arguments in a marriage have started because one of the partners begins yelling at the other as a result of her misunderstanding. It is so easy to get defensive and yell back without thinking. This kind of response can result in a full-blown war. Look carefully beyond the initial outburst and see what is the underlying issue or what is really troubling your spouse before you yell back. If you begin to argue or criticize as soon as your spouse opens his mouth, he will learn that it is easier not to talk about any issue, let alone issues as difficult as those *sacred cows*. In our interviews with successful couples, they often brag about feeling safe when they unload their troubles, talk about difficult issues, or argue from different points of view, in environments that are non-threatening, non-judgmental, and empathic.

6. **Pay particular attention to non-verbal messages from your spouse.** Our body language can sometimes tell more than the words that are spoken. Take the time to notice your spouse's body language to see if it matches the verbal messages she is giving you. If it doesn't match, ask your spouse if that is how she really feels about the subject. Misunderstanding leads to further misunderstanding. Clear up any problems immediately. Don't let them build up. If you thought you understood something that was said, and it proves to be wrong, go back and clarify it right away.

One of the most important times to watch for non-verbal signals is when greeting each other at the end of the day. Have you ever noticed how your spouse entered the house after one of those perfectly wretched days? It was clear from the minute he walked in the door that nothing had gone right that day. You could see the anger and frustration hanging over him like a black cloud. If you said or did the slightest little thing he jumped on you like a tick on a dog. He yelled at you, threw things around, and was apparently blaming every bad thing that happened to him that day on you. So guess what, you yelled back. Then the argument started. Perhaps you even went to bed mad at each other. Think about it though, was he really yelling at you? Probably not. Something made him mad that day and you were the safe target. He can't yell at the boss. He can't yell at the secretary, the cab driver, or the children's teachers. If you really "listened" to his non-verbals you would have understood that he wasn't angry with you. Instead of returning anger in kind, maybe you should have said, "Darling, you obviously have had a bad day. Why don't you tell me about it? I'll be glad to listen. Get it off your chest. I want to help." This is a clear case of why understanding is so important to your communicative relationship with your spouse. Many marriages that fail do so because the parties involved listen but do not understand. Misunderstanding can generate a vicious cycle. Misunderstanding leads to further misunderstanding, and can cause a further deterioration of the communicative relationship between the two of you. Don't allow this to happen to your relationship!

7. **Keep a notebook with the dates of all of the important marital events.** The list should include your anniversary, each other's birthdays, the day you met each other, the date you moved into your home(s), and the like. Sit down together and brainstorm to ensure that no important date is left out, then organize the dates by month. Each of you should consult the notebook of important events at least weekly.

Forgetting something or failing to observe important things about your spouse are not vitally important in and of themselves. It is the message these omissions send to your spouse. When you do not remember important information about your spouse or important events in your lives together, frequently your spouse interprets this behavior as your thinking these events are not worth remembering or observing. Your spouse's perception of your action is much more important than your intentions.

At least once a week, talk about a significant or memorable event in your lives together. For example, talk about one of your most memorable moments from your last vacation together or about when your children were born. The point is, discussing memorable events reminds each of you how full and exciting your lives together have been.

Pick out the ideas from this advice section that you both wish to start working on and post them in a prominent location. Begin today!!! You cannot afford to let another day go by without improving this most critical characteristic of successful marriages. The pleasure you will feel as you put these ideas into practice will make it all worthwhile. In successful marriages, talking, listening, understanding, observing, and remembering become habitual. They become part of the fabric of the relationship. And in the end, they allow successful marriages to have *No Sacred Cows*!

CHAPTER 9

Seven Surprising Secrets #3: The Golden Rule

*Discovering the secret of how to grow mutual respect
and understanding over time is one of the
foundational ingredients for successful marriage.
The Golden Rule, while simple to understand
for some, seems to be quite difficult for others
to apply consistently in their marriages.
Examples of mutual respect between partners
abound in successful marriages.*

NO PERVASIVE CHARACTERISTIC applies more to a successful relationship than the *Golden Rule* and we have found no substitute for mutual respect and kindness in a successful marriage. While respect for each other is almost always a part of the vocabulary of newlyweds, it fades quickly in failing marriages but grows deeper over time in successful ones.

At the moment you both said, "I do," your level of respect for each other was soaring. Love, passion, and unabashed excitement form the perfect climate for respect. "Honey, let me open that door for you?" "Darling, you look simply ravishing!" "Your idea is terrific!" "Sweetheart, is it warm enough for you?" Phrases like these flow easily from a newlywed's vocabulary because newlyweds are tentative in their relationships and are careful to be polite, considerate, and caring so their new partners will cherish them fully. Taking note of every detail of word and appearance, newlyweds demonstrate the ultimate in respect for their new partners. Discovering the secret of how to grow mutual respect and understanding over time is one of the foundational ingredients for successful marriage.

The *Golden Rule*, while simple to understand for some, seems to be quite difficult for many to apply consistently in their marriages. As we say repeatedly, the little things matter in love and marriage. Do the little things and your marriage or loving relationship will prosper.

Charley learned his lesson some 40 years ago! He grew up in a rural area of Missouri back when outhouses were more prevalent than toilets that flushed! When we first got married some 43 years ago, Charley, "the consummate gentleman" as Liz refers to him, had to learn an important lesson about toilet seats.

As it turns out, toilet seats are designed to protect women and save marriages! There are four kinds of husbands when it comes to *Toilet Seat Love*. Here they are, briefly described.

First, husband number one goes to the bathroom. He lifts the seat and goes, then replaces the seat in its down position. Wife loves husband when he does this! The marriage is saved!

Husband number two fails to lift the seat and, therefore, goes ON the seat. But, being a kind and respectful husband, he cleans up his mess with a handful of Kleenex. Wife still loves husband but not as much.

The third kind of husband goes to the bathroom, doesn't lift the seat, goes ON the seat, doesn't clean the seat, and wife sits in his mess later that day. Wife is not happy with husband! Trust us on this.

The fourth kind of husband raises the seat before he goes, but leaves the seat in the upright position when he is done. Later that day, wife sits in the toilet bowl and the impact splashes toilet bowl contents on the floor. Occasionally, she gets stuck in the bowl and needs assistance in getting out. Wife does not love husband when he does this. The marriage is in jeopardy!

We hope you enjoyed the levity of this little story but, more important, you find its meaning to be helpful as you think about the little things that make your loving relationship with someone else thrive. It describes just one of those little things that really shows respect for your partner. Always remember that lasting relationships and successful marriages are built on an accumulation of the little things that demonstrate your respect for each other.

Examples of mutual respect between partners abound in successful marriages. These couples form a kind of mutual admiration society that builds on each other's strengths. They treat each other with kindness and dignity. Their roles in their relationships are determined out of respect for each other's talents and their life circumstances, not by gender and tradition alone. They enhance their communicative relationships by respecting their occasional individual needs for privacy and aloneness. So how do successfully married couples develop the level of respect that makes the *Golden Rule* a pervasive characteristic of their relationships?

Each marriage begins with an established level of respect, both for each other and oneself. Respect is the foundation for all types of communication within a loving relationship. Respectfulness, in its simplest form, is the way we show consideration for others, or the way we treat another person. Yet, people are often more likely to express respect to friends and acquaintances than to their own spouses.

It amazes us every time we see a gentleman open the door for a perfect stranger, while letting his wife get the door for herself, or when a woman thanks a waiter very politely for handing her a fork, yet never acknowledges or thanks her husband for passing her the salt. Why on earth do we forget to treat our spouses with the same degree of respect we treat others?

When was the last time you "ordered" your spouse to get you something? Perhaps it was a cup of coffee. "While you're up get me this … or get me that." Now stop and think when you last "ordered" a friend of yours to get you something while they were up. Maybe you order your spouse to take out the trash or water the lawn. Both kinds of orders effectively demonstrate a feeling of disrespect that would not be tolerated in a friendship. Why should it be any more acceptable in a marriage?

Another form of respect in a successful marriage is the honor we show our husbands or wives. What is his worth to you as an individual? Believe it or not, you demonstrate your true feelings about her worth every time you make contact with your spouse. Each marriage has its own unique feelings. It is a relationship that builds its feelings of love over a long period of time. The ingredients of all marriages may be similar, but its unique blending makes a special one-of-a-kind marriage.

Try spending just 15 minutes writing down all of the special qualities, talents, or skills your husband or wife possesses. If you were not able to finish the list in 15 minutes and your 8.5- by 11-inch paper is already full, congratulations! You probably do not have a problem in this area. However, if 15 minutes have long since passed and your paper is nowhere near full, you need to spend the next several days carefully observing the special person that you married and look for all of those qualities, talents, or skills that make him so important to you and others.

Love is too important to notice only your spouse's shortcomings and miss the gifts she has to offer. You will be surprised by the number of good things you can observe about your spouse if you spend several days blocking out his negative points and only letting your mind take in his positive qualities. Life can immediately become much more enjoyable if you are looking for strengths and not weaknesses. Building upon those strengths will not only enhance those strengths, but it will also minimize the impact of the weaknesses. Show honor to your spouse when you make contact with her by letting those positive thoughts come through.

Dean and Nancy learned that lesson early in their 54-year marriage. When Dean first spotted Nancy studying in the college library, it was love at first sight. Dean immediately made the advances needed to secure a date with Nancy. The two just seemed to attract attention everywhere they went together—they were an amazingly striking pair. Dean swears that Nancy is still the same "hot looking lady" that he first fell in love with 55 years ago. Nancy, beaming from ear to ear, informed us that heads still turn when Dean walks into a room. They were the most polite and loving couple toward each other that we have interviewed. So, naturally, we had to ask the obvious question—was it always that way or were there times when things broke down, causing them to lose their respect and politeness toward one another?

Dean immediately said that he could never be anything but respectful toward Nancy, because he owed his very existence and self-worth to her. As they told us their story we could understand why Dean felt that way. It seems their first five years of marriage started out in a normal, uneventful manner. Dean secured a management position with a national store chain and was doing extremely well. Nancy was very content to manage the home front and do the entertaining for his business connections. For Nancy and Dean, it was the idyllic 1950s marriage. Unfortunately, a large national chain bought the company Dean worked for and eliminated most of the mid-management positions in his company. It was part of the massive cuts made immediately after the takeover.

How would they make their house and car payments if Dean couldn't get another job immediately? Dean started to worry about everything. They had very little in their savings account and their families were not in any position to help. Dean said that it came as quite a blow to his ego to lose his management job.

As the weeks of looking for a new position turned into months, things got extremely stressful for the two of them. Dean's already bruised ego took another tremendous beating when Nancy was forced to go to work as a waitress because he couldn't find a job. It didn't pay much, but they could pinch pennies and survive for a while on her meager earnings. Dean told us his frustration level was so high at that point that he lost his temper when even the littlest thing went wrong. There he sat without a job, and his wife had to waitress at the local café to just make their house payments each month. He applied everywhere for management positions, but nothing was available. Too many unemployed former managers in the area hit the market at the same time.

Then the beauty of their story became crystal clear to us. Dean explained that the deeper he went into depression about their situation, the more Nancy talked him through it. Every night she would tell him that he needed to be patient and just wait for the right position to come along. He just had to hang in there and keep his options open while he continued to search. Nancy would repeat Dean's strengths to him every time he felt like there was no hope. She constantly told him how amazing he was, how he could figure out anything, how good he was at managing people and what a kind and honorable gentleman he was. Dean said that without Nancy's daily reminders of his strengths, he would only have concentrated on his weaknesses and his inability to find a job. After six months, he was ready to take any job and not wait for the right position.

It was then that Nancy told him the butterfly story. Nancy said that if you try too hard to catch the butterfly, you can never do it. However, if you sit still and let the butterfly come to you, it will light on your shoulder. Dean was so stressed about not having a job right away and letting Nancy down that he was not doing his best in the interview process. Nancy decided to make a note for Dean's pocket with each of his strengths beautifully written down for him to look at right before he went into the next interview. She was convinced that all he needed to do was relax and allow the person doing the hiring to see Dean's amazing talents and he would surely be offered the job.

Within a week, Dean secured an interview with a prestigious national chain for which his education, past experience, and talents would certainly be a perfect match. This time, right before the interview he carefully reviewed the note Nancy placed in his pocket, which skillfully highlighted his strengths. Dean went into the interview confident, knowing all of the talents he could bring to this company. Needless to say, he secured a management position. In fact, it must have been just the right position for Dean, because he was promoted through the management ranks until he became vice-president of operations with the same company. He said that when it was time to retire, it was difficult for him to leave such a terrific company that had recognized and rewarded his talents for so many years.

To this day, Dean is absolutely convinced that Nancy's positive attitude and focus on his strengths is what made the difference. Dean said that the respect Nancy demonstrated every single day of that terrible seven-month ordeal will never be forgotten. Then he asked us, "How could I treat Nancy any other way than with dignity and respect?" Dean went on to explain, "She took me through the lowest time in my professional career and brought me out of it every single day by only concentrating on my strengths and never once mentioning my weaknesses. Life has meaning and purpose when you have a relationship like the one I have with Nancy."

It was at that point that Nancy broke in and said, "Life is a short venture. If you take time to focus on the negative, you might miss the most important positive thing of all—the potential for lasting love. When we celebrated our Golden Anniversary a few years ago, all I could do was think about just how lucky I was to have married Dean." As she continued telling us all of the wonderful things about Dean, it was obvious that they had formed a mutual admiration society. They respected each other's talents and strengths. What they learned about each other during those stressful seven months when Dean was without a job has sustained them throughout their 54-year marriage. They are a shining example of the importance of respect in successful marriages.

Unlike Dean and Nancy, many couples find it difficult to consistently treat their spouses with respect and courtesy. Ask yourself another question, "Do I express myself in a courteous manner to my spouse at all times?" If the answer is no, imagine the message you are communicating! "I don't respect you enough to treat you with the same courtesy I would give to a friend." You've seen this behavior in others. If you're like us, it makes you feel very uncomfortable.

Let's look at some common examples. Did you ever get up from watching television to get yourself a drink or a snack without offering one to your spouse? Not very courteous, is it? Did you ever yell at your spouse in public? Or embarrass your husband or wife in public by telling everyone within earshot a "family secret"? Or worse, share in intimate detail about a recent bedroom activity? Unfortunately, most human beings react instinctively by returning this same kind of discourteous behavior. It becomes almost a one-upmanship situation.

A couple of years ago, we attended a New Year's Eve party with another couple. We suspected for some time that Debbie and Mack's marriage was on the downhill slide, and their behavior at the party confirmed our suspicions. From the time they arrived, the attitude they displayed toward each other was a perfect example of non-respectful communication—no evidence of the *Golden Rule* in their relationship.

Instead of enjoying the festivities and dancing like the other 20 celebrating guests, Mack and Debbie were eating everything in sight. As Mack nibbled on a piece of cake, he leaned over to Debbie and said, "Boy, I sure wish you could cook like this." Not to be out-done, Debbie glanced over at one of her friends from work and said to Mack, "You and Bill are the same age. How come Bill looks so much younger?" Mack retorted, "Look who's talking!" He then commented on how beautiful Jenny looked by saying, "She sure takes good care of herself. I've been telling you for years to exercise more." On and on the put-downs went. Mack put Debbie down. Debbie put Mack down. We never heard them say a nice thing to or about each other all night long. Frankly, we were embarrassed to have come with them to the party. Instead of celebrating New Year's Eve with 20 exciting people, we were trying to lighten the tension between Mack and Debbie so that the rest of the guests would not have their festive moods adversely affected.

Through the first few years of Debbie and Mack's marriage, they displayed a great deal of respect for each other. However, in recent years it became increasingly clear that something had gone wrong. Their once humorous little jabs toward each other were now laced with poisonous hostility. As we were riding home with them after the party, we couldn't help but comment to them about their behavior. The surprising thing was, they honestly didn't realize how they had been acting. They did confess that they had been feeling hostility toward each other for some time, but neither was sure why. We didn't know if drawing it to their attention would have any positive effects, but we just had to try. Both Debbie and Mack were wonderful individuals, who were destroying each other with every jab and negative comment they made. They certainly had a lot of changes to make if their marriage had any hope at all of becoming successful. Breaking the negative cycle was paramount. They might have had a chance if they could have broken the negative cycle by treating each other with the same degree of respect as they would have liked to be treated. The point is this—communication begins with respect for each other. There is just no substitute. In this case, Debbie and Mack didn't learn the lesson. Their marriage failed.

When you do not communicate respect for each other, you put up an iron curtain between the two of you. If you don't feel and show respect for each other, none of the other forms of communication we describe in this book matters—communication begins with respect.

Your marriage may be a "traditional" one where only the husband works outside of the home and the wife cares for the children and the household. That's great—there is nothing wrong with one person taking care of the home needs and the other providing the financial support, so long as this is a mutually agreeable arrangement and both roles are equally respected.

However, if you are like us, and more than two-thirds of this country's married couples, you are balancing two sets of jobs, careers, and educational endeavors. If this is the case, you cannot maintain the same roles as in a "traditional" marriage. You cannot have it both ways. Respect for the needs and demands inherent in each of your roles becomes highly important. It is impossible for both marriage partners to maintain careers outside the home while expecting only one person to still assume all of the routine responsibilities of keeping up a household, taking care of the children, managing repairs, etc.

Our best illustration of this point comes from a happily married couple that experienced both types of marriage—one with only one spouse working outside of the home and a dual career marriage. Having been married for 44 years now, Susie explained to us that both arrangements had their advantages and their challenges. The challenges of dual careers had to be overcome if the arrangement was to work for both of them. Back in 1967 when Devin was pretty well established in his career as an investment banker, they decided that financially they could afford for Susie to quit her job to focus all of her time on raising their three-year-old son and one-year-old daughter. Everything went along just fine until both of the children started school. Faced with the ever-increasing expenses of the larger house, children's school clothes, dental work, and doctor's bills, the couple decided that it would really help out their financial situation if Susie would return to work.

Susie's excellent real estate skills were in high demand, so it was not surprising that she found a job within a week. Suddenly, what seemed like such an easy solution to their financial concerns caused an even greater set of problems for Devin and Susie. With the increase in income came a decrease in time to devote to home and family. Who would take care of their two children when Susie or Devin could not get there to pick them up from school? Who would cook dinner? How would all of the household chores get done? Who would clean the house? How would the dog get along in the house without periodic attention? All the little items that had not even been considered during the discussion of Susie's returning to work now loomed menacingly on the horizon. Devin understood Susie's new time demands from work since he had relied so heavily on Susie to take care of the household when he was working and she was staying at home. Devin respected her new role as a real estate agent and the added responsibilities for her that came with the new job.

Susie and Devin quickly worked out arrangements for after-school care for both of their children on days when neither of them could get home early enough. Their pressure and worry immediately eased just a bit by allowing both of them to finish their work before rushing away to care for the children.

Not surprisingly, even with the after-school care, their previously smooth home life was continuing to fall apart since neither Susie or

Devin had enough time to take on one more burden. And worst of all, the kids added to Devin and Susie's problems by constantly misbehaving in order to gain the needed attention from their parents. The first two months of the transition seemed like a nightmare since even their children's teachers were calling home with school related problems. Apparently, the change did more than create monsters at home. Both children were bringing their need for attention to their classrooms.

Something had to be done immediately, if this was going to have any chance of working. So, the next thing they talked about was how to solve the pressures of the basic household chores that were piling up. Together, Devin and Susie determined what things someone else could do and what they wanted to reserve for themselves. They agreed to have the shirts taken to the cleaners and have the house cleaned twice a month. Devin and Susie were scared to death that they were in over their heads and they could never afford to pay for this kind of help. But they knew that they had to find a solution if both of them were going to continue working outside of the home.

The first couple of months were such a struggle financially that Susie almost quit her job and returned to the management of the house. They were both feeling that it wasn't worth it. However, wisely, they made an agreement to hang in there for four months and then see how they were doing at that point in time.

When they sat down to analyze how things were going after four months, both concluded that while it had been a rough change, things were working much smoother now. The financial relief that came from Susie's successful re-entry into real estate sales was much needed and made any challenges worth it. But, when they looked at it honestly, the best part of the change turned out not to come from the financial advantage. The best part of the change turned out to be the change in their two children. Before Susie returned to work, the children were demanding and seemingly helpless when it came time to do any kind of household chores. However, when Susie and Devin made the decision to hire outside help, they also recognized that the children needed to learn responsibility and become a part of the solution instead of part of the problem. Devin and Susie did a great job of investing the extra time during the transition to help their two children learn to take responsibility for their share of the chores. It added to their feeling of togetherness. The children's pride was unmistakable when they received their allowances each week!

Through the challenges of this transition, Devin and Susie gained a greater appreciation and respect for each other, and their children learned from their parents' respectful behavior toward each other. They watched and learned how to solve problems together.

It is easy to see why Devin and Susie have been happily married for 44 years and raised two highly successful children, both of whom report being happily married. They practiced the *Golden Rule* until it was a pervasive characteristic of their marriage. Devin and Susie told us that they only hoped that they had provided a strong enough model of respect for their children so that they would be able to pass it on to their five wonderful grandchildren. How could it be any other way? What Devin and Susie did seemed so easy when they were telling us their story. Unfortunately, it is very difficult for many couples to follow this model. They find it hard to understand that mutual respect is the basis for working through the tough transitions in a marriage. Devin and Susie's example illustrates the power of the *Golden Rule* in ensuring lasting love.

Unfortunately, not all marriages are like Devin and Susie's. We remember so well watching our neighbors Ken and Lisa move in while they were still on their honeymoon. Ken was in his second year of medical residency and Lisa was a nurse's aide. It seemed to be a marriage built on common interests and convenience, rather than deep emotion. Neither of them displayed an overabundance of affection toward each other from the first time we met them. Ken and Lisa had what many would call a stormy marriage. Lisa put up with Ken's constant verbal abuse for the first six years of marriage. He never had a good thing to say about her. Ken certainly never acknowledged that Lisa was worth anything to him other than as a slave, a verbal punching bag, and someone to earn an income so he could attend medical school. She was, in Ken's eyes, "stupid" and "incapable" of doing anything useful. His favorite expression was "get me." Get me this or get me that. Lisa's purpose, it seemed, was to fetch like a dog.

Needless to say, Ken's lack of respect for her was driving Lisa crazy. Even with Ken's entry into the medical profession and Lisa's ability to quit her job as a nurse's aide, the verbal abuse continued from Ken. The problem was she would never say anything to him about the way she was treated. Lisa, like many in this type of situation, just took it.

Surprisingly and suddenly during the seventh year of their marriage, Lisa began to change. She rarely complained to her friends about Ken anymore. She even appeared to be happy once again. This abrupt change in her behavior made her friends curious. Was Ken beginning to treat her with respect after all these years? Lisa confided, "No, Ken is still the same old jerk, but I've learned how to deal with him." Lisa's method for handling the situation was shocking, but not at all surprising after six and a half years of torment.

Lisa had decided that Ken was not going to change. The only alternative in her mind was to get back at him. So, every morning after Ken went to work, Lisa would go secretly off to the local university to take classes. She decided to finish her degree in business using Ken's hard-earned money. Since he always made fun of and discouraged her attempts to finish her degree, Lisa was certain that this would be a surefire way to get back at him for his abuse. One day, in the not too distant future, Lisa planned to casually invite Ken to her graduation ceremony. Wouldn't that just be the ultimate revenge?

However, while pursuing her degree, something exciting began to happen to Lisa. One of her professors took a very special interest in

Lisa's abilities, and began to build up her deflated ego and poor self-image. The professor showed Lisa that she was a very capable person. At first, Lisa could hardly believe that a dashing, brilliant professor like Alex would take the time to notice her, let alone provide her with extra help and encouragement. Little by little over the next year Lisa's self-worth began to blossom. New discoveries about herself seemed to be occurring each day. Lisa found that she even enjoyed debating the merits of economic theories. She gained the self-confidence needed to stand up to others when she believed strongly in something.

All the years of verbal abuse, put-downs, and insults began to fade into the past. No longer could Ken destroy her self-confidence. Alex had rekindled the enthusiasm for life and knowledge that lay dormant in her for the past six years. Suddenly, everything in life was exciting and new. Each and every moment she spent with Alex was enlightening.

A new kind of feeling overcame Lisa just as soon as Ken left for work each day. What had begun as a spiteful act turned into something very exciting and fulfilling. Lisa finally found true dignity and self-worth. She discovered that she was capable of maintaining a lasting relationship based on mutual respect.

Needless to say, it took only a year and a half of experiencing true mutual respect before Lisa filed for divorce. The last time we spoke to her, Lisa and her dashing professor were still married and getting along just fine. The only loser in this story was Ken, who never did understand the true meaning of respect. Unfortunately, sometimes the only escape from a horribly degrading relationship is divorce.

Treating your marriage partner the way Ken treated Lisa communicates not only a lack of respect for the marriage but also an incredible lack of respect for the person you married. You cannot imagine the irreparable damage such irresponsible action has on a marital relationship. When you don't follow the *Golden Rule*, when you treat your partner disrespectfully, you can cause your spouse to feel defensive, lower his self-esteem, and even cause him to withdraw from the relationship.

There are many marriages in the world characterized by this kind of behavior. You don't have to have well-developed observation skills to notice marriages lacking respect. Our guess is that you and your spouse have occasionally shown some type of disrespect toward each other. The point is, everyone is human and can be disrespectful at times. Just don't let the lack of respect creep into your marriage on a regular basis because it can quickly destroy your relationship with each other. The barriers caused by mutual or unilateral disrespect are difficult to bring down. The cement in the barrier becomes harder over time and tougher to crack. The only way for the *Golden Rule* to become a consistent part of your marriage is to practice it often enough to make it an everyday habit in your relationship.

In our interviews we discovered a most interesting aspect of the *Golden Rule.* We have yet to find a successful couple that hasn't told us about their respect for each other's individual need for privacy and aloneness. Privacy is, as one psychologist put it, "The opportunity to belong only to yourself." Without question, human beings are social animals. But that very need for sociability creates in each of us an occasional need for privacy. There are simply times when we must be apart from everything and everyone. In the successful marriages we have studied, the absolute need for privacy and aloneness is respected, honored, and encouraged.

Clyde and Monica learned about the need for privacy very early in their 32-year marriage. Both of them said that this was such a difficult issue for them that it almost cost them their marriage. During the first year together, Monica talked non-stop to Clyde. Now, Clyde didn't always answer, but Monica still talked and talked and talked. Clyde felt like he could not get away from Monica's need to engage him in conversation whenever they were together, so he was seeking places to go just to have a few minutes of quiet. Clyde's need for privacy and aloneness was increasing steadily as they were approaching their first anniversary. Monica literally wouldn't leave Clyde alone for even a minute when they were together. To make matters worse, she followed him around the house everywhere he went, causing him to begin pulling away from their relationship. While Clyde knew how difficult it was becoming, his attempts to discuss it with Monica or have her understand had not been successful. He had approached the subject with Monica so many times and in so many ways that he had finally given up trying to talk about it with her at all.

They both hoped that their anniversary trip to Gulfport, Mississippi, would ease the strain. Booked into their favorite hotel, they were certain that this would be just what they needed. Instead, Monica's incessant talking continued the entire first day of their trip. Her obsession with interrupting Clyde also persisted until he was thinking of drastic measures to help her understand.

That evening when Monica asked him to go for a walk with her on the beach, he knew he had his opportunity for some much-needed seclusion and quiet. After a great deal of convincing, Monica agreed to go for a walk by herself and let Clyde read his book alone in the hotel room. Reluctantly, Monica started out for the beach. After about 15 minutes, she felt so lonely and guilty for leaving Clyde that she turned around and headed back to the hotel. So as not to startle Clyde, she knocked gently on the door before entering. To her surprise, Clyde did not answer. Monica knocked a bit harder. Again, Clyde did not answer. Then she noticed the DO NOT DISTURB sign on the door. What was this? Monica pulled out her room key and turned the knob. To her amazement, as she opened the door the chain caught and the door jolted to a dead stop.

All she could think to do was call out Clyde's name. No answer. She called louder. No answer. After two or three minutes of trying to get him to answer the door, she got scared. Maybe something happened to him. Down to the front desk she scurried to ask for help. As the security guard came with her to the room, he kept reassuring her that everything would be all right. He said that her husband was probably just in the bathroom or really sound asleep so he didn't hear the knocking.

The security guard's hard bang on the door would surely get Clyde's attention, if he could hear anything at all. No answer. Then the security guard announced loudly, "Security, open up now." To Monica's amazement, she heard Clyde coming to the door. He slowly unlocked the chain and opened the door with his head lowered. He explained that he just needed a little privacy; so he put out the DO NOT DISTURB sign hoping that Monica would leave him alone for a few minutes. The guard smiled nicely and said, "Haven't been married long, huh? You two will learn." Then off he went.

Monica immediately broke into tears and began yelling at Clyde about not answering the door, about the scare he gave her, and finally about her embarrassment in front of the security guard. Then it seemed to hit her—why did Clyde do that to her? Was he just playing a cruel joke or did he hate her so much that he wanted her to leave? Clyde seized the moment by taking Monica in his arms while trying hard to explain just how desperate he was for privacy and aloneness. He loved her very much, but he couldn't handle her obsession with talking to him all of the time. Monica took a deep breath and slowly tried to process what Clyde was telling her.

After what seemed like an eternity of talking, shouting, crying, and angry silence, they began to understand just how desperate the situation had gotten for them. Even though they loved each other passionately, there was an insurmountable wall between them that had to be knocked down quickly if they had any chance at all of finding lasting love.

They finally decided to work through it together. Clyde promised to tell Monica outright when he needed quiet time. They soon developed a signal that both understood. While it was a difficult issue at the time, both Monica and Clyde laughed a lot as they recalled their first couple of years together. They still have that DO NOT DISTURB sign hung on the doorknob of their bedroom 31 years later!

We have witnessed time and time again marriages in which one or both partners failed to understand the importance of being alone, not only for themselves, but for their spouses as well. When we first introduce this concept to others, the reaction is usually one of surprise. Many couples are of the mistaken notion that they are to be constantly attentive to their spouses. While their intentions are good, their desire to be attentive causes them to, in fact, interfere with the quality of their communicative relationships with their mates. The desire for too much closeness can inadvertently drive a wedge between husband and wife. Isn't that ironic?

In all probability, many couples believe that quantity of time together is the most important characteristic of their relationship. Instead, the "law of diminishing returns" comes into play here. The economists would explain it something like this. Let's say you buy a case of your favorite cola and decide to drink it in one setting. The first cola tastes great. Perhaps the first two or three taste good. But after about four or five, the quality of taste begins to diminish. If you were to drink the whole case in one setting, you would like each cola less and less until you reached a point where you began to absolutely hate your favorite cola. The "law of diminishing returns" seems to appropriately describe many marriages, doesn't it? More is not always better. Give your spouse some privacy … the opportunity to be alone. Expect the same opportunity for yourself. Don't allow communication in your marriage to fall victim to the "law of diminishing returns."

In our interviews, we have been continuously reminded of the importance of privacy and aloneness to the success of a marriage. After one of our early workshops, a young man who had been married for seven years confided in us that his short marriage was failing.

Adam's response was clear when we asked him why. We had heard it so many times before. His marriage was failing because he never had a chance to be alone. The feeling of suffocation was overwhelming him. Adam said, "I feel an obligation to be with my wife all the time when I am at home. When I try to get the time for myself that I so desperately need, my wife thinks I am angry with her. To keep from making her angry, I give up my private time." As a result, Adam was spending more and more time away from home. He would stay later at the office, go for long drives by himself in the car, and make up any excuse he could think of to literally steal a few minutes away from his wife and everyone he had to deal with all day long at work. It was apparent to us that Adam could not get his need for privacy and aloneness satisfied at home so he was doing everything he knew how to get his needs satisfied somewhere else. We have a feeling this little scenario describes the situation in the homes of many people reading this book. It is really quite a common problem, especially during the first few years while couples are learning to adjust to living together.

Here is the advice we gave Adam based upon our many interviews with successfully married couples. First of all, recognize the need for privacy and aloneness in yourself. In addition, relieve yourself of the guilt complex you have developed for that need. Next, talk openly to your wife about your needs and your feelings. It will not be an easy conversation, but it is vital if your marriage is to stand a chance of being successful. Help her understand three important things. One, each of you has a need for privacy and alone time that has to be respected. Two, it is okay and normal in successful marriages to have this need. And three, you love her very much. That conversation will lay the groundwork to begin working out an effective solution for providing seclusion when needed. The next thing you and your wife can do is set aside a mutually agreeable time each day during which each of you can be alone. (If you have children, involve them as well. They have this need, too). And most important, remember not to get jealous of each other's time alone.

Several months after we talked to Adam we received a card in the mail. Can you guess what it said? His message was simple and to the point, but powerful nonetheless: "All is well. My wife and I have developed a deeper and more loving level of communication than we have ever had before. The short time we take for privacy and aloneness each day is worth its weight in gold. We are going to make it after all." And they have. They just celebrated their 31st year of marriage.

About 20 years ago, a lady we met at a restaurant told us a poignant story about the importance of respecting the need for alone time and privacy in a marriage. She was dining by herself at a table next to us. Throughout the meal she kept looking at us as if she knew us. Finally, she came over to introduce herself. She apologized for staring at us. It seems she recognized us from a picture she had seen accompanying an article about us in one of the local newspapers. We invited her to join us.

In the course of the conversation she informed us that she had been married for 11 years, she had two children, and her husband worked for one of the major employers in the city. Rather innocently, Liz asked her why she was dining alone. Instantaneously, tears gushed from her eyes as she began telling us her story illustrating the dual concepts of marital privacy and aloneness about as well as any story we have heard.

Libby met her husband, Stan, at college in one of their finance classes. It was love at first site for both of them. Through their final two years of college they were inseparable, even studying together to make sure they both excelled in all classes.

With only one semester left before they completed their degrees, Stan and Libby were married and ready to go job hunting in earnest. By mutual agreement, Libby and Stan decided to return to their hometown of Seattle to look for work. They were both successful in landing terrific jobs within the first two months of their searches.

In June Stan graduated with a degree in accounting and Libby completed her degree in marketing. They headed off to Seattle to begin their careers and establish their lives together. Everything went smoothly for the first five years of their marriage. In fact, so smoothly that Libby and Stan decided they were ready to finally have children. They had been saving all of Libby's paycheck each month by living economically in a tiny apartment and continuing to drive their old cars from their college days. They had a sizable nest egg set aside to make a down payment on a real home.

With their decision made to begin their family, the first thing they did was to move out of their apartment into a house they found in their old neighborhood. It was a three-bedroom house needing just a bit of fixing up to make it absolutely ideal for their new family.

After getting pregnant with their first child, Libby quit her job to stay at home. One year later, she had another child. This was just how they had planned it. Both babies were healthy and beautiful. Libby and Stan thought their lives must be as close to perfect as any two people could ever hope for.

Libby loved the idea of staying home to raise their children and fill the role of homemaker. And she was good at it! The children were well adjusted, the house was always impeccably clean, and Libby rather enjoyed the role of hostess for Stan's many dinner guests since his promotion at work. The problem she unveiled for us was all too familiar, however.

As the children entered the toddler stage, Libby would generally get up at five o'clock in the morning, feed the children and her husband, do the wash, clean the house, do the shopping, and the like. She never seemed to "have a moment of peace." It seemed that the children, who were with her constantly, were always demanding more and more from her. They had boundless energy and were in continuous motion, creating new challenges for Libby on a daily basis.

Each evening about the time her normal routine was nearly completed, Stan would arrive home from work, often with a dinner guest. By the time dinner was over, the children put to bed, and the house straightened, it was usually ten o'clock at night. Then Stan wanted to talk. At about 11 o'clock, he was ready for bed. When Stan was ready for bed, he expected that Libby was ready for bed as well. He just couldn't go to sleep most nights unless he and Libby made love. Being a "dutiful" wife and loving Stan intensely, Libby would comply. By the time sex was over and Stan was asleep it would usually be after midnight. Now it was Libby's time to be alone, but she was too tired to care.

Libby confided in us that the routine was about to kill her. The physical exhaustion was bad enough she said, but the virtual absence of private time was hurting her the most. Her whole day involved attending to the needs of others. Worse yet, Stan did not understand because, after all, "now she was only a housewife after she had worked for a high-pressure marketing firm!" She had, according to Stan, plenty of time to be alone during the day. Libby's need for privacy and aloneness had reached the point of desperation. Now we were beginning to understand why she was dining out by herself. For Libby, this was the only time she could be alone with her own thoughts.

The point is this … Libby's need for privacy and aloneness was not understood by Stan. In desperation, Libby did the only thing she could … run away! To make matters worse, because Libby had taken several evening outings to get away from the children and the pressures, Stan had recently accused her of cheating on him. She was certainly in a "catch-22." She was damned if she did and damned if she didn't … a lose-lose situation!

Could we give her some advice, she asked? We talked for a long time about the need for an open conversation with her husband about her need to find privacy and alone time. Libby confided in us that her husband treated her with great respect in all other situations, but she hadn't been able to find the right words to help him fully understand just how desperate she was feeling. We told Libby about the critical roles privacy and aloneness play in successful marriages and how those needs must be respected. Suffice it to say, it apparently worked out for her and Stan. We got a thank you card from them several months later, a portion of which read as follows: "We now recognize how important it is for us to allow time for just ourselves as well as each other. The newly found high quality of our respect for each other is testament to the soundness of what we initially thought was strange advice … communication can be improved through occasional non-communication." Thirty-two years later it is still working for Libby and Stan, as they are one of the successful couples who took part in our study.

What is the message here? First of all, it seems to us that we must begin by recognizing the need for privacy and aloneness in ourselves. When we recognize the need in ourselves we are more likely to recognize and understand the need for privacy in others. We are doing others and ourselves a great disservice when we do not provide for ourselves the opportunity to cleanse our minds. Respecting that need is critical to achieving the *Golden Rule* present in all successful marriages.

Each individual has a different level of need that can change at different stages in her life. Understanding and recognizing the level of need can be quite difficult at times, especially for a person with a low level of need for privacy and aloneness. Being alone with your thoughts provides for you a periodic psychological renewal. A few moments alone with your thoughts each day free the spirit and cleanse the soul. Do not deny yourself these moments together with yourself. You know what we are talking about, don't you? Remember to recognize that your spouse also has these same needs.

Second, and just as important, is assuring yourself and your spouse that it is natural to have this need and that everyone has this need. In other words, feeling guilty about needing and wanting alone time is not appropriate or healthy. Recognize the need and embrace it.

If you and your spouse allow each other time for privacy and aloneness, think of the possibilities. The quality of communication can only be enhanced between the two of you after refreshing your minds and spirits with alone time. Did you ever notice how hard it is to talk and listen to someone else when your mind is overflowing with thoughts about work, home, children, and the like? No matter how hard you try, you listen but you do not really hear. And you want to know why? It is because you have denied yourself those moments of belonging only to yourself. What kind of real communication goes on between the two people in a marriage within this context? We believe the evidence is clear—not much!

Isn't it interesting that at the root of successful communication with your mate is no communication at all? You'll have to admit, this is an interesting notion with considerable merit. While we were quite taken with the idea in our early interviews with successful couples, it was not until some of their stories and examples so poignantly illustrated the concept that we fully grasped the importance of the need for privacy and aloneness. Sometimes we try so hard to be great communicators that we end up with results opposite from our intentions. Because of our social nature, we have been misled into believing that we must always socialize. You only have to consider this for a moment to see the fallacy in this kind of thinking.

If we were pressed, we would probably admit that privacy and aloneness have been at the top of our list of needs many times in our marriage. We live such hectic lives at work that the time to be alone with our own thoughts is paramount to our engaging in any meaningful communication with each other. The recognition and respect for these dual needs are fundamental to successful communication in a marriage. If we are unable to communicate, nothing else matters.

You have to belong to yourself before you can belong to others. Do not miss the opportunity. As the song goes, "Even lovers need a holiday … time away … from each other!"

— *Advice* —

There are numerous ways in which a husband and wife can develop a quality relationship based on mutual respect. Most of the advice that follows came to us from the successful couples we have interviewed over the past 25 years. The couples that gave us this advice have marriages we hold in high regard, ones that are characterized by mutual admiration and respect, ones that thrived for more than 30 years. It is common sense advice, yet often it is not followed because individuals forget to take the time to support their own spouses and use the *Golden Rule*. They get too busy with their own needs, and forget that respect takes time and love.

The *Golden Rule* means that you take the time necessary to demonstrate respect for the one you love. Here are some ways to develop the important feelings of mutual respect in your marriage.

1. **Remember the *Golden Rule* of respect: "Treat your spouse the way you would like to be treated."** Courtesy and politeness should always be on the front burner. Whenever you and your spouse are together, be the nice, wonderful person you really are. For instance, use the words "please," "thank you," and "you're welcome." These

simple courtesies mean a lot. Habits can be formed either way, good or bad, so why not make it a habit to always treat your spouse the way you would want to be treated. Make it a pervasive characteristic of your marriage.

Respect the complexity of your marriage partner. Your partner is a complex entity with many interests, ideas, desires, habits, and experiences. Don't narrowly define your mate's capabilities. Show interest in your spouse's work, his hobbies, and in the multitude of activities in which he is engaged. Find out what your partner's strengths are and take time to make compliments about those strengths. Graciously help your spouse when she needs to work on one of her weak points. Care deeply about what is important to your spouse, from the littlest things to the major issues.

Do nice things for each other. Treat your spouse like the special person he is, not as your personal slave. Periodically, slip your spouse a little note under her pillow that describes some of your favorite things about her. Leave him a little sticky note of good cheer for the day that can be placed in his wallet. Find unique ways to tell your mate just how special she really is to you. Make this a habit in your lives together.

2. **Respect yourself individually.** You can't respect someone else unless you show respect for yourself. A good example of this would be to look for your own strong points and build on your strengths. As your strengths become solid, negative aspects fade into the background. Don't put yourself down, instead recognize your strengths and strive to enhance them. The point is, if you recognize and build on your strengths, the negative habits become easy to overcome.

3. **Never share in a public forum any private family matters.** Why do you think they call them "family secrets"? Once said in public, the words can never be taken back. The damage is already done.

4. **Respect your spouse's opinions.** You can't always be right. Your spouse has a set of experiences that form the basis for his opinions. Those experiences are uniquely different from yours. At the same time be careful not to put your spouse on a pedestal. She possesses human frailties just like you. If you think she can do no wrong, you set both her and yourself up for ultimate disappointment. Your spouse makes mistakes just like you. Respect him for it.

5. **Begin by recognizing the dual need for privacy and aloneness in yourself and your spouse.** The recognition and practice of the absolute need for privacy and aloneness is, in our judgment after analyzing thousands of interviews, a fundamental predisposition of successful marriages. The amount of time available to satisfy these two needs varies from one marriage to another and from one marriage partner to another. But one thing is clear, all marriages will stand the test of time only if these dual needs are recognized and respected. How do you and your spouse improve the quality of communication based on this notion?

   Discuss with your mate why the need for privacy and aloneness is important and necessary for both of you. Talk about the need to cleanse your minds before meaningful communication can occur between the two of you. Identify for each other the ways in which these needs can be satisfied, such as by reading a book, taking an uninterrupted snooze on the living room couch, spending time staring out the window, or puttering in the garden.

Attempt to recognize the alert signs for needing time alone. In other words, what verbal and non-verbal messages does your spouse emit when she needs to be alone? Can you agree on a signal or statement that would be a cue to allow your spouse some time to be away from you just for privacy and aloneness? What kind of DO NOT DISTURB sign can you work out between you so you will know when to respect that need?

6. **Do not continually follow your spouse in lock step every time they move throughout the house.** We are reminded of the wife who would even follow the husband into the bathroom, sit on the floor, and talk to her husband as he was sitting on the throne reading his favorite magazine. As the husband told us his story, he kept saying how much this felt like an invasion of his privacy in the worst way. Privacy arrangements within your own house may need to be worked out between the two of you. The conversation about this issue will need to be handled most delicately.

   Another way of invading your spouse's privacy is by asking your spouse a lot of pointless questions just to hear yourself talk or make conversation. Say something when you have something important to say. Say nothing when you have nothing significant or important to say. Sometimes, silence can be golden. Learn to appreciate silence and give your spouse the space he needs during his alone time.

7. **Do not, we repeat, do not ever get jealous or angry with your spouse when she needs to be alone.** If she senses your displeasure, she either won't allow herself the opportunity to be alone or she will resent you for being jealous or angry because of her need to be alone! This is one area that takes

understanding and respect from both partners in a marriage. Whatever you do, never feel guilty because you spent time alone. If you feel guilty, you cannot be expected to follow through on your own need for time alone. Remember that the absolute need for privacy and aloneness is a fundamental predisposition of every human being, so feeling guilty about it is illogical.

Our research with successfully married couples tells us that marital communication is enhanced and expanded when the minds of the respective individuals in the marriage have been given the opportunity for cleansing. When a person is at peace with himself or herself, he or she can feel free to communicate. He or she is capable of effective communication. If you do not occasionally allow yourself the opportunity to belong only to yourself, you will never be able to belong to someone else.

When the *Golden Rule* becomes a pervasive characteristic of your marriage, you and your spouse will be a part of a mutual admiration society that builds on each other's strengths. You will treat each other like each of you would like to be treated—with the kindness and dignity you deserve. Your roles in the marriage will be determined out of respect for each other's talents and your life circumstances, not by gender and tradition alone. You both will respect each other's occasional need for privacy and aloneness, bringing you an enhanced communicative relationship.

The true value of a relationship is measured not by what the two individuals think about respect, but how they show respect for each other. The *Golden Rule* is easy to understand but many times more difficult to practice consistently. Every person is special, and you selected one to cherish forever. Make that forever filled with respect and love, so you two can celebrate your Golden Anniversary together. Start today!

⋖⋗

CHAPTER 10

Seven Surprising Secrets #4:
Your Body Is Your Castle

The message is a simple one, really. What you eat,
how much you eat, and how you care for
the appearance of your body can affect
the relationship you have with your spouse.

E DON'T KNOW WHAT YOU
had for breakfast this morning, but it may well affect the way you feel
and act for the rest of your day. Your feelings, the way you emote, your
anxiety, your productivity, your ability to engage in a loving relationship, are all affected by what you put into your mouth and how you
maintain the health and appearance of your body. The effects can be
quite dramatic—for good and for bad. Successful marriages long ago
recognized that you must manage your mind and mood through
food, exercise, and attention to your appearance, since *Your Body*
Is Your Castle.

Interestingly, in our early interviews with successful couples they talked about the importance of what they ate and drank, but didn't relate it directly to their psychological well-being. That has changed for successful couples over the last ten years with the knowledge gained from research demonstrating that changes in mood can be directly attributable to what foods, additives, drinks, and chemicals you put into your body.

What's the message here? It's a simple one, really. What you eat, how much you eat, and how you care for the appearance of your body can affect the relationship you have with your spouse. Pardon the pun but this notion really is "food for thought." Simply put, you can enhance your relationship with your spouse if you pay careful attention to the link between food and mood. Over the years we've come up with a formula that improves the way we feel psychologically and, thus, improves the way we communicate with each other.

Have you ever heard the old familiar saying, you are what you eat? More importantly, we believe, you are psychologically what you eat. And if you do not believe this, did you ever notice how lethargic you feel after you have eaten a large evening meal? Your tummy is full, you feel drained, and you are filled with this overwhelming desire to sleep. When people talk you find it hard to concentrate enough to comprehend what it is they are saying to you. As a matter of fact, you don't really care what they are saying to you. You would rather head to the recliner and settle in for the evening.

Another excellent example of food affecting a person's psychological state is the change in behavior of a child who "lives" on candy and other sweets. They are hyperactive, erratic, and are characterized by dramatic and rapid mood swings. Simply put, the sugar affects the way they psychologically react. Sugar sets in motion chemical changes affecting the metabolism of their bodies.

It has been discovered through research that greasy or high-fat foods also affect you psychologically. Greasy foods, in a real sense, "weigh you down." Too much of this kind of food changes the way you react psychologically. If you eat low-fat, high-energy, multi-grained foods, you will not only feel better psychologically, you will also look better. It is a nutritional fact that increased body weight does not come from diets rich in low-fat, high-energy, and multi-grained foods. So take time to watch the number of grams of fat in prepared foods and begin limiting your fat intake so you will improve both your appearance and psychological health. You will be healthier in both body and mind.

This notion that what you eat or do not eat affects your moods and behaviors is a principle that is generally accepted by the person on the street. We have all lived too long to believe otherwise! But if you want to get frustrated, discuss this issue with many medical professionals. Talk about 17th century thinking! These professionals are quick to agree that smoking is related to lung cancer, that cholesterol is associated with heart disease, and that moderate exercise promotes good health. However, try presenting the notion that proper eating habits and vitamin and mineral supplementation affect us in a positive way *psychologically* and, thus, affect the way we communicate with others. Well, get ready for a heated discussion. Our experience is that the mention of this notion causes most of the medical professionals we know to turn us off like a water faucet! Trust your instincts and the latest research results on the link between foods, additives, and drink on psychological health. Intuitively, you know there must be a strong positive correlation between proper eating habits and good psychological health. Over the last several years the research is proving that to be the case.

It has taken us many years of research and experimentation, but we do believe that our formula improves the way we feel psychologically and, thus, improves the way we communicate with each other. Taking into consideration what we have learned from nutritional research and the research linking foods and additives to psychological wellness, we formed our recommendations for areas of focus that can improve your psychological health as well as your physical health.

First, become familiar with the basic tenets of proper nutrition. Go to the your local bookstore and look in the health section to find a basic nutrition book to read. Next, read a thoughtful book about vitamins and minerals. You can also check out the USDA website www.MyPyramid.gov as another resource. When you have acquired the basic foundational knowledge of nutrition and vitamins, you are ready to begin further exploration of this subject.

In continuing the exploration of how nutrition affects you, try a little experiment. Over the next three weeks, eat the way you and your spouse normally eat, keeping a detailed daily record of everything you eat, when you eat it, and how you feel after you have eaten. Incidentally, doing this together also provides each of you with the opportunity to sharpen your focus on the potential effects of the important characteristic of *Your Body Is Your Castle* to your marriage.

After the three-week period, analyze your eating habits according to your newly acquired basic knowledge of nutrition. If you are like us, you will make several profound discoveries. Most of you will discover you do not often eat well-balanced meals. You eat too much sugar, salt, and greasy foods. You probably rely on fast or already prepared foods, which are devoid of nutritional value in many cases. You probably also eat way too rapidly and drink too many things that are not good for you—too much alcohol in particular. The point here is simple. We all have a lot of poor habits. It is difficult to make changes in your lifestyle unless you take the time to realize how your bad habits affect your physical and psychological health. When you come to that realization, you are ready to improve in this important aspect of your marriage.

After doing our first set of interviews with successfully married couples, we heard so much from them about taking care of each other's health and good eating habits that we thought we should look more carefully at our own habits. So, almost 25 years ago we did this very same exercise to analyze our eating habits. Talk about poor eating habits! Since we were on the move constantly trying to gain a foothold in the early stages of our careers, we never took the time to prepare well-balanced meals, let alone worry about what the food did to our moods. It was more a question of throwing together whatever we could as fast as we could when we both got home from work completely worn out. When we analyzed our eating habits over a three-week period, all we were sure we were getting was a large number of calories and precious few nutrients. No wonder we didn't seem to feel at our peaks psychologically.

With considerable study and much effort, the two of us drastically changed our diet. We prepared a salad every day and worked hard to vary the ingredients. One day we would accent it with tomatoes and cucumber, another day with dried cranberries and toasted almonds, another day with carrots and cooked beets. Changing the salad dressings has also often added to the variety of our meals. We have included several of our favorite fresh salad recipes in the Appendix (p. 288), creating for you a different recipe to try each day over the next two weeks. By then you will be ready to pick out your favorites, vary the ingredients of others, or create your own new recipes. The important thing is to develop the daily habit of adding a salad with fresh ingredients to your diet.

Back in the early days of our change in diet it was tough to find the fresh ingredients, plus everything had to be prepared from scratch. However, in most grocery stores today you can find lettuce cut and ready to serve, small, bite-size tomatoes, carrots and radishes already sliced, and beets already cooked and ready to be put directly into the salad. It makes salad recipe creation and preparation a lot more enjoyable.

Another part of our plan was to cut down on the sugars, fats, and white breads. The fats and white breads were especially difficult for Charley to cut down on while the sugars and white breads were difficult for Liz. We did lower our intake of these eventually, but we had to make a concerted effort to steadily reduce all of these until our normal diet contained more fish, multi-grains, fruits, and vegetables, substituting for the sugars, fats, and white breads. This is an area we still continue to work at even today.

Our normal diet has been filled with good nutrition, fun ingredients, and interesting menus for the last 25 years. Almost every day we still eat a salad we create from fresh ingredients. We learned a lot from the successful couples we first interviewed more than 25 years ago and our study of the importance of food and mood. We are convinced that we have added to the fullness and longevity of our lives together by changing our eating habits through the knowledge we gained from our research. In a sense we love each other so much that we owe it to each other to eat right and take care of our psychological health as well as our physical health.

Improvement comes by designing a program to eliminate, or at least diminish, the frequency of eating the foods which you have discovered adversely affect you. In addition, we recommend that you take a daily vitamin and mineral supplement appropriate to your body build and lifestyle. Why, you say? If you believe that you get all the proper nutrition you need by simply eating the proper foods, then we have some swampland in Arizona we would like to sell you! With today's lifestyles and fast-paced existence, taking a vitamin and mineral supplement ensures that you do not miss some of the basic needs that you did not have time to expertly plan for in your diet.

Extending the concept one step further, since you are psychologically what you put into your body, consideration should also be given to eliminating some of those other bad habits. Quit smoking, cut way down on the alcohol consumption, and eliminate any unnecessary over-the-counter medications you take. Develop a moderate exercise program the two of you can enjoy doing together.

What's the message here? It should be obvious. Namely, you can do a lot to improve the way you feel physically and psychologically. When you do this you naturally improve the way you communicate. Give it a try!

While these changes are not easy, they are really worth it. Of course, if you are unwilling to make the necessary changes, then you are going to greatly restrict your ability to find lasting love with your spouse and celebrate your Golden Anniversary together.

There is another aspect of the communicative relationship involving food that we would like for you to consider. When was the last time you and your spouse cooked a meal together? When was the last time you ate a meal together without the newspaper providing a barrier between the two of you? What about the television? It is rather difficult to communicate with each other or your children when your conversation is constantly interrupted by the events in Iraq, or Washington, or … you see, there are things you can do to control the conditions under which food enters into your lives. You can control what you eat. You can control when you eat. You can control where you eat. Yes, you can control the quality of your communication by controlling what, when, and where you eat. A marriage does, to a large extent, survive on its stomach, and the conditions surrounding each meal need to enhance the psychological atmosphere. Remember, you are psychologically what you eat!

The dramatic impact of the relationship between a person's psychological state and the food he or she eats became quite evident to us many years ago. One of Charley's students, Randy, came to him complaining of dizziness, a high level of anxiety, and constant irritability. The student had been recently married and was concerned that his frequent outbursts of irritation were driving a wedge between him and his new wife. A simple case of "newly married jitters" thought Charley. A few sessions of counseling with Randy and all his problems would go away, right? Wrong! Counseling did not work.

Nothing seemed to work for Randy. Perhaps we were dealing with a physical problem of some sort. Maybe a check-up by a doctor would be in order. After a series of tests, the doctor concluded that Randy had nothing wrong with him. Needless to say both Randy and Charley were relieved.

You guessed it, even though Randy had nothing medically wrong with him, he still had the same symptoms he came to Charley with in the first place. Well, Charley had been doing some research into the nature of the relationship between eating and drinking behaviors and psychological state. (People who study these kinds of things are called orthomolecular psychologists). So, as a last resort, Charley decided to ask Randy to keep a daily log of everything he ate and drank for one week. Randy was instructed to record everything! Randy was so desperate, he would do anything, even something as ridiculous as keeping a daily log of his eating and drinking patterns.

When Randy brought in his log for Charley's review, everything seemed normal except one thing. Randy drank 30 to 40 cups of coffee per day! Poor old Randy, he was suffering from the "coffee crazies." To make a long story short, Charley assisted Randy in establishing a program of coffee withdrawal. Within four weeks, Randy was down to only two cups of coffee per day, and decaffeinated coffee at that! Randy reported that his emotional distress seemed to have completely vanished. He and his wife were doing great again. Coffee had become a psychological poison for Randy, due to his extraordinarily large consumption of coffee. Without it Randy was now calm and relaxed. His dizziness, irritability, and anxiety disappeared. Randy really had become psychologically what he drank and the impact was dramatic.

Just as too much of something like coffee can cause dramatic psychological and relationship issues, too little of the proper foods can also cause unusual psychological effects. Several years ago we interviewed a couple that had been happily married for 37 years. When

Myrtle and Wally were asked what was the most difficult time in their marriage, they looked at each other and Myrtle immediately blushed. Wally started to explain. They had been married for about ten years when Wally noticed Myrtle was acting very strangely. Instead of her jovial self, Myrtle was grumpy, depressed, and argumentative. Even the slightest difference of opinion caused her to go into a rage that resulted in arguments nearly all of the time. Myrtle had been yelling at everybody, especially Wally. He had no earthly idea what had gotten into Myrtle and didn't know how to help her. This was such a drastic change, which had lasted for over a week, that Wally wanted Myrtle to go to a professional for help.

It appeared to Wally that Myrtle was on another of her famous 12-times-a-year diets, but she had never been this crazy when dieting. Myrtle was only about 30 pounds overweight since the baby was born, but she worried about it constantly. So, periodically she would get frustrated with her weight and decide to diet. Her diets usually lasted about three days before she lost her willpower and started to consume her regular quantities of food again. Myrtle explained that this time it was different—she really stayed on her diet.

Myrtle said that she didn't feel like her jolly attitude would ever return. She felt grumpy all of the time. No problem, Myrtle thought, dieting is hard work. Myrtle explained that no one seemed to understand that she really did feel totally grouchy and irritable all of the time. Neither of these feelings were normal experiences for her. She knew there was something terribly wrong with her but did not relate it to her new diet.

Myrtle resisted going to a professional for the next couple of days, but nothing seemed to work. She was the one who normally put a spark in the air with her laughter and kept the marriage constantly on an even keel. Now, Myrtle was becoming clearly psychotic, and even lapsed into hallucinations. Her constant distortion of reality was just plain spooky. Sweet, lovable, gentle, and competent Myrtle was even becoming a danger to herself. Myrtle said that Wally didn't know the extent of how bad things were at first, but she finally told him. Myrtle explained that she really didn't want to live with those feelings any longer and had thoughts of running away or doing something terrible to herself.

Wally took a couple of days off work to start watching Myrtle's every move, trying to see if he could figure something out or at least protect her from herself since she refused to get help. The first thing he did was prepare Myrtle a nice breakfast. Instead of eating it, she just played with the toast and drank only her hot tea. He figured it was just the depression, so he decided to fix her favorite dish for lunch. Sure that Myrtle could not resist shrimp pasta, he called her in for lunch. To his amazement, she just sat there and again drank only her tea. Due to their conflicting work schedules, Myrtle and Wally had only had one meal together in the last week, so he never thought about what she was or wasn't eating. Wally immediately asked Myrtle about which diet plan she was on now. The answer told the entire story. Myrtle said, "Her own plan—a total water and liquid diet."

Ah, the truth be known! It became blatantly apparent to Wally that Myrtle was starving herself. She wanted so badly to lose those 30 pounds that she had gained after the baby was born that she literally quit eating. After reading about the wonderful results of a water diet, she committed herself to drinking only water until she returned to her ideal weight. Of course, the water diet was only intended for one day of body cleansing, not as a long-term weight reduction method. But Myrtle was so desperate after trying so many different diets that never seemed to work that she came up with her own crazy plan. No wonder Myrtle was a psychological wreck—there just is not enough nutritional nourishment in water by itself to keep anyone's health intact.

Wally talked sense into Myrtle, so she understood that it was all right to eat something. He worked with Myrtle to educate her about low-fat diets and the advantages of consistently good eating habits.

And while Wally was at it, he decided that he and Myrtle ought to take daily multiple-vitamin supplements. He went to the local store to buy a natural vitamin supplement that both of them have continued taking to this day.

With Wally's help, Myrtle began by eating three small and well-balanced meals per day. To ensure that she was getting the proper nutrition, Myrtle continued to supplement her diet with the vitamins Wally bought for her. Within just four days, Myrtle returned to her old self. Her psychosis disappeared. It seems that Myrtle's emotional and mental state improved dramatically through proper nutrition. Orthomolecular psychology strikes again! And incidentally, Myrtle lost the 30 pounds slowly and steadily with proper nutrition and a regular exercise program. She looked great... and she felt great again! Wally and Myrtle both said they learned a great deal from that terrible experience. For them, it was why they understood and paid such close attention to the characteristic of *Your Body Is Your Castle* in their relationship.

All married couples need to have a better understanding about the relationship between nutrition and psychological health. You need to become aware of how a change in nutritional regimes can influence behaviors and consequently your relationship with your spouse. Think of all the married couples of the world that think food and drink are for the physical body only. The way you feel psychologically influences the way you communicate with your spouse. And the way you feel psychologically is, to a large extent, dependent on what you eat and drink. While not all psychological problems are a result of poor nutrition, the next section will give you a few very obvious food influences that can be avoided or enhanced to make you feel different within just a few days time.

Did you ever hear of hypoglycemia? Well, first of all, it's the opposite of diabetes. Basically, it is an excess of the sugar-related hormone released by the pancreas in response to a rapidly rising blood sugar level. When blood sugar levels are driven below normal by this hormone, a person will develop a craving for sweets. More importantly, a number of mental and physical symptoms can occur as a result of this low blood sugar problem. For example, have you ever suffered from depression, dizziness, headaches, fatigue, cold hands and feet, insomnia, or crying spells? We bet you have. If you ingest an overabundance of sugar or seem to crave sugar, there is a chance that these symptoms were caused by the vicious cycle of too much sugar ingestion, followed by a lowering of the blood sugar level, followed by more intake of sugar, followed by … and so it goes. For many, the cycle is never-ending.

Did you know that almost all processed food has sugar in it? According to Carlton Frederick, a well known author of books and articles about the relationship between nutrition and psychological health, the average American swallows 1 and 1/3 teaspoons of sugar every 35 minutes, 24 hours a day! And you thought you only got sugar when you put a scoop in your coffee. Start reading the food labels, looking for the words sugar, sucrose, fructose, maltose, glucose, syrup, or dextrose. You will be amazed at the high levels of these sugars in your commonly prepared foods.

Remember the coffee crazies? Did you ever suffer from coffee nerves? Caffeine in coffee stimulates the central nervous system. This in small amounts can make you more alert and ready to think. However, for heavy coffee drinkers the caffeine level can be at an extremely high level, directly affecting the psychological system. What is worse, if they do not continue to consume large amounts of caffeine, a heavy coffee drinker can become irritable, intolerant, dizzy, and full of anxiety. Like sugar, the cycle can be vicious.

Nicotine is another chemical additive agent related to emotional problems. As a matter of fact, heavy smoking can rob the body of blood glucose, its major fuel. Heavy smoking can create a desire for more sugar and caffeine. Talk about vicious cycles! If you do smoke, don't just think about the adverse effects of smoking on your lungs.

Consider the psychological impact and maybe it will provide you with the necessary reason to seriously think about quitting.

What about alcohol, you ask? There are more adverse effects on your body from alcohol than just the obvious ones reported by the media. Did you know that alcohol destroys vitamins and minerals in the body? Talk about biting the hand that feeds you! Too much alcohol can actually cause malnutrition. And we know from Myrtle's story what can happen when malnutrition strikes. While research indicates a glass or two of red wine can have positive effects on your psychological and physical well-being, too much of a good thing can have the same negative effects on you as other alcoholic drinks.

As you determine how to alter your food and drink input to improve your overall psychological well-being, another possible area to investigate is food additives. There is much research indicating the possible effects of food additives and preservatives on some people. If you are one of those sensitive individuals who are affected by preservatives or artificial coloring or flavors, you need to become a label ingredients reader and rely more heavily on fresh products. They are better for you anyway. Think back to all those quickie foods you eat, or worse yet, feed your spouse. Quickie foods are foods that have been refined and processed, contain food additives, often have high sugar content, and contain many chemical pollutants without much nutritional value.

It is not our purpose to scare you to death when we talk about your nutritional intake, substance behaviors, and psychological health. It is our purpose to convince you of the importance of the direct linkage between your nutritional habits and your psychological wellness. The quality of your relationship with your spouse is directly linked to how you feel. If you quit smoking and if you control your use of coffee and alcohol, then you can exercise greater control over the way you feel, or for that matter, the way you make your spouse feel.

The successful couples we interviewed made the food and mood aspects high priorities in their lives together. They learned the importance of taking care of their psychological and physical health through good nutrition and exercise.

Long ago we established the tradition of scheduling our respective annual physicals on the same day. Why, you ask? It's simple really— we love each other from the bottom of our respective hearts and want to be around each other for as much as we can for as long as we can.

Think about it—beyond your own health, whose health do you concern yourself with the most? We bet it is the one you love the most. In the loving relationships we have observed over the years, including our own, we note how much happier people are in their lives when they are personally healthy and when the one they love the most is healthy as well.

Frankly, and in our humble opinion, we have a mutual responsibility to each other to do our best to maintain our health. We eat well, take our vitamins, are religious about taking our medications every day, and riding our bikes on the many trails in St. Louis has become nearly addictive. We encourage each other to do all of these things and then top off our year by having our annual physicals. It is always better to catch a health problem in the very early stages, so a physical exam is a must. Oh, and the good news is—we passed our physicals this year with flying colors!

Doing our best to stay healthy for ourselves and for the ones we love is the best way we can think of to say, "I love you." And being healthy makes that "physical love" all the more fun and exciting!

Another important aspect of the characteristic of *Your Body Is Your Castle* in successful marriages is the care of your physical appearance. Do you remember the impression you had when you met your spouse for the first time? You probably stopped dead in your tracks and stared because they looked so good! With a sparkle in their eyes, successful couples often describe the notion of looking good quite eloquently as they brag about their mates. In our interviews, we continually hear statements like, "My wife is the sunshine of my day." "My husband makes me feel good all over when he gets dressed up just to take me out to dinner." "She is still the same hot chick I married 48 years ago." "He lost 25 pounds just for me." "She is beautiful, don't you think?" "He is the most dashing man I've ever met!"

Successful couples brag about how much effort their partners put into making their physical appearances look terrific just for them. They talk about trying to look their best for each other and they work hard at presenting themselves in the most positive light. The fascinating part to us is that even the most "unattractive" or "ordinary" looking happily married couples find each other most appealing. It isn't about their natural beauty. But rather, it is in the eyes of the beholder that they are good looking, beautiful, or handsome. Even the most gorgeous or handsome person who becomes an unwashed slob at home on a regular basis tells a lot about the general lack of regard for his or her spouse. Caring enough to look your very best for your mate is the essence of this aspect of *Your Body Is Your Castle*.

The point is this. We do form impressions of people by the way they present themselves to us. If they generally look nice, wear clean clothes, are nicely manicured, and smile, we view them differently than if they are normally sloppy and not well groomed. We have a more positive feeling about them. That is just human nature. It is a pervasive characteristic that came through in successful marriages. Happily married couples take great care to look nice and smile for their spouses.

There are times when we all do "let our hair down." Thank goodness we occasionally have that opportunity. But what if that happened nearly all the time? Does the following describe the scene at your house? Nearly every day you are running around the house in a worn out, ten-year-old bathrobe. Your hair is dirty and messy. You are lounging around in your underwear. You're unshaven. You went to bed dirty last night because you were just too tired to take a shower. Sure, you say, "If I can't relax at home where am I going to relax?" Valid point! What if, however, that describes the way you normally look around the house? That doesn't qualify as the occasional "letting your hair down." Did you ever wonder what message you are communicating to your spouse?

You see, taking care of your personal appearance is an important characteristic in a successful marriage and is a powerful form of communication. Think of the beautiful messages you are sending out when you look great. You simply must take the time to put your best foot forward when you are around your lover. And if you don't think the way you look makes a difference, consider this. Do you remember the last time you and your spouse got all dressed up to go out to a party or your anniversary dinner? She looked lovely and sexy in her gorgeous evening dress. Her makeup was on just right. She looked like the next Jennifer Aniston, Halle Berry, or Jessica Simpson. He looked tall and handsome in his neatly pressed suit—kind of a James Bond look-alike. As a matter of fact, you turned each other on. Cold chills ran up and down your spine. Suddenly, the thought of going out lost some of its appeal. The thought of staying in gained in its appeal. Thoughts of a cold bottle of champagne, candlelight, and a burning fireplace suddenly caused you to be overwhelmed with romantic urges. The aspect of looking good for your spouse was in full swing.

Much of the time, how you look also determines your mental attitude about how you feel and vice versa. When you do not look good and in turn do not feel good about yourself, it becomes very difficult to communicate good feelings toward your spouse. One of the best illustrations of this concept is characterized by the relationship between Paul and Betsy. They were the best of friends throughout their high school years. Both Betsy and Paul were chosen by their high school classmates as the most likely to succeed. So on to the university they went.

Those two vibrant, good-looking college students turned their friendship into a blossoming romance. By their junior year at the university, they had decided they could not wait until graduation to get married. Both sets of parents were delighted with their decision since they were sure Paul and Betsy were perfect for each other. Betsy's parents were totally excited about planning for the wedding. In fact, the planning process was unlike any of the horror stories their friends had warned them about. The in-laws got along famously and the wedding planning went smoothly from start to finish. They were actually ready for the wedding the week before it was scheduled to happen.

At the wedding we could not get over what a beautiful couple Paul and Betsy were together. Heads would surely turn, no matter where they went. Paul and Betsy just seemed to radiate health, beauty, and love.

Every time we saw them for the first six months of their marriage, they were hand in hand, gazing at each other like they were still on their first date. We were convinced that they must certainly be the perfect couple. When they decided to continue with their education right into graduate school, everyone celebrated, knowing this couple was bound to accomplish great things together. However, as the academic demands became greater, all of their time was spent studying. While studying late into the night Paul and Betsy consumed just about every snacking food in sight. Almost overnight they seemed to blow up like balloons being rapidly inflated with helium gas.

By the end of their second year together, each gained well over 50 pounds. Needless to say, out the window went the good looking wardrobe, the slinky dresses, the tapered suits, and the sexy nightgowns. Unfortunately, out the window also went their hand holding and moonstruck gazing at each other.

We tried to get them to come for walks with us or go for a swim or take a bike ride—anything that would help Paul and Betsy start to reverse the pattern of junk food eating, lack of exercising, and sloppy dressing cycle that they had gotten into. Nothing we suggested seemed to work. Instead, by the end of their third year together, each of them seemed to gain another 50 pounds and dress even sloppier. It appeared that they had also given up on bathing, since we never saw them when they didn't look or smell like a dirty old sock.

By the time they earned their master's degrees neither Paul nor Betsy had any joy within them to give to each other. We watched what we thought would be a marriage of true perfection turn into a dismal routine rut of lackluster images. Neither of them ever dressed up for each other, or for that matter even bothered to put on clean clothes. Smiles toward each other just never seemed to appear anymore.

After we all said our goodbyes at their graduation and parted to go our own separate ways, we talked for hours about how painful it was to see two such terrific people so very sad. What could possibly have caused them to change so drastically in such a short period of time? We guessed that we would never really find out the answer.

As it turned out, we did not hear from Betsy or Paul again until 20 years later at an alumni reunion. Much to our total surprise, the two people that came up to give us the warmest of greetings were Betsy and Paul, looking just like we remembered them from their wedding picture. That is to say, each had lost all of the excess weight; they had reestablished their old sharp, well-groomed dressing habits; and were back to moonstruck gazing at one another. We were absolutely delighted and just had to hear all about how they had accomplished this miracle and what had caused them to do it.

Since they were staying in town for the weekend, we set up a dinner date for the following evening. Our anticipation was almost more than we could bear. Here was our ideal couple back to their true form. How could they possibly have both accomplished such a drastic transformation?

Dinner was splendid, even though the next day neither of us could remember what we had eaten or anything about the restaurant we had gone to. It was the wonderful story that Paul and Betsy had to tell us that made the evening so spectacular.

It seems that Paul and Betsy left college to pursue the careers of their dreams, and nothing seemed to work out. No real good job opportunities seemed to open up and nothing worthwhile had happened to them in the five years after they left college with their master's degrees. Their relationship had deteriorated so far that the only thing Paul did at home was watch football games and drink beer. Likewise, the only thing Betsy did was to stay in the bedroom reading magazines and snacking on junk food.

The real critical turning point for them came when even the minimal job Betsy had landed was eliminated due to the company's financial difficulties. It was then that she had to go back to job-hunting in the open market.

After a very frustrating six weeks, Paul and Betsy had another one of their famous shouting matches. This time, however, Paul struck the arrow painfully close to the problem's heart. Betsy said that she wanted to die when Paul told her that she would never be employed again because no employer wanted an unwashed, fat slob to work in their business. Paul said that as soon as the words were out of his mouth, he knew the hurt and damage he had done. Not only did it cut Betsy to the bone at a very difficult time for her but it also brought up something that the two of them had NEVER before discussed—their respective weight problems. Betsy knew that the only thing slender about either of them now was their ability to smile.

Their weight problems had so adversely affected the way they felt about themselves and the way they dressed that their entire lives had been altered. Now it was so coldly and openly before them that they both just stood there staring at each other. Betsy obviously could have screamed right back those same words to Paul, since the words were just as true in his case. However, the pain she was feeling temporarily overwhelmed her into silence. Suddenly, Betsy realized just how far down the tubes each of them and their marriage had really fallen.

Paul told us that for the first time in years, they held each other and just sat there crying. "It probably did us more good than anything else," Paul said. "You see, we found out that we still loved each other very much. We had just spent so much time being defensive about how we looked that our love had gotten hidden away and pushed out of sight."

Betsy said that the first thing they did was go shopping for some decent clothes. Only two outfits apiece, since they made a pact with each other that the last five years of weight gain would be shed together, the same way they had gotten it. A rejuvenated sense of purpose took hold of both of them.

The next thing Betsy did was schedule a haircut appointment. Even 100 pounds overweight, Betsy felt beautiful when she walked into her job interview the next day. Betsy said that she approached the interview with a feeling of renewed confidence that successfully landed her the job. She has since received several promotions.

After Betsy's success, Paul worked up enough courage to begin searching for a new job to hopefully end the torment he felt working in an unskilled, minimum-wage position when he had so much more to offer. After about a month of interviews, Paul landed the job of his dreams. At long last, he was going to use all of his years of education in his work.

Betsy and Paul began exercising at least three times a week, completely changed their diet to incorporate fruits, vegetables, and fish, while cutting down on sugars, fats, and carbohydrates. They kept their promise to each other that the junk food would no longer enter their house. While they described the considerable difficulties they had with the transition to a healthy lifestyle, both Paul and Betsy admitted to the excitement they felt whenever they shed another ten pounds. They were doing it together and nothing could stop them.

Within a year and a half, they both were down to their normal weights again. Each time they changed sizes, they would treat themselves to two new outfits. This way, both of them felt that they could look very respectable during their weight loss program and stay within their meager budget.

Slowly, as the weight came off, and their pride in themselves returned, their love affair began to take on its same old vibrancy. Their thirst for life and each other flourished again. Paul and Betsy became the perfect example of the importance of looking good for yourself and your spouse. Their story, we are happy to say, is a true success story. We only wish that all of the life stories we have heard could have been as successful as Paul and Betsy's story.

Another aspect of the characteristic of *Your Body Is Your Castle* in successful marriages is all about how you dazzle your spouse on a regular basis. Melinda and Artie spent most of our interview time talking about this aspect of their 36-year marriage. They called it their spice of life. Here is how they explained it to us.

Melinda and Artie were two ordinary looking people. Artie told people he was 5 foot 11, as he liked to stretch the truth just a bit. He was actually only 5 foot 8. Melinda, however, was 5 foot 10 with bare feet and 6 foot 1 in heels. While she wasn't overweight, Melinda was a big-boned woman. The fact of the matter was, they were an odd couple at first glance. The thing that made them stand out strikingly from other couples was the radiant smiles they had for each other. We observed them for many years before conducting our interview with them. Whenever their mate came into view, Melinda or Artie always seemed to light up immediately with a glowing smile.

What was the attraction to each other? What gave them that radiant glow? As Artie explained his fascination with Melinda, it quickly became obvious. Melinda seemed to know just what clothes to wear and how to fix her hair to accentuate all of her positive features and make Artie's head turn. When we asked Melinda how she knew what to wear, was it natural or did she get assistance, she simply replied that she asked Artie and then listened for his reactions. Melinda studied not only his verbal reactions but his non-verbal ones as well. Melinda concentrated on experimenting with slightly different clothes and hairstyles until she found exactly what elicited that radiant smile from Artie. Artie also demonstrated great taste and knew what looked good on Melinda, since she seemed to get many more compliments when she wore Artie's favorites to work or to a social event. Melinda was so successful with her study of Artie's reactions that she soon learned which clothes she should buy if she wanted that immediate radiant smile from Artie and she knew which clothes would be met with an unresponsive, lukewarm smile if she selected to wear them. This made such good sense, but reading the non-verbal signs to that degree had to be a special talent for Melinda. She said it was more about questioning and really listening for the answers because of her overwhelming desire to elicit that beaming smile from Artie.

After a few years, when Melinda felt confident in her skill, she said that the next step was a great deal more difficult for her. Melinda was intent on helping Artie learn how to dress and look in a way that would make her have that same instant radiant smile when she first saw him. Melinda said that she fell deeply in love with Artie because of his intelligent, caring, and humorous personality. But unfortunately, Artie paid so little attention to his appearance that at times she knew people had to underestimate him just because of the first impression he made. They just couldn't get past his short, sloppy exterior. Melinda loved and appreciated him too much to let that continually happen, so she was determined to help him learn a new skill. But what a delicate operation this had to be. Working to let someone you love know how to look his best without damaging his ego in the process can be a difficult challenge.

Melinda began with a birthday present. She spent almost a week's salary to buy Artie a beautiful black cashmere turtleneck and grey trousers. Having carefully shopped the sales at Macy's, she was quite proud of the value of his gift. However, while she just knew Artie would look terrific in this style, it was nothing like what he usually wore. Preparation before the opening of the gift was going to be in order. Melinda made comments about how nice several actors on television looked wearing similar types of clothing. She showed Artie several magazine pictures with the same clothing and made positive comments. When it was finally time to open his present, Melinda thought she had perfectly set up his acceptance of the change. To her amazement, Artie seemed to breathe a sigh of relief when he saw the sweater. What a strange reaction. Why would he have reacted that way? Even though he verbally told Melinda how terrific the present was, she couldn't help pondering over what she read in his face—it was relief. So she asked, "What were you thinking when you saw the sweater and trousers?" Artie was silent for a long time. Then, he tentatively started his explanation.

Artie took Melinda's comments about the actors and the magazine photos as criticism. He was afraid Melinda was unhappy with him and interested in others. Artie explained that he had always wondered how he could have been so lucky to have such a beautiful and wonderful woman like Melinda love him when he was short and not at all attractive. What Melinda thought was the perfect set-up for easing into change had in fact hurt Artie in a different way. This was the start of their real two-way communications that enhanced the characteristic of *Your Body Is Your Castle* in their marriage. Melinda explained to Artie how she worked to figure out just what to wear and how to look to make him sparkle. She confided in Artie that she wanted to help him do the same thing because she knew that if she felt that same sparkle about the way he looked, other people would give him a chance to show his real personality and his talents might have a better opportunity to be more appreciated.

After much open discussion, Artie agreed to let Melinda help select his clothes and critique his appearance without feeling defensive. The first few times were obviously painful for Artie, but the reaction at work was so positive that it reinforced Melinda's selections.

Slowly but surely, Artie began to feel comfortable with Melinda's selections and advice about his clothing and style. His self-confidence was bolstered by Melinda's continual positive comments and the radiant smile he saw on her face when she looked at him.

Artie always thought he was less than good looking, but the reactions he was getting from Melinda and his co-workers made him think otherwise. He embraced the change and had no intentions of ever going back to the stained white shirt, wide-striped necktie, pocket protector, and his favorite worn-out blue sport coat.

Melinda and Artie found the characteristic of *Your Body Is Your Castle* to be an important part of their lives individually and together. Its effect was obvious by just seeing them together. But what may have been even more impressive is that their attention to this characteristic in their marriage spilled over positively to their work. Both Artie and Melinda say that they felt more confident and were more accepted by others at work. No wonder they talked about this as such an important part of their 36-year marriage.

Just as looking nice for your spouse can be an important aspect of the characteristic of *Your Body Is Your Castle*, so can a simple smile. You can express pleasure, amusement, affection, and approval with the simple curvature of your lips and without even uttering a word. Think back over the times you have tried to express these feelings verbally. It's occasionally very difficult to do, isn't it? There is an old adage that says, "You can express more feeling in a smile than with 1,000 words." Smiling is such a powerful method of expression. It has been said that a smile is the sunshine for the soul. According to the experts, it takes fewer muscles to smile than it does to frown. And it is certainly easier to smile than to verbalize the same emotions you are feeling when you smile.

Have you ever watched someone smile? A smile is a pleasant expression characterized by a sparkling of the eyes and the upward curvature at the corners of the lips. Smiling gives a person a favorable, pleasing, and agreeable appearance.

Several years ago we were enjoying a speech by a renowned psychologist that drove home the important role of smiling. He said, in effect, that it is biologically, physically, chemically, and humanly impossible to sprout an ulcer and smile at the same time. It seems that when we smile and laugh, our body produces a set of chemicals that block the production of another set of chemicals that produce ulcers. This notion may well be one of the most important laws of the universe!

If smiling is so powerful, so easy, and so healthy, why don't we smile more frequently? Better yet, why don't we smile at our mates more often? Our guess is, we would be healthier and so would our spouse. And friends, think of the wonderful communication possibilities smiling would afford you in your marriage. How many times have you smiled at your mate today?

For us, the best part of the day is when we awake, look at each other, and smile. You know what that smile says to the two of us? It says we're alive and in love. It says, go forth and conquer the world—I'm behind you. A simple smile says so much. It communicates more than 1,000 words could ever say.

However, many marriages we have observed are smileless. The two people occupying the relationship learned somehow never to smile, going through the day with their smiling muscles on hold. Maybe they are just saving their smiling muscles. However, we cannot for the life of us figure out what they are saving them for. An old wives' tale seems appropriate here … "Use them or lose them."

It is a fact that happiness is a learned feeling. Have you ever seen people in the worst of situations laughing through what you would consider terrible conditions? On the other hand, we have all read about wealthy, successful, beautiful people committing suicide. How does one individual react so differently to the same conditions? It is a learned behavior. In other words, you can learn to smile, laugh, and be happy by learning to accept and adjust to any conditions life throws at you. With a little practice almost anyone can learn how to smile. When you smile, the whole world smiles with you. When you frown, you really do frown alone!

We've got a little game for you. Sit eyeball to eyeball with your spouse. Now smile at each other. Do it again. See how long you can hold your smiles without breaking into laughter. We won't ask you to do it again because you both are probably laughing yourself into oblivion. Smiling is easy to do and it brings forth a very positive reaction from the person you are smiling at. It brings instant warmth to the feelings in the room.

Starting today, every time you pass by your mate give them a great big smile. They'll love you for it. A smile can be your umbrella. It keeps the rain of sadness, anger, and misunderstanding away. A smile is the easiest form of communication to implement. All it takes is practice. It immediately increases the chances for the characteristic of *Your Body Is Your Castle* to become a habit in your marriage. Practice today and every day of your lives together. When you're down, bring forth the image of your lover's smile. When you do, life's little problems seem to float away and life's big problems get a little easier to handle.

Always remember to take time out from the hassles of life to look nice and wear a smile. Surely, even with all you have to do in life, you can still find the time to communicate to your spouse all of the positive feelings and emotions that smiling and looking nice can generate.

— *Advice* —

What can you and your spouse do to control those nutritional and substance habits that affect your behavior and consequently affect the way you communicate with each other? Our experience and research would suggest that we are able summarize the major issues with the advice tips listed below. While the list is by no means all-inclusive, it can start you on the right path to feeling healthy both physically and psychologically. It is offered in the hope that you and your spouse will become more cognizant of factors that affect your communication on a psychological level. Successful couples care about what they eat because they understand the importance of managing the health of their bodies as well as their minds.

They also care about the way they look for each other. When you smile and look nice you are sending beautiful messages to your spouse that increase the chances for the characteristic of *Your Body Is Your Castle* to happen and become a habit in your marriage. Taking the extra time to put your best foot forward whenever your lover is around is definitely worth the effort it takes.

Try a few of the ideas we learned from research and some of the happily married couples we interviewed to help you on your way to eating right, smiling, and looking nice for your spouse. This advice can make the characteristic of *Your Body Is Your Castle* become a natural part of your relationship, just like it is for successfully married couples.

1. **Read a good book or google some of the excellent websites about nutrition and vitamins.** In the health or psychology section of your bookstore the shelves are filled with excellent books on the subject of how different foods affect your psychological health as well as your physical health. A good website to start your nutrition education is www.MyPyramid.gov provided by the USDA. This website provides basic information about

the food groups, what each does for the body, and recommendations for proper nutrition. The more you understand about the effects of different food and drink, the better chance you have of changing your habits. Remember, successful couples pay particular attention to their nutrition because of the effects on overall mental and physical wellness.

2. **Eat lots of fresh fruits, vegetables, and whole grains that are rich in nutrients while cutting way down on foods containing salt, refined sugar, white flour, food preservatives, coloring agents, artificial flavoring, hydrogenated fat, alcohol, and nicotine.**

In the Appendix (p. 288) we provide some of our favorite fresh salad recipes for you to try over the next two weeks. We are able to add fresh vegetables to our diet with the salads we make and eat each evening with our dinner. Try some of these recipes with your dinners. They are really quite easy and a delightful way to add fresh vegetables to your daily meals.

Did you know that canned vegetables have a 239,000% increase in sodium over fresh vegetables according to one researcher? (That was not a typographical error; it really was an astounding 239,000%!) Read the labels on the food you buy. Know what the heck you are putting into the bodies of you and your spouse. There is a wealth of information on product labels that will probably shock you the first few times you study the labels of your favorite prepared foods.

Stay away from white bread and other foods that have had the nutrients and fiber content pounded out of them. That "enriched" white bread you bought yesterday only means that the vitamins had to be put back in because the processing destroyed or removed the content that was there previously. Try multi-grained breads that have not been processed to death. The grocery stores are full of already prepared fresh fruits and vegetables that can be eaten on the spot. Try new and interesting varieties to add to your meals.

Neither alcohol nor nicotine has any nutrient value whatsoever. As a matter of fact, both of the drugs actually destroy the nutrients stored in your body. Studies have indicated that red wine, as an antioxidant, is an exception to this and does have positive effects on your physical health. However, the positive effects are limited to one or two glasses per day.

3. **Relax and eat slowly.** The body digests food much easier when you relax and allow time to eat slowly. An added benefit of eating slowly is the increased chance of time for successful communications. Some of the best communicating time occurs at relaxed meals.

4. **Just use common sense about what you put in your body.** Do not get obsessed with health foods and just the "perfect" diet. Instead, gain an excellent knowledge of foods and nutrition, and then make good nutritional choices at the time of purchase, while limiting the intake of things that you know can have adverse effects on you.

Much of the advice we have given you does not sound much different from what you read in the newspaper or hear on television. The difference is this ... they are talking about the physical body as if it had nothing to do with the psychological state of a person. The equation is simple. What you eat and ingest affects the way you feel. The way you feel affects the way you communicate! Pay much more attention to the aspects of food and mood in your relationship and remember that a marriage, to a large extent, does survive physically and psychologically on its stomach.

5. **Update your at-home wardrobe.** Ditch your favorite nightgown from 1995. It might have been sexy when you bought it, but it lost its sex appeal a long time ago. Surely there is a sale going on at Macy's, Kohl's, or Dillard's that can economically land you an updated, sexy nightgown. Guys, put some decent clothes on when you watch television. Honestly, do you have to watch television in your worn-out underwear or your old jersey filled with moth holes? If your friends came over to watch football with you there would be some thought put into what you were going to wear. So, why sit there in front of the television with your wife in your old ratty underwear or moth-eaten jersey?

Find out what turns your spouse's head so you can look that way. Like Artie and Melinda, ask and listen for the answers to what makes your spouse take notice. Make the extra effort to figure it out carefully until you know exactly what looks good and what will take her breath away when you first come into view. Nothing can say more to your spouse than the effort you make to look especially appealing just for him. We guarantee you will recognize the awesome look on your mate's face and in her eyes when you hit it right.

6. **Endeavor to practice good hygiene around your spouse.** Do you remember the old saying, "I take a bath every Saturday night whether I need it or not"? Don't believe it. There is nothing as unpleasant as a person with a strong body odor, dirty hair, and dirty clothes trying to be romantic. The way your face looks is part of

the way you dress. An unshaven face or one without a touch of makeup detracts from your good looks. It's the effort you make to be appealing to your mate that counts. It is not being a supermodel, but rather being the best you can be that matters. You will be amazed at the difference it makes when you feel clean and sparkling fresh.

Also be careful with the smells. Too much of a good thing can be obnoxious and certainly not romantic. Check out the level of perfume or aftershave lotion that you put on. There is nothing worse than the lingering smell of someone in a crowded place who applied too much perfume or aftershave lotion. Ask your spouse what he or she likes and dislikes about the perfumes or aftershave lotions. You might be totally surprised by the response.

7. **Smile and laugh together often.** Remember, it takes more muscles to frown than to smile. Save your energy— smile at your spouse instead of frowning. It is the simplest of expressions with the most powerful effects. You can change the entire atmosphere with a simple smile. Greeting your spouse with a warm smile at first glance can transform even the worst of moods. Nothing makes life more enjoyable than being around a warm, smiling person. A smile is a terrible thing to waste, so practice using your smile as often as possible.

Laugh together often. Laughter is just an exaggeration of a smile. It can come from seeing a funny movie, hearing a good joke, or just sitting at a shopping mall watching the strange things people do when they don't know someone is watching. Laughter is good for the body and soul. When you sense your partner is down in the dumps, do whatever it takes to support her, until she is able to laugh or smile again. The problems of the world are easier to handle or can even disappear entirely when there is a friend at home whom you can count on to pick you up.

These ideas can be implemented immediately. They can change the atmosphere of your marriage almost instantly. Yes, the power of eating right, smiling, and taking care of your physical appearance is that great! Your whole relationship will be more productive if you feel good. Feel good about yourself by taking the extra time to look your best and spend more of your time with a smile on your face rather than a frown. It is just downright hard to be sad or crabby when your lover treats you to a warm, glowing smile, which says, "I love you so very much." And yes, the characteristic of *Your Body Is Your Castle* in a marriage causes people to smile and increases the potential for achieving a long and happy marriage together.

CHAPTER 11

Seven Surprising Secrets #5: Filing a Joint Return

Filing a Joint Return is symbolic of how happily married couples deal with their finances.

*W*E CAN AT LEAST SAY ONE good thing about the IRS: the IRS allows married couples to file a *Joint Return*. Now we all know that married couples filing a joint return generally pay a higher rate of taxes than if they were not married and filed separately. However, that's not what we are talking about here. *Filing a Joint Return* is symbolic of how happily married couples deal with their finances. Successful couples have learned to communicate about their finances and make decisions *together*.

If a couple wants their marriage to succeed, they must come to grips with the important role financial communication plays in their marriage. Married couples must talk sense when dealing with their dollars. We are convinced that one of the major causes of divorce is the breakdown in the communicative link between husband and wife over the financial aspects of their marriage. These financial strains cause tension and arguments that lead to a deterioration in the strength of their communicative bond. Because of the severe financial burdens placed on their marriage, many couples argue, blame, scapegoat, and, in effect, destroy their marriage.

Perhaps the biggest test of the strength of our relationship with each other came in our 16th year of marriage. Frankly, we thank God we paid attention to the importance of making our major financial decisions together. If we hadn't, our marriage would have been in shambles a long time ago. The story starts out well enough. After living in our house for a number of years, we decided it was time to build a new home. This house would be our "dream home." Off we went to the local supermarket to pick up an armful of those delightful magazines that are full of pictures of all those wonderful homes that everybody dreams about but nobody can afford. What the heck, shoot for the stars, we thought. Over a several-week period, we looked at those books, filled our heads full of ideas, then sketched floor plans, exterior shapes, where the bathrooms should be, and so forth. We mutually agreed that we would draw all of the floor plans ourselves and then take it to a builder for an estimate of cost. If we could not get the house we wanted at a price we could afford to pay, we would not build it. And we knew what we could afford to pay because we spent endless hours playing with figures. We wrote a nice mathematical spreadsheet that would tell us exactly how much our monthly payments would be. We even figured out what the annual taxes and insurance would be.

With the floor plans in our collective hands and armed with our computer printout detailing our payment schedule, we went off to the bank to see if we could get financing. As we expected, the bank approved the loan. You see, our analysis clearly indicated what we could and could not afford. The principle was simple. We would be in control of our destiny. If we could not afford our dream home at a price we were willing to pay, we would not build it. We had a desire to vacate our home of 11 years but not a need to do so. We were in control.

The next step was to find a reputable builder. After two weeks of asking around and seeking advice from people who had recently built a new home, we decided on a builder. Boy, were we lucky (or so we thought). The guy we found was a partner with, perhaps, the best builder in town. Moreover, they could get us the building site we wanted in the part of town we wanted. Wow, a double play! We invited him over, showed him our plans, and apprised him of the amount we could afford to invest in the new home. The question was, could he build the house we wanted at the price we could afford to pay? He would look over the plans, prepare an estimate, and get back to us in a week or so. A week passed. Yes, they could build the house we wanted at our price. This was a deal too good to be true! As it turned out, that's just what it was.

In hindsight, we should have been suspicious when the builder's estimate for the house we wanted exactly equaled what we told him we could afford to pay. But, we were so enamored with the idea of building our dream house, the thought that this was more than a coincidence never occurred to us. In hindsight, we have concluded that he didn't really want to defraud us. He just wanted to build the house for us so desperately; he let his desire get in the way of his judgment. At least that is the perspective we still choose to believe.

The day ground was broken for the foundation we took off work so we could be there to watch the bulldozer take those delicious slices of sweet earth. That day was a glorious day. However, the days that followed were not. It seemed that every time we got a bill for something, it was higher than the estimate. No, it wasn't just 2% higher … it was 20% … 30% … often 50% more than the original cost estimates for each stage of the project. Heck, the house was only two-thirds finished and was already darn near the total estimate we had been given! We were a little nervous to say the least. On three different occasions we went to the builder's office to discuss the situation only to be told, "Oh, don't worry about it. Things will be less expensive from this point on. Why, we may even come in under the estimate."

Not only were we becoming convinced that the price of the new home was getting beyond our means, but our realtor had been unable to sell our old house for the six months it had been on the market! Guess what, we needed the equity in our old house in order to make the down payment on the new one. We were beginning to sense that we were on a treadmill to financial ruin. The only saving grace was the fact that we had excellent credit and friends who were willing to help. The banker understood our problem and decided that no payment would be due on the new house until our old one was sold. The interest would be rolled into the total final cost of the house. Thank God for that!

By the time the house was finished it would have ended up costing us nearly 40% more than the original estimate and be more than three months late! Our lawyer friend understood the situation we were facing. The decision to threaten a lawsuit was a painful one for us. But we had to do it. The lawyer drew up the paperwork, made a few phone calls to the builder's lawyer, and was able to cut our losses in half. You see, the builder, in order to avoid going to court, "ate" all of his profits on the house.

It would be tough, but we could cut all of our other spending and maybe we would be able to make the new house payment—if only the old house would sell. So, we decided to go to a different realtor. The new realtor sold our old house within just six short weeks!

What's the point of this story, you say? Remember, we are the ones who preach the virtues of effective marital communication. We talked over all aspects relative to the planning and building of the new house, and the selling of the old house.

There wasn't a thing we didn't talk about. When the nightmare unfolded, we couldn't cast aspersions in each other's direction. There was no blame to assign. We got into this mess together and we would get out of it together. We were so accustomed to financially communicating with each other that to do otherwise wasn't even in our thought processes. During this whole ordeal, we never yelled at each other or cast blame. The funny thing about this experience is that now, looking back, we're somewhat glad it happened. Why would you say that, you ask? Simple ... we had proven to ourselves once and for all, effective communication is at the heart and soul of our marriage. We survived a most painful financial experience from which it took us almost eight years to recuperate.

There have been times in our marriage when the sun seemed like it would never shine on our parade again. We have eaten popcorn as a steady diet in order to feed our daughter and worked four jobs between us to pay for our college debts. You know the dilemma of the young married couple ... always scratching to make ends meet and still coming up short.

Even through the hardest of times, we have always held together because we worked hard and communicated about our financial situation. We planned together and worried together, and then made it work together.

The need for open lines of communication regarding finances has also been a common characteristic throughout the interviews we conducted with long-time successful couples. One of the most unbelievable stories we have encountered during our interviews was about financial communications between a husband and wife who had been happily married for 41 years. As Connie and Jeff tell it, when they had been married for about 20 years things were feeling quite comfortable for them financially. They were not too worried about everyday expenses any longer, since they seemed to be able to pay the bills when they came in. To them, they considered that to be living on easy street. Both Connie and Jeff were doing wonderfully well with their career advancements. Connie was now a senior department head at the local bank and Jeff received the top regional sales award from the insurance company he worked for. While both Connie and Jeff were busy with their careers and the care of their son, they still seemed to find enough time to enjoy each other's company and entertain their friends. In almost all regards, they felt quite good about their marriage, their relationship, and their lives.

As Jeff and Connie began telling us about the most challenging experience of their marriage, what we heard was totally unexpected from two such reasonable and responsible individuals. Jeff explained that back in 1986, Connie's 45th birthday was coming up and he wanted to make it special. He had been really involved with some major business clients and was feeling enormous guilt about the time he had been spending away from the family. He would also use her birthday present as his way of making amends for not paying greater attention to her over the last several months. Jeff knew exactly what would make Connie's eyes pop out—the new black Ford Thunderbird that she had been talking about non-stop. It was a two-door coupe with power everything, leather seats, and even a tilt steering wheel. They were doing great financially, so he didn't even give a second thought to talking to Connie before actually buying the car. On Friday he took off work early and made it to the dealership just in time to sign the papers they had already prepared for him. He would drive it home to surprise Connie that evening. What could be better? Jeff knew he had the perfect present and he knew they could afford the payments. But what he didn't know was what Connie had been doing over the past week.

Connie was bound and determined to have that new car she had been dreaming about. She had driven her car for nine years and it had become an unreliable piece of junk. Over the last several months, she had tried to engage Jeff in conversations about a new car, but to no avail. As a department head at the bank, financing would be a breeze. She knew they could afford the payments, so it was time to just go ahead and talk with the dealership. Connie told them everything she wanted in the car. She decided to save a few bucks and eliminate most of the power equipment, but she had to have the leather seats in her new black Ford Thunderbird. Yes, that's right, **her** new black Ford Thunderbird! Now you are beginning to see the picture. Jeff had been listening, but didn't give Connie any clue about the surprise he was planning for her. Connie had been talking, but not seeing any evidence that Jeff had been listening. So, being an independent spirit, Connie moved forward with the purchase of her new car for arrival on her birthday.

As you can imagine, Connie's 45th birthday will never be forgotten by either of them. Jeff and Connie broke out in uproarious laughter before continuing their story. Connie arrived home first. She was so excited that she put the car into her garage slot and just sat in the car awaiting Jeff's arrival. She knew him so well that she was certain of his excitement over her initiative. Jeff always bragged to others about how much he valued Connie's initiative. He was going to be so proud of her.

As soon as Jeff opened the garage door, his stomach felt instantly queasy. Oh my, what had Connie done? Connie, on the other hand, was patiently sitting in her new car and felt overwhelming excitement with the sound of the opening garage door. The other new car had not yet come into view. Then it happened, Connie saw the car Jeff was driving into the other slot in the garage. It was the same car!!! Connie now felt instantly like she was going to throw up. What had she done? What had Jeff done? The beauty of the situation did not dawn on them. Only the financial devastation of having two new car payments hit them both when they saw the other car. Jeff stepped out of the car first. Connie felt almost paralyzed. She just could not seem to move out of the driver's seat of the new car she had just purchased. Jeff gently opened her car door and put out his hand to assist her. It was at that point that she burst into tears. How could they fix this? What would they do? We knew they must have found a solution, since both of them burst into hearty laughter again before continuing their story.

Jeff said that he immediately started apologizing to Connie, who seemed too stunned to move, let alone talk. He didn't know what else to do. This was the first time they hadn't sat down together to discuss a major purchase. Each was so sure it was the right decision; Connie and Jeff just went ahead individually with their purchases. After a long and painful evening, they decided to go back to the dealership first thing in the morning to see if anything could be done. Funny thing, Connie and Jeff worked with two different salespeople at the same large dealership. Jeff had ordered the car special, but Connie's version of the black Thunderbird was straight off the lot. Maybe that would help. All they could do was go back to the dealership together and attempt to work something out. But what would that be? The owner of the dealership was amazing. First, he said that in his 28 years of owning the dealership he had never heard of such a thing happening. He seemed almost amused, which struck Connie and Jeff as a weird reaction to their terrible situation. The dealership owner then explained that when the paperwork went in on the second car, he figured out that there might be a problem or that there was a really special surprise coming to two people. Since only one car was a special order and the other was off the lot, he figured that he could work something out on the car purchased off the lot if it was really a mistake. That sure explains his lack of surprise at seeing Jeff and Connie there first thing Saturday morning. Jeff explained that it took almost a week to straighten out all of the financial details, but everyone was wonderful to them. Connie said that they laugh often about the hard lesson that birthday taught them, but it was anything but funny while they were going through it. They were asking themselves, how could they have been so dumb … why didn't they talk about it before making their purchases, etc., etc., etc.

Married couples usually don't tell us funny stories like Connie and Jeff's story about their financial learning experiences. Usually they don't see much humor in situations that can produce traumatic financial outcomes. The lack of open lines of communication about finances was unfortunately evidenced in a couple we met recently. They had gone far beyond the point of reason with their own commitments. Trina had worked for four years putting her husband through school and paying for William's expensive medical costs from an improperly healed shoulder injury not covered under their insurance plan. Their long struggle seemed almost over. However, when William finished his under-graduate degree in June, he dragged his feet on job hunting. Instead of encouraging him to seek employment, when July rolled around Trina gave her two weeks notice at her job. She only had kept the job to pay the bills until William earned his degree. That had been their agreement. Trina couldn't wait even another day to be free of the torture from the job she hated every minute over the past four years. For her, it was now over and she would finally be free. Trina decided it was her turn to attend school, regardless of the financial consequences for their marriage.

After putting four years of hard work into their marriage, how could their communicative link deteriorate so completely that a decision of such major importance could have been made without discussion or agreement? There they were, facing a marriage with no income, stagger-ing bills, and no discussions—just arguments. If Trina and William had only followed the first rule and kept open the lines of communica-tion about finances, the situation could be vastly different now. Had they talked about their financial matters for the past four years, maybe William would have been much more sensitive to the needs of the family and made an immediate attempt to seek employment. Had they talked about her extreme desire to return to school immediately and the effect it would have on the financial status of the family, maybe Trina would have understood the situation and waited until William secured a job before quitting. Instead, two stubborn people took their own paths, jeopardizing the future of their marriage.

Trina and William spent the next year arguing, blaming, and being angry at one another over their financial situation. Trina refused to quit school and return to work. William finally found a job he was willing to take, but that was almost 11 months later. In the meantime, since they couldn't make their house payments the bank was threatening foreclosure; they didn't have enough equity in the house to refinance; and they had reached the limit on all of their credit cards. They stood to lose their house and all of their possessions. Unfortunately, with all of the pressures and their habit of non-communication, Trina and William could not find a way to rebuild their relationship. Sadly, their marriage ended in failure.

When a husband or wife comes to us desperately seeking advice, all too often the root of the problem is their financial situation. Raul and Ellie are a perfect example. They had been married for 12 years. By and large you would have to judge their marriage a happy one, except for one serious recurring problem that they could not seem to resolve. They were always broke before the 20th of the month and argued constantly about their financial shortfall during the last ten days of each month. As we both knew, there could be a lot of different reasons for this kind of problem. But, in this case, it was the same old story we had heard so many times before.

Raul tried to economize in every way that he knew how. He bought used tires for the car, did the repairs on their home himself, bought the cheapest clothing he could find, and put on hold his dream of purchasing a motorcycle. Ellie, on the other hand, loved to shop. She never saw a pair of shoes she didn't have to have. Whatever Ellie wanted, Ellie purchased without concern for the family's budget or financial security. Ellie was beautifully adorned for every occasion. Since Raul paid the bills, Ellie seemed to have no idea where the money went or how much there was. Near the end of every month, they got into blistering arguments about their finances. Needless to say, their financial communicative link had broken down, if it had ever existed at all.

We gave Raul and Ellie lots of encouragement and these seven financial tips:

1. Keep open lines of communication regarding your financial status.

2. Be a one-checkbook family.

3. Pay all of the bills together.

4. Never make a major purchase without talking it over with your spouse and sleeping on it.

5. Mutually agree on your routine spending habits.

6. Make a realistic budget.

7. If all else fails and you are in over your heads financially, seek professional financial counseling.

We corresponded several times with Ellie and Raul over the next several months. They worked very hard to repair the broken link in their communication regarding their finances. Raul and Ellie said they were determined to stop their financial problems from growing any bigger and possibly destroying their beautiful marriage. They found out that if one is doing all of the spending and the other is trying to economize and pinch pennies, it is time to sit down and talk turkey. Some type of compromise needed to be worked out. They just had to find a way to agree about their spending habits. The good news, Raul and Ellie figured it out before it was too late. Unlike many marriages, Raul and Ellie figured out how to talk sense when dealing with their dollars and have now been happily married for 31 years.

Not too long ago a television talk show host was talking to his "expert" guest about the "ideal" marriage. According to him, two-thirds of married couples in the United States today both work outside the home. So far so good. His next "statistic" sent us climbing the wall, however. His comment went like this: "In families where both husband and wife work outside the home, the happier marriages have a two-checkbook arrangement." In other words, without any research data he was suggesting that when both earn a wage, they should each keep separate checkbooks, pay separate bills, and the like. How absolutely ridiculous! **This is the opposite of what successful couples reported to us about their finances.** Since when is the money earned in two-wage-earner families your money, my money, your bills, my bills, your house, my house? In our research, the money earned by married couples is "our money." It is most unfortunate when couples take a two-checkbook attitude, since it is probably indicative of other divisive issues in their marriage as well. Such a notion communicates a lack of trust.

During a recent interview with a happily married couple, Darrin explained that Melody had inherited a considerable amount of money after her mother's death. He made the mistake of asking Melody what she would like to do with her money. Melody snapped back in an irritated voice, "What do you mean my money? It has been our money for almost 50 years and that isn't going to change now!" Their conversation is indicative of the attitudes about finances shared by the thousands of successful couples we interviewed over the last several decades.

Don't let the "expert" cited earlier lead you down this primrose path. If you are following the advice of this "expert" perhaps you should take a long hard look at where your relationship is and where it is going.

Probably the more appropriate "experts" should be a couple we interviewed who were married 59 years. Bruce and Louise started their marriage on the right foot using one checkbook and talking about their financial decisions together. However, when Louise got her first job in the second year of their marriage, she fought long and hard with Bruce to let her open her own account and keep their finances separate. After two tense and challenging years of fighting over finances and never being able to figure out which bills came out of which account and never balancing the totals correctly, something had to change. The tension in their marriage had increased to the point that it started to damage their relationship and stifle their communication with each other. What they decided after many hours of conversation was that it wasn't Bruce's money or Louise's money, but rather it was their money. The decisions had to be theirs together. The responsibility had to be theirs together. And the checkbook had to be theirs together. They have now been successfully using the one-checkbook approach for the last 56 years. We think they qualify as the real "experts."

If you are not feeling comfortable with the financial situation in your marriage, then it is time to talk. Things never magically get better with regard to finances. It takes a joint effort and a lot of hard work. A perfect example of just how difficult it can be for some couples to handle their finances came from our interview with a couple happily married for 33 years. Ben explained that when he and Felicia were first married, his job at the factory provided what both of them thought was a wonderful income. They could afford a nice apartment, a car, clothes, and living expenses. What more could two young newlyweds want? During the first five years, Ben's income increased while their expenses remained about the same. Everything was going along fine until their first child was born. Little did they realize the added costs associated with raising a child. Even though it was a struggle, they managed to make ends meet each month until the second child was born with severe medical needs. While the insurance covered the majority of costs, there always seemed to be extra expenses that were not covered by their plan. No longer could their meager income support Ben's family.

As they moved deeper and deeper into debt, the tension between Ben and Felicia steadily increased. The finance company was in the process of repossessing their only means of transportation before Ben could swallow his pride long enough to seek professional help. The financial counselor at the factory was able to secure help from a charitable organization to pay for most of the costs associated with their baby's medical needs that were not covered by their insurance plan. Then the counselor worked with all of their creditors to arrange payments that they could afford on Ben's take-home pay. But the most important step the counselor took was to enroll Ben and Felicia in weekly financial counseling workshops. Ben and Felicia said they learned to budget, economize, and live within their income. Ben was able to secure some much-needed financial relief through over-time work at the factory.

Ben and Felicia said that they would never have made it without professional guidance and help. They told us that they learned valuable lessons during the horrible two-year period it took them to get their finances back in good shape. Today, both of their children are healthy and have graduated from college. Ben is now the day shift foreman at the factory and they own their own home. Ben explained again that none of this would have been possible without the counselor's help and what they learned from those weekly sessions.

Unfortunately, many couples realize that they are in financial trouble when it is too late to easily turn things around and they are unwilling to take the painful steps necessary to solve their financial problems. The successful couples we interviewed reported to us that they learned the lessons of *Filing a Joint Return* early in their marriage. It was their stories about learning the hard lessons of how to manage their finances together as a team that successful couples shared with us.

∽❦

— *Advice* —

In analyzing our own marriage, as well as in our interviews with successful couples who have been married for more than 30 years, we discovered seven key elements absolutely essential to effective financial stability in a marriage. We believe couples can avoid the financial communicative breakdowns if they simply follow these seven basic rules. These are the foundational requirements before the characteristic of *Filing a Joint Return* can become a natural part of how you deal with finances in your marriage.

1. **Keep open lines of communication regarding your financial situation.** In a marriage you must share both the joys of financial success and the burdens of financial setbacks. Never argue and get angry at each other over finances. Casting blame and calling your spouse names will not solve your financial problems! If you keep in touch regarding your financial situation you are much more likely to avoid commitments that place a strain or burden on your relationship. Remember, an ounce of prevention is worth a pound of cure.

2. **Be a one-checkbook family.** In other words, even if both of you work, put all of your money together into one shared checking account. We are reminded of the psychologist whom we recently saw on a television talk show. He indicated that his best advice to a husband and wife who both worked was to put their separate earnings into separate checking accounts—his and hers—in this way, each would retain their separate "financial identity." We reject his notion entirely! Marriage is a shared financial responsibility, as well as a shared financial joy. The two earnings go together in one pot to meet those obligations that were entered into jointly.

3. **Pay all of the bills together.** In this way, each of you knows where your money is going. That doesn't mean both of you have to actually sit down together to pay the bills. Rather, it means that both of you need to know exactly what the bills are, what is being paid, and what are the outstanding financial commitments. Placing the entire burden of financial responsibility on one person just isn't fair or wise. When both husband and wife have full knowledge of the financial situation, it prevents one person from becoming the scapegoat in discussions about money problems. Without this type of arrangement, it is too easy for one of you to say, "If you hadn't paid that credit card bill in full, we would have enough money to buy food until the end of the month. It is all your fault."

4. **Never make a major purchase without talking it over with your spouse and sleeping on it.** Couple communication on this matter will insure to a large extent that you both agree on the purchase, thus preventing a serious fault-finding session later if the decision was a bad one from a financial point of view. This notion also promotes sharing. What you own in a marriage should be yours together … not yours and mine. We are often asked, "What is a major purchase?" Excellent question! Major varies from one couple to another. Obviously, a house, an automobile, or a large appliance qualifies as major to most couples. After that, the definition runs the full gamut. There have been times in our marriage when making a $10.00 purchase was a monumental decision, and other times when we felt that a $200.00 purchase was major. The notion of "major" varies from couple to couple and depends to a large extent on your financial situation. You will have to decide … but you must decide together!

Realize after you both have decided to make that major purchase that it may not be easy to shoulder the financial burden for a while. Often lifestyles need to be altered slightly and money usually spent on frills will have to be put toward financing the major purchase. Discuss this fact before the purchase so that you both can decide where and how the spending will have to be cut.

When you think that you both have made the decision and know how it will effect your financial situation, sleep on it. You would be surprised at the number of purchases you don't make if you sleep on it! The bright and shiny car you felt you just had to have on Wednesday isn't nearly so bright and shiny on Thursday when you figure out what it is going to cost you each month! This method has worked so many, many times for us. We would certainly be in debtor's prison if we bought everything that we fell in love with and wanted to buy right on the spot. We now save those kinds of love affairs for the $10.00 items and use our rule of "sleeping on it" for anything over $200.00. Oh, we can hear you now … "but it may be gone by tomorrow!" There is a very slim chance of that occurring. In 43 years, the only thing we lost that way was a 1972 baby blue Mustang. (However, we later found a 1973 baby blue Mustang that we drove and loved for almost ten years.)

5. **Mutually agree on your routine spending habits.** Taking the time to analyze what each of you routinely spends money on can be just as important as making decisions about major spending issues. If one of you is regularly purchasing new clothes, hobby supplies, recreational items, etc. while the other one is skimping on everything to make ends meet, open discussion and

changes need to occur immediately. Many times we have observed routine spending habits to be problematic and often overlooked because each purchase doesn't seem like it amounts to very much money by itself. However, if it is a regular pattern of spending, the amounts can add up quickly to large financial problems.

6. **Make a realistic budget.** Take out a sheet of paper and write down all of your regular monthly expenses, including housing, food, cars, etc. Then in the next column write down your monthly income. See what is left after the fixed expenses (i.e., food, housing, etc.). Then decide what kind of limits you both will put on the spending of the money and what kind of priorities you both feel are important to maintain. If your expenses are greater than your income, you need help immediately from a bank, a financial planning group, or a financial counselor at work. Don't take too long in resolving this type of dilemma. The kind of stress this puts on a marriage can be extremely damaging.

7. **If all else fails and you are in over your heads financially, seek professional financial counseling.** Don't show so much pride that you can't or won't seek help. Your marriage is worth saving! We would suggest that you talk to your banker (he or she wants you to succeed financially, it is in his or her best interest), a financial planner, or an accountant, or get a referral from a friend. Most financial problems are solvable! Don't bury your heads in the sand and pretend that the problems will disappear. There is one thing that always seems to be true … financial problems do not go away; they only get worse if you don't take steps to solve them. Establishing an effective financial communicative link just makes good sense!

Sometimes, good old common sense is the best way to deal with finances. Whatever decision you both are trying to make, apply the good old fashioned test of common sense. When logic tells you that it just isn't right, listen to that logic. So many times we have heard from people who say, "We really knew that it didn't make sense to get in so deep, but we both just went ahead anyway." That's why we added an extra activity in the Appendix on finances (p. 297). You will find a short quiz to get the two of you doing even more thinking about your finances.

When financial problems exist, work very hard together to find solutions. If it means an extra job or two on a temporary basis, do it. In other words, do whatever is necessary to find solutions to the problems you are having, and then don't let yourselves get into the same kind of mess a second time.

We guess what it all boils down to is the same philosophy that our entire book expounds: keep your wits about you, communicate, and do whatever the two of you need to do to make your financial problems solvable. But for heavens sake, don't allow finances to unravel the beautiful relationship you have with your spouse. Make sense of your dollars … start today!

CHAPTER 12

Seven Surprising Secrets #6: The Loving Touch

*Touching becomes kind of a **Morse Code**—*
a substitute for language and the expression of feeling.
Successfully married couples have mastered
*the **Morse Code** of marriage—*
it's called touching.

WE HAVE BEEN MARRIED FOR **43** YEARS
and simply can't keep our hands off of each other! For many years,
we thought we were unique. Then we started our research for this
book, and did we get a big surprise — virtually every happily married
coupled we interviewed reported the same condition! Over time we
have come to call it the "tactile response." Literally translated, it
means, "I touch you here, I touch you there, I touch you everywhere!"

During our interviews with married couples we pay a lot of
attention to their tactile interactions. More often than not, they sit on
the couch during the interview and hold hands or place some part of

their body on their mate's body. It is their way of saying, "I love you so much I simply must touch you." So why all of this touching?

As part of our interviews we asked the couples to tell us what they believe to be the most endearing and important characteristics of their spouses. We continued with the following questions: "How would you describe your spouse? What adjectives would you use?" Here are the words we most often heard: encouraging, positive, loving, honest, has integrity, beautiful (or handsome), understanding, wonderful, patient, loves life, loves me, unselfish, giving, caring, trusting, generous, helpful, conscientious, and humorous. Words to live by in a marriage, wouldn't you say? And they said these things unabashedly, without apologies.

Those in a successful marriage know nearly everything about each other. They have studied in infinite detail how their spouse looks, feels, and acts. They know what makes the one they love tick and can recite in scripture and verse their best qualities. They brag about each other all the time. They love each other for a whole bunch of reasons and don't mind telling you what they are.

What do their words about each other have to do with touching? Here's what we observed during our many interviews—when couples told us something special about their spouses in response to our questions, they would touch each other as if to emphasize the importance of the words. Touching was like an exclamation mark! Over time, we believe that these couples, like the two of us, say these words with a touch without always saying the words out loud. Touching becomes kind of a **Morse Code**—a substitute for language and the expression of feeling. Successfully married couples have mastered the **Morse Code** of marriage—it's called touching.

A wise person once said that if you pass your spouse 100 times a day, you should touch them 100 times a day. When you touch someone, you are acknowledging his presence and expressing your love. In effect you are saying, "I love you so much I simply must touch you."

Touching ... let us count the ways. The most obvious forms of touching are a simple tap or pat on the body, hand holding, and kissing. A kiss on the lips, the cheek, the hand, or the forehead makes your partner feel good. How about a good hug? Have you hugged your mate today? And of course, the intimacy of a sexual encounter to many is the ultimate touch.

There is one fundamental rule in our house. If you come close enough to each other to touch—then touch. Try to walk down the hallway at our house and not get touched. We touch each other so much during the day it's a good bet that if Guinness kept touching records, we would surely hold the record!

Oh, to be sure, we have our detractors about this characteristic of a successful marriage. We hear them all the time. "It's embarrassing to touch in public." "Isn't it a little childish for grown-up and mature adults to hold hands and kiss in public?" Where is it written that "mature" adults can't communicate affection by touching? Perhaps, if we practice communicating love and affection through touching maybe our children will also grow up to be wonderful artisans of touch. We seriously doubt that the world would be a more dangerous place because people spent more time touching! Quite the contrary, we bet the world would be a better place to live if it were full of people spending time touching their loved ones.

A number of years ago, Ryan and Carman were students in one of Charley's classes in counseling. In almost every way, Ryan and Carman were the same as every other student in his class—except for one important difference. You see, Ryan and Carman are both blind. Ryan has been blind since birth and Carman since she was about eight years old. They met at a school for the blind where they were both students. Carman says jokingly, "It was love at first sight!"

Now in their last year at the university, Ryan and Carman were enrolled in an introduction to counseling psychology course Charley was teaching. Upper level undergraduate students and graduate students who were interested in careers in the helping professions, particularly counseling, typically took this as their first course in the field. One of the many things the students do is participate in a simulated counseling experience. The best way to use your learning and knowledge about how to be a counselor ... is to be one! The best way to learn how to empathize with a client ... is to play the role of a client!

An important part of role-playing and simulation is the study of non-verbal communication. Counselors need to be aware of the non-verbal signals emitted by their clients. In one of the exercises, Charley required members of the class to pair off and attempt to communicate messages to each other by touching. They were told to keep their eyes closed and touch only at or above the shoulder levels of their partners.

On the class day when the students were to practice this exercise, Charley intentionally asked Carman and Ryan to pair up. For nearly 20 minutes, Charley watched a class of 70 people touch and feel each other with their eyes closed. What a sight to behold. As you might have guessed, muffled laughter filled the room during the first few minutes of the exercise. You haven't seen anything until you've seen a bunch of nervous people with their eyes shut touch and Braille each other.

After about 20 minutes, a strange thing happened. The class got very quiet; everyone was finished except one couple. Nearly all eyes were fixed on Carman and Ryan. You see, being blind, they had become experts on the art of touching! To watch them communicate love and understanding to each other through touching was, well ... awesome! There was incredible love in their eyes. Yes, in their eyes!

Everybody in class that day learned a great deal about touching and marital communication from Carman and Ryan. There are none so blind as those who will not touch. That day we all thanked Ryan and Carman for giving us a glimpse of the power and art of touching. They were true artisans of touching.

We learned another important lesson about touching from a couple sitting next to us at a recent banquet. We are tempted to call them "Touch" and "No Touch" … but we will not do that even though the titles fit so beautifully.

The thing that struck us as funny about this couple was the fact that Juanita touched everything in sight. Juanita would touch Charley. She would touch Liz. She would touch the waiter. Juanita would touch just about everyone she talked to as if to accent her words.

On the other hand, her husband Miguel would touch no one! Not even his wife, Juanita. Being constant observers of people, we could not help but notice their opposing behaviors. No one has ever accused us of being shy, so toward the end of the banquet we asked both Miguel and Juanita if they would like stay for a while and have a drink with us. They were a little curious, however, about why people they just met for the first time at dinner would make them such an offer. We told them that we were writing a book about successful marriages and we would like to interview them. Incidentally, we have discovered over the past several years that most couples jump at the chance to be interviewed and are wonderful about sharing their personal stories and experiences with us. That is how we gained such rare insight into the nature and characteristics of successful marriages. Like other couples, Juanita and Miguel readily agreed when they discovered why we wanted to talk with them.

After the four of us ordered our drinks, we broke the ice by commenting about what we had observed during the banquet concerning their touching behaviors. Juanita indicated that she was raised in a family of touchers. She grew up accepting the belief that to communicate, express love for people, or simply acknowledge their presence, you had to touch them. Her father and mother were both great touching teachers. Juanita said that she never remembers a time when her mother and father weren't touching each other or one of the children. It was just part of who they were as a family.

Unlike Juanita, Miguel was brought up believing that touching another person, except for an occasional handshake, was something you did only in private. The male of the family was to be strong and tough, showing no emotion or intimacy of any type in the presence of others. His father used to say, "Only sissies touch. Real men don't." At any rate, Juanita and Miguel admitted that this touch/no-touch problem had created more than its share of tension during the 12 years they had been married.

Miguel commented that he had observed the two of us spending a lot of time holding hands and touching each other. It made him feel quite nervous. We explained to him that touching was simply very natural for us. We did it all the time! It was a part of who we were and an important part of our relationship. Since Miguel brought up the subject, Juanita followed with the statement, "Look at him (referring to Charley), he's a big, tall man and he touches his wife constantly. He doesn't look like a sissy to me!" Charley was holding his breath waiting for Miguel's response. To Charley's relief, Miguel agreed that he didn't think Charley looked like a sissy, but Miguel knew that he would look like one if he did the same thing. It was just how it was.

After quite a little bit of coaxing by us, Miguel finally relented and held Juanita's hand, right in front of us! Don't laugh; this was a very traumatic event for Miguel. We asked him how it felt to hold Juanita's hand in public. Other than making him a little nervous, he confided in us that it felt pretty good. Judging by his reaction, we followed up by asking him if that surprised him. "Yes, it does," he confided. Miguel went on to explain that while we provided a comfortable and reassuring environment for him to feel safe enough to touch Juanita in public, it was still quite difficult and uncomfortable. We let him know that it would take time and practice to overcome the uncomfortable feeling that was etched in his mind from his upbringing.

Miguel and Juanita's situation illustrated perfectly how painful touching can be for some couples. But touching is like most other forms of communication ... you have to try it out, practice it, and before you know it, you have it mastered.

We asked Miguel and Juanita to drop us a line in a couple of months and let us know how they were doing. It was not a surprise at all to hear in their letter several months later that Miguel felt quite comfortable occasionally touching Juanita in public and felt he was now mastering a whole new way of expressing his caring and concern for Juanita. Their communicative relationship had taken on a whole new dimension. This new dimension can be a part of your marriage as well.

By now, you have spent a few hours reading our book and are probably still wondering, "Why haven't they talked about S-E-X?? After all, isn't sex a form of touching and marital communication?" Probably no one loves good, wholesome sex better than us. We would suspect that our sexual relationship over the 43 years we have been married is very close to perfect. A loving, sexual encounter with someone you deeply love is, perhaps, the ultimate form of touching and communication. The joining together of two bodies, the warmth of a naked embrace, and stimulation of someone you love to the point of delirium is a wonderful experience. These are the kinds of moments that you keep stored in a wondrous reservoir of memories that lasts throughout a successful marriage.

Older adults between the ages of 57 and 85 make sex an important part of their lives! Those are the results of the first comprehensive national survey of the sexual attitudes and behaviors of older adults as reported in the *New England Journal of Medicine*. And, as you might have guessed, our 25 years of research with successfully married couples found the same conclusions.

For sure, every happily married couple we have interviewed over the last 25 years reported at least a reasonable degree of satisfaction with their sex lives. But you know what, **NOT ONE** of the couples we interviewed who had been married for 30 to 77 years reported that their sex life was central to the overall success of their relationship. Not one! Sure it was important, but if you think anybody's marriage is going to last 30 or more years just because they have good sex—well, forget it! It isn't going to happen.

Lasting marriages are characterized by frequent moments of intimacy and bliss. Like we said, over the years we have had a wonderfully healthy sexual relationship with each other. Sometimes our sex is so good ... well, we won't bore you with the details!

We could wax on and on about the role of sex in a marriage, but others have done that over and over. Those who write about sex all the time might have contributed to much of the dysfunctionality surrounding sex in relationships. Frankly, some of the popular books on the subject we have seen hold up a standard of sexual performance and gratification that hardly any couple could achieve. And worse yet, couples that can't live up to the "standard" think they've failed. Many times their relationships suffer.

Our message should be clear to our readers—in a successful marriage sex can be fun, important, and a healthy way of being intimate with your partner. Just because you get older and have been married for 30 years or more does not mean that your sexual life has to be less active. On the other hand, based on our research and first-hand experience, we think sex is grossly overemphasized in terms of its centrality to successful and long-term marriages. So much more is present in those relationships that pass the test of time. Sex is only one of them and is certainly not the most important for couples with long-lasting, successful marriages.

If sex were the most important part of a marriage, Towanda and Shawn would never have made it to their 31st anniversary. They spent the last four years without even thinking about sex because of a drunk driver. As they were returning home from a lovely evening at a local fund-raiser, a drunk driver hit their Toyota head-on at well over

50 miles per hour. Luckily neither of them has any memory of the accident after seeing the car coming straight toward them. They were spared the pain and horror of the hours immediately following the crash.

Towanda and Shawn were transported by helicopter to the trauma center at Baptist Hospital. Within about three days, Shawn was able to sit up in the hospital bed, but it would be several months before he would regain his strength and have full movement of his legs and his left arm. However, Towanda was not as fortunate. She had sustained major head trauma and had internal bleeding, leaving Towanda in a coma. The doctors were not optimistic about her recovery, indicating that Towanda had been in a coma for three days with no signs of improvement.

The impact of the doctor's prognosis for Towanda was beginning to sink into Shawn's consciousness even though he was battling his own physical and psychological problems from the accident. How would he ever survive without his love of 27 years? It just wasn't possible to think about. Shawn felt like he had been knocked off balance and was unable to process mentally what was happening. Their perfect life was in ashes as they both lay in their separate hospital beds, two floors apart due to the nature of their injuries. How could this be happening to them? They loved each other so much, yet in one instant a drunk driver could destroy everything. Shawn tried to figure out what he should do.

It took about a week before Shawn was able to get into a wheelchair long enough to visit Towanda in her hospital room. There she lay—still and silent—not even breathing on her own. She had so many bruises on her face that Shawn hardly recognized her. The first thing Shawn did was to get close enough to Towanda's bed to get hold of her hand and just hold it tight in his own. He spent the next hour just sitting there talking to Towanda while continuing to hold her hand. Shawn was looking for any signs of movement or recognition in her face, eyes, hands, or anywhere. Nothing!

Each day while Shawn was working hard to recover himself, he would find a way to wheel himself down to Towanda's room to hold her hand. After a week, he gained enough flexibility to be able to lean over to kiss her on the cheek. Each visit was longer in duration and allowed him the opportunity to touch Towanda's hands, arms, and cheeks as he kept telling her how much he loved her and what they were going to do when they left the hospital together. Day after day, as Shawn slowly regained his own strength, he saw no signs of change in Towanda. Yet, he spent longer and longer amounts of time just holding her hands and touching her face, as he talked to her about their wonderful lives together.

One day as he was rubbing her arms, one of her doctors came in and sat down to visit with him. Shawn's fear was that he wanted to discuss the eventual removal of the life support systems. Instead, the doctor spoke very softly about the power of touch. It seems that he had spent valuable time with eminent doctors from other countries who had witnessed first-hand the miracles of recovery when the patient was given no hope of survival. The doctors were convinced that some of their patients with a medical prognosis of no hope had been reached through the power of touch from a loved one. The doctor told Shawn that love and touch can have great healing powers at times when medicine provides no more answers, so he should not give up yet.

Little did the doctor know just how critical his timing had been for Shawn. It was just the encouragement he needed. Instead of taking the prognosis as a sentence of impending doom, Shawn set out to produce one of those miracles the doctor had talked about. He continued touching Towanda as often as he could get up and out of his own hospital bed.

After 15 days, Shawn was ready to be released from the hospital. He needed six to eight weeks of heavy-duty physical therapy before he could return to work even on a very limited basis. However, he knew that his release meant it would be more difficult to spend the needed time with Towanda since they lived almost one hour away from the hospital and he would not be allowed to drive for at least another month.

When the physical therapist and counselor came into his hospital room to talk to him about the plans after his release, he broke down from the overwhelming hopelessness of what he thought would be an impossible situation. Shawn credits these two caring individuals with turning Towanda and his entire situation around. After several phone calls, they arranged for Shawn to stay at a residence home for family members who needed to be close to their loved ones and had no means of transportation. With that placement came a full support system of other caring individuals for everything he would need. At that moment, Shawn was sure that things were going to work out okay for both him and Towanda.

Each day as soon as he had endured the pain of the physical therapy session, he would move his wheelchair into Towanda's room. There he sat touching her arms, legs, shoulders, neck, and face. As he brushed her hair, he would tell her that he couldn't wait until they could begin doing things together again. It had been 19 days and still no sign of any type of recognition or movement. Yet, Shawn was sure Towanda knew he was there and that she would not give up on life.

Shawn told us the next part of their story with such an exaggerated smile on his face that we knew it would certainly be inspiring to hear. It was the morning of day 20 following that fateful accident. The day was going to be filled with thunder, lighting, and heavy rains, so Shawn intended to spend the entire day with Towanda. He knew that she had always been a little afraid when bad weather hit and he just wanted to be with her. As soon as he entered the room, he felt a change. He wasn't sure what, but he swears that he knew things were different. Over to Towanda's bed he rolled in his wheelchair and immediately took hold of Towanda's left hand. He gave it a big squeeze and said he felt Towanda react. He was so excited that he hit the call button continually for anyone to come in to see. Then it happened, her eyelids slowly started to open. He was sure of what he was seeing, but when the nurse came in Towanda was still. Shawn began shouting at Towanda to open her eyes while continuing to grasp her hand as tightly as he could. Then the nurse got even more excited than Shawn as she went running down the hall to fetch a doctor. Towanda had moved her hand. Both of them saw it at the same time. It was really happening. Towanda was coming back to them.

Over the next two days, Towanda slowly came out of the blanket of darkness she had been in since that awful night when the drunk driver crossed the path of their lives. It took another three days before Towanda could return a kiss from Shawn. After four full years of physical therapy and speech therapy Towanda has regained all of her functionality and swears to this day that she pulled out of the darkness of her coma only because she felt Shawn there waiting for her. No one in the world could ever convince Shawn or Towanda that the power of touch was not the most important characteristic of their successful 31-year marriage and their lives together.

The importance of *The Loving Touch* in a marriage is only too well illustrated with another story that was told to us by a couple enjoying their 33rd year of marriage. Cathy had tried everything during the 7th year of their marriage to get her husband to take the time to pay attention to her. For almost a year, Cathy's husband had been doing his paperwork every evening and on the weekends at home. It seems he was so focused on work that she had taken a back seat. In fact, as she tells it, she didn't feel like she even lived in the same house with George. She was beginning to get suspicious and frustrated because she couldn't remember the last time George had touched her in a loving way. Rather than talk to George about her concerns, she would pout, and conjure up in her mind all sorts of awful things. Was his lack of interest in her due to his having an affair? Was she no longer exciting and attractive to George? Was he mad about something? For week after week, she thought these dreadful thoughts.

Cathy finally decided to do something. She had a plan. That night when George got home from work, she met him at the door with her apron on. Yes friends, just her apron on! As he came in the door, Cathy turned and walked into the kitchen with George close behind. Needless to say, her entire posterior was fully exposed for George to see. But nothing happened. He didn't even notice her. He grabbed his stack of paperwork and sat down in the living room to read it. Cathy was frustrated to say the least.

After a few minutes, she served George a drink. In total frustration, Cathy turned and walked away. Again, George didn't even notice her exposed posterior. She began to wonder if George had gone blind or maybe it was true that he was having an affair and he no longer had any interest in her. Let's face it—Cathy was a very attractive and shapely woman in her early 30s. Any man in his right mind would have noticed her shapely posterior, but not George. He had his paperwork in his lap and was totally absorbed in his own thoughts. What had happened to their romance? Where was the spark that fired their passion?

When Cathy completed the dinner preparation, she called George in to eat. As usual, he buried his head in reading his paperwork while he ate, totally oblivious to anything going on around him. She served him wine: filled his plate for him, talked to him … nothing phased good old George. Now Cathy was furious. After all, was she so unattractive, even in the partial buff, that he was simply not interested in her anymore? She would make one last attempt.

Into the kitchen she went. While there, she took off the apron, leaving her stark naked. Surely even George would have to notice her now. She picked up the desert tray and proceeded back into the dining room. Up to George she walked in her completely naked state, served him his dessert, and waited for him to notice her. Guess what? George didn't even look up from his paperwork! At that point, Cathy had two choices—either get totally mad or try out her old sense of humor on George. She decided to go for the humor.

Cathy stood there totally in the buff and said, "Coffee, tea, or ME?" At that question George looked up and opened his mouth to gasp. Instantly, she simply leaned over to give him a great big kiss. He quickly forgot about his paperwork, dessert, and everything other than Cathy. George told us that they quickly cleared the table and made good use of the space for the next delicious hour. While both of them were blushing as they explained how delightful that evening turned out to be, they pointed out that the most important part of the evening was really their conversation. Cathy finally unloaded all of her fears and concerns to George. He sat there in amazement that he had been so preoccupied with his problems at work that he had gotten out of the habit of touching Cathy. In fact, he realized just how long it had been since they warmly hugged, touched in any stimulating way, or engaged in intimacy. George was suffering from "Out of touch, out of mind." He promised to work on it and asked Cathy to tell him when she was feeling neglected. Cathy explained that she let her imagination, fears, and emotions take control of her logic. Together they learned an important lesson before it was too late for their marriage to be successful. Their romance blossomed again as they worked hard to rekindle the fire and passion they had in the first few years of their marriage.

As you can see from these personal stories from long-time happily married couples, the act of touching each other is a most effective and powerful form of marital communication. When you and your partner have practiced touching for a while and get in the wondrous habit of touching, you'll discover just how marvelous this form of communication can be. And we ask you, how could you possibly spend even a minute angry with someone who just said, "I love you so much I simply must touch you."

From the thousands of interviews with successfully married couples came the understanding that just as important as the act of touching is the underlying reason for the touching. They use touching as a substitute for language or a kind of **Morse Code** because they know nearly everything about each other. Each couple has studied in infinite detail how their spouse looks, feels, and acts. They know what makes them tick and can recite in scripture and verse their best qualities. They brag about each other all the time. Happily married couples are masters at completing each other's sentences. They understand their spouse's hot buttons, their cold buttons, their moods, and what they are feeling in their heart. Making this aspect of *The Loving Touch* characteristic an integral part of your marriage requires that your spouse become your favorite subject.

❧

— *Advice* —

It is our sincere hope that you and your spouse have accepted what our research says about the importance of touching in marital communication. But understanding and accepting this is only the beginning. You have to put the concept into routine practice before it will become a characteristic of your marriage. After analyzing the advice about touching offered by the long-time happily married couples we interviewed, we offer the following ideas that can help you and your spouse establish and maintain *The Loving Touch* in your relationship.

1. **Make a point of touching your spouse in some way at least ten times a day.** Give your spouse a hug, a kiss, or a tap on the fanny. However you touch, do it at least ten times a day—more often if possible. When you touch him, you are acknowledging his presence. Be sure to tell your spouse how you like to be touched. Tell her what makes you feel good and why, so your mate will be encouraged to continue. Give it a try. This is one time where practice makes perfect. And what the heck, if you don't get it exactly right the first time you will still have a lifetime together to improve it. We'll just bet there will be a great deal of appreciation from your spouse just for trying.

However you touch lovingly, do it often. There really is no excuse for not communicating with your mate in ways that you can convey only through a touch. Every time you touch your spouse you are saying, "I love you so much I simply must touch you." When you and your mate get into the wonderful and glorious habit of touching, you will discover how truly special communication can be. Get into this habit today. Perfect the art of touching. You will, in reality, touch the heart of the one you love the most. Happy touching!

2. **Sit and face your spouse using Braille to discover all of his intricate features.** Take turns holding your partner's face in your hands. Caress it. Braille it. Memorize it. Take a good close look at that wondrous creation you hold in your hand. Study and memorize your mate's eyes, nose, and curvature of the lips. Let your spouse know just how much you have observed about her face. When you have this exercise mastered, you can create your own touching exercises. Try out a new one each week.

3. **Find various ways to get close enough to be able to touch each other.** From time to time, when you watch television or read a book, sit next to each other. Make sure the two of you are touching next time you are sitting on the couch together. And every once in a while, sit real close to each other in the car. Why not, you used to! Why should now be any different from then?

Any time you leave the house, whether for a walk or shopping, you should make a concerted effort to hold hands ... if only for a short period of time. When you are walking, it is a real shame to let your arms and hands flop needlessly by your sides. Put them to good use—

hold hands! Did you ever notice what wonderful and expressive hands your spouse has? If you have not held hands today, well … why haven't you?

4. **Endeavor to kiss your spouse in the morning, before the evening meal, and before you go to bed.** You would be surprised at how many couples fail to kiss even once during the day. Remember, it was a kiss that awakened Sleeping Beauty. Use your kiss to awaken the loving flame within your spouse.

5. **Make a point when you go to bed of taking turns playing the "S" game.** Try this with your mate tonight. When you get in bed play the "S" game. Have your lover lay on her side with her body shaped liked the letter S. Once she is in position, you squeeze your body close to hers by forming an S around her. Wrap your arms around her. Feel the warmth. After a while, reverse positions. This little game is guaranteed to make you feel warm and secure. We bet that you will sleep better too. Who knows, you might even spend the night that way. It sure beats the heck out of an electric blanket in the winter!

6. **Use touching as your *Morse Code* to make an exclamation mark of your love.** Touch your spouse as you compliment what you really like about the way your lover looks. This little habit forces you to pay careful attention to your spouse. Do the same thing in the evening. One of the things Liz does often is leave Charley a little Post-It note on his wallet with a special note about him or his day and gives him a big hug or touches him to accentuate the meaning of the note. Charley carries the latest note in his wallet with him all of the time.

7. Engage in intimacy often. It is the ultimate form of touching. Find new ways to enjoy the special closeness it brings to your marriage. When simple touching is a routine part of everyday living with your spouse, those little love taps can lead to stimulation and intimacy. Successfully married couples report that having the characteristic of *The Loving Touch* as a natural part of their marriages enhances their possibilities for sexual intimacy—the ultimate form of touching.

Critically important to a successful relationship is the art of touching. Successful couples have studied in infinite detail everything about each other. They know what makes each other tick and can describe the best qualities and virtues of their spouses. They brag about their spouses, constantly focusing only on each other's strengths. Successfully married couples communicate this deep knowledge of each other through their touching. Touching for them has become a kind of **Morse Code**—a substitute for language and the expression of feeling. When you and your spouse become great artisans of touch, the characteristic of *The Loving Touch* will be a natural part of your marriage.

CHAPTER 13

Seven Surprising Secrets #7: Beyond Boring

Frankly, marriage should never be boring!
The successful marriages we have studied
are characterized by variety, adventure,
laughter, excitement, surprises,
and doing the unexpected.

YOU'VE HEARD THE OLD SAYING, "VARIETY IS THE SPICE OF LIFE." That saying is an apt description of a key element in a successful marriage. Frankly, marriage should never be boring! The successful marriages we have studied are characterized by variety, adventure, laughter, excitement, surprises, and doing the unexpected.

Your love affair with your spouse can grow beyond any possibilities you ever thought imaginable when variety stimulates and delights the normally routine and mundane moments of life together. While predictability is part of any successful marriage, couples can strive so hard to be predictable in the interest of maintaining harmony in their relationships that they allow their relationships to become stale and without variety. They run the risk of making it a perfectly boring experience.

True love should also be full of surprises! On our 18th wedding anniversary we decided to go out to the most exclusive restaurant in town. Decked out in our best duds we set out for a marvelous evening of dining and dancing. Liz already knew she wanted the lobster, and Charley only had thoughts about a big steak with a side order of jumbo shrimp. A bottle of some good Cabernet Sauvignon wine also had to be a part of our celebration dinner. After dancing away the night, we would undoubtedly head home for a little fun by the fireplace (you can figure it out). So here we are, at the best restaurant in Columbia, Missouri, our hometown, having a pre-dinner glass of wine in great anticipation of a lovely, romantic anniversary dinner. The waiting line was longer than usual, since they didn't take advance reservations and it was a Saturday night. We knew the wait would certainly be worth it, even though we were both extremely hungry.

However, we were struggling with the hunger pains after 45 or 50 minutes of small talk waiting to be seated. Our conversation focused mainly on the delightful and funny memories of our wedding night— we had spaghetti from a carryout restaurant that night because it was the only available food when we finally were freed from the wedding party.

We had long since finished the glass of wine we paid for and there were still 15 parties to be seated ahead of us. Hunger finally over took us and the impulse struck. Liz grabbed Charley by the hand and out the door we went. We hopped in the car and drove across town. Charley, as you might guess, was beginning to wonder what kind of adventure Liz was taking him on this time. He found out soon enough as Liz pulled up to a little fast-food taco restaurant. Out of the car we hopped, into our favorite fast-food stand we went. We each ordered two tacos and a burrito along with a glass (paper cup) of ice tea. We took our order outside to sit together at one of those little metal tables with an umbrella to enjoy our anniversary dinner. To top it off, the table was positioned right next to one of the busiest intersections in town!

We don't ever recall having so much fun on our anniversary. We were eating what were arguably the best tacos in town, so the stares and horn honking just added to the evening's fun. It doesn't take much imagination to figure out why people would be staring when they saw us all dressed up with no place to go, sitting at that little round metal table in front of the local taco stand. We laughed; waved at people we knew who honked their car horns at us; and, in general, felt kind of like juvenile delinquents. We shall never forget that anniversary. This, friends, is what we mean by "upending expectancies"! This was one of those wonderful spontaneous surprises that make our marriage such a gas. Ah yes, true love is full of surprises.

We had just finished relating our anniversary story to a group of participants at one of our workshops, when a couple boldly stated that they had a better example of the real importance of variety and surprise in a marriage. They were both so eager to talk that we decided to let them have a go at it. It seems that Phil and Nancy started out their marriage, as all married people seem to do, very much in love. However, after three children, the demands of Phil's successful legal career, and 11 years of marriage, things had gotten stale.

Nancy would constantly suggest things that they could do together. She even arranged for babysitters, tickets, etc., to no avail. Phil always had the perfect excuse for not getting involved. It was usually an excuse about having too much work to do in preparation for his upcoming legal battles—all true and understandable. However, Phil never seemed to be off from work. It was a growing beast that slowly, but surely, took over his entire personality. Nancy even tried purchasing jeans and sweaters for Phil to wear, hoping that it would help him learn how to unwind and become a little less stuffy. Nothing she did had any effect on him.

As the years passed on, Nancy just kind of gave up on most of her ideas and came to grips with the fact that her gray, pinstriped husband had no excitement left in him. His pizzazz had all dried up somewhere along the way.

She had two choices, either discuss divorce or put her energies into something other than their marriage. Either way, something different and exciting had to be added to her life. Nancy could not just sit there and die of boredom for the rest of her life.

Right before one of Phil's many out-of-town trips, Nancy brought up again the same old subject of boredom and the need for a change. Phil gave his same old grunt and continued packing. This discussion had been repeated 100 times in the last several years. However, this time Nancy mustered up all of her courage and continued on with the discussion. She explained to Phil that she could not continue with their marriage if something did not change. This time Phil heard. He sat back in the chair and froze in silence.

At that point, Nancy was very sorry that she had continued the discussion so far. Why was she risking her safe, routine kind of life? There were lots of marriages in worse shape. At least Phil was a good provider for her and the kids.

Instead of sticking in there and explaining to Phil how desperate she really felt, she immediately backed off and said, "Forget about it. It is just because you are leaving again for another week. Oh well, have a nice time and I will see you when you get back."

At that Phil finished his packing, kissed Nancy goodbye, and departed. Nothing was really settled between the two of them. All they had accomplished was to peek over the edge of a deep crevice that had been separating them for years. Neither of them could sleep that night because the conversation that they had left unfinished loomed large.

Nancy was determined this time not to feel sorry for herself so she made delightful plans for each night of the week. If Phil would not join her for exciting engagements, she would at least take herself out for a bit of fun.

It was the second night of Phil's trip that started the wheels turning. He spent the evening trying to call Nancy. Each time he tried, the phone was busy. His frustration level was rising. Didn't Nancy know by now to stay off the phone when he was gone, so that he could get through? To his surprise, when he finally did get his phone call through, a babysitter answered. She very carefully explained that Nancy was at the ballet and would not be home until 11:30. How many times had she asked him to take her to the ballet? His first thoughts flashed back to their conversation just before he left home. Was she alone at the ballet, or had she gone there with someone else? Phil's adrenaline started to flow. No, that's stupid. Not his Nancy! He immediately dismissed the idea as pure nonsense.

Most of that evening Phil spent standing in front of his hotel room's mirror very carefully analyzing what he saw. There in the mirror was an ultra-conservative, 39-year-old man with wire-rimmed glasses, wearing his normal pinstriped gray flannel suit. The more he stared, the more he realized that he had been in his own hotel room for more than four hours and had not even loosened his tie. Maybe Nancy was right. Maybe he really was all dried up and stuffy.

He tried to go back and recollect when he had changed. He just couldn't remember changing; however, he could remember back to those first few exciting years of their marriage together. They never had a dull moment. The question nagged at him all night, as he thought about what happened.

The next day, Phil conducted his business in his same professional manner, but his thoughts kept wandering back to Nancy. He wondered if she were really right about him. Had he been too blind to see it? Was it too late for them?

As soon as he returned to the hotel room after his meeting, he immediately called home. Nancy's reassuring voice would make all of those doubts fade quickly away. Instead of reaching Nancy, Phil again reached the babysitter. Oh my God, where was she this time? It seems that Nancy had arranged to go to dinner and then to a concert. She was expected to return this time at about midnight.

After hearing that, the doubts became more than Phil could stand. This was his wife of 11 years. What was she doing? Two nights in a row … she must be with someone else. Phil could hardly control his temper or his mind. His thoughts of rage and guilt were rising so fast that he could not wait until midnight to yell at her over the phone. This kind of thing had to be done in person.

He canceled his meetings for the following day, packed his bags, and checked out of the hotel. If he drove straight through he could be back in San Francisco and home, standing in their living room by 11 o'clock. When he arrived, the children were sound asleep in bed and the babysitter was napping on the couch. He took care of paying the babysitter, so she could go on home.

There Phil stood, waiting to do mortal battle with whoever walked through his living room door. For the next 45 minutes, Phil frantically paced every inch of the floor. He had imagined his wife doing every conceivable thing in the world. Then it hit him … if only he had listened; if only he had realized that Nancy was really bored, maybe this would not be happening to him now.

As the clock struck 12, he heard the car pull up into the driveway. If he had any rational thoughts left, he would have figured that if it were her car, she must have been driving it. Therefore, Nancy would have to be alone. However, he was far beyond rational thoughts. To his surprise, Nancy walked in by herself, yawned, and said that it was nice to have him home so soon. It turns out that Nancy was quite alone, only going to the events to eliminate some of the boredom that she was feeling. She did not even have a very good time. There stood Phil, feeling like the biggest fool in the world.

From that night forward, Phil was a different person. Nancy just could not believe the change. Overnight he seemed to enjoy life again. They went to dinner, concerts, movies, and vacations. The romance and spark was back in full swing. It was a miraculous transformation. Nancy wondered for many years what caused the change, but was content to just appreciate the revitalization of the husband she so deeply loved. It was not until their 25th wedding anniversary that Phil told Nancy what he was really doing home from his business trip that night.

Nancy and Phil were right—their story was a perfect way to illustrate how important it is not to get stuck in a boring rut because of the daily grind. They have been happily married now for 32 years and told us that they never loss sight of how important it is to "spice up" their marriage often with variety and excitement. They go *Beyond Boring* as often as possible.

Surprise and adventure are so important to a great marriage.

One of the funniest stories we ever heard was from a couple who explained to us that their 57-year marriage was a "real hoot" because of the unusual tricks and pranks they played on each other when things seemed to be getting in a rut or when one of them needed a pick-me-up. Even with that explanation, we were not prepared for what we heard when Rodney and Esther shared their story with us.

It seems that Rodney was approaching his 85th birthday with much dread because he had it in his head that 85 years old sounded so old. Esther tried to explain to him that 85 may have sounded too old when they were 60 years old, but now that they were both almost 85, it was 100 years old that sounded so old.

Esther told us that nothing she said or did budged Rodney off his fixation with getting too old. She had to think of something spectacular. Then the perfect idea came to her. Instead of presents or flowers, she would surprise Rodney by showing up in a new bikini. Esther intended to purchase a bikini herself and wear it for Rodney's 85th birthday.

So off to the shopping mall she went. At 84 years old, she knew the salesclerk would probably laugh out loud when she asked to see the bikini swimsuits, but this was the only surefire surprise that she could think of to change Rodney's mood. So she braved what she knew would be a lesson in humiliation.

Into the swimsuit department she went and to her amazement, the salesclerk immediately took her to the bikini section without even cracking a smile. It was not until she asked what size did her granddaughter need that things turned in the expected direction. Esther calmly replied that she needed a size 12 or 14 for herself, not a granddaughter. The well-seasoned salesclerk burst into a big grin and then checked her reaction quickly by managing to ask, "And what color were you thinking about?" They settled on hot pink, since it was Rodney's favorite color.

Bikini in hand, she was now ready for the real challenge—where and how to surprise him. Esther said she had so many ideas, but settled on going out of the back door and coming around to ring the front doorbell. Rodney would certainly be surprised with that approach. Esther said the one obstacle she could not control was the unpredictability of the weather in March. So, she developed a back-up plan just in case it turned bitterly cold or snowed.

Rodney's birthday turned out to be simply beautiful. It was 58 degrees with a crystal clear sky. Perfect! Esther was all set.

At 6:00 pm Esther donned her hot pink bikini and wrapped herself in her warm winter coat. As she headed out the back door, she worried for a split second about the neighbors seeing her. However, she dismissed that thought immediately because Rodney was too important to her to care about what the neighbors might think. She just had to get him out of his funk.

As soon as she rounded the front corner of the house, she dropped her coat over the fence. There she was, 84 years old, in a hot pink bikini in their yard—too late to turn back now. Luckily, the street seemed to be deserted. As she reached the front porch, she waited a minute to catch her breath. Then, she rang the doorbell. After what seemed like an eternity, Rodney opened the door. The expression on his face was worth its weight in gold. He was totally stunned. Esther certainly had surprised him.

When Rodney finally regained his composure, he reached out to grab Esther's arm, pulling her into the house. As he shut the door, he burst into the biggest grin she had seen on his face in at least a month. They both began to laugh and talk about how she came up with the idea after worrying about his fixation with turning 85 years old. Then Rodney said it hit him—Esther looked amazingly sexy to him standing there in her new hot pink bikini. They didn't explain any more about their evening together, except to say that Rodney didn't seem worried any longer about turning 85 years old. Considering the enormous grins on both of their faces, we could only imagine what the rest of that evening involved—surely surprises of a special kind.

Sometimes creating surprises and adventure can take a lot of hard work to accomplish, but that's what can make it so special for your spouse. Angelo and Gayle said the surprise vacation Angelo worked out 18 years ago was the first big adventure they experienced together. Angelo bought several raffle tickets his UAW group was selling as part of a fund-raiser for disabled area children. He felt obligated to join his group in helping the children. The prize was a fully paid vacation to Anchorage, Alaska, for two. Now, that was certainly something he and Gayle would never in a million years think about doing, but what the heck. He never won anything anyway, so what did it matter?

About a week after the drawing, Angelo received a call at home saying he was the grand prize winner of the fully paid trip to Alaska. Since it was his union group that worked out all of the arrangements, Angelo knew it wasn't a joke. The vacation was theirs! Now what? Would Gayle even consider going to Alaska? Neither of them were adventurous or outdoor people, so what would they do in Anchorage?

As Angelo started to investigate the arrangements and possibilities he couldn't believe what he had won. Included in the package were seven nights of hotel accommodations, round-trip plane tickets for two, and money for meals. This was unbelievable. Angelo and Gayle would have had to save for several years to be able to afford a trip like this. Not only was he starting to get excited, he was also trying to figure out how to tell Gayle in a way that would cause her to share his excitement. Angelo wanted it to be a total surprise for Gayle because it had been two years since their last real vacation.

When Angelo finally figured out what would get Gayle hooked on going to Alaska, he knew it was going to take a bit of research to make it happen. First, he went to the bookstore to secure a travel guide for the Anchorage area, containing all of the contact information for wildlife explorations. Within a week, Angelo was able to set up a boat excursion to see 26 glaciers and do whale watching on the way. Next he arranged for a scenic train ride from Anchorage to the boat docks on the Anchorage Whittier Rail. The tour guide indicated that there would be plenty of opportunities to see wildlife and the countryside from the slow-moving train. The last part of his plan was the very best. Angelo was going to splurge. He arranged with K2 Aviation to fly out of Talkeetna, Alaska, in a little six-seater plane to Mt. McKinley. This was it—the last piece of the plan. He was sure that when he told Gayle they were going to land on a glacier on Mt. McKinley she would be thrilled … or maybe on second thought her reaction would be an instant panic attack. No, he was sure she would be thrilled. Anyway, this was his best plan and he was ready to spring it on her.

Angelo and Gayle arrived home that evening about the same time and began the usual hustling around to get dinner on the table. As soon as they both sat down and started to eat, Angelo started into his well-rehearsed presentation about the opportunity he won for both of them to go to Anchorage, Alaska. As Angelo moved into the explanation of the boat and train trips, it was obvious that Gayle was anything but thrilled. Continuing, undaunted, Angelo finally got to the plane trip to Mt. McKinley and landing on a glacier. Just as he thought, Gayle's expression turned quickly to what he thought was excitement. All of a sudden she caught her breath and said, "Oh my goodness, you are crazy! You want me to do what?" Angelo and Gayle were both laughing as they told us about her first reaction. Gayle said she was scared to death. It wasn't as if they were going to do one new thing, they were going to do everything new and different in a one-week period of time. She had never even ventured out of the state, so the thought of going so far away from home to the unknown was terrifying at first.

However, Angelo was right about what would hook her into his plan. Gayle had always been fascinated with mountains. She would read any article she could find on mountain expeditions around the world. The thought of flying up to Mt. McKinley and landing on a glacier was too thrilling to allow the fear to stop her. Gayle warmed up quickly to the trip and helped Angelo with the final planning.

It took them about a month to plan the final details of the trip and make all of the arrangements. While still somewhat apprehensive, when the big day came to depart for Alaska both of them felt as prepared as possible for this new adventure.

To their delight, Anchorage was nothing like the wilderness outpost they had anticipated. Anchorage turned out to have many wonderful restaurants, museums, and little shops; a zoo; and the scenic Tony Knowles Coastal Trail. They immediately rented two bicycles and headed off for the trail. Since the sun was out for almost 23 hours in July, they had plenty of time to return to the hotel before dark. Their arrival day was an absolutely unexpected success. They had ridden ten miles on the bicycles and had seen a moose, several small animals, and magnificent wild flowers.

The next day was spent relaxing aboard the Alaska Railroad en route to the docks. Once there, Angelo and Gayle boarded the Glacier Discovery Excursion Boat to go whale watching and glacier gazing.

Angelo said he knew the trip to Alaska was a great success already when he saw Gayle's face as she heard the roar of the ice breaking off a massive glacier and falling 100 feet straight into the bay. Gayle said she felt like a real explorer seeing something most people never get to experience, let alone see first-hand from a boat deck. Before the excursion boat arrived back at the docks, Gayle and Angelo saw whales, sea lions, black-legged kittewakes, and dall sheep—none of which either of them had ever seen before.

Back on the Alaska Railroad for their return to Anchorage, Angelo and Gayle talked non-stop about what they had just experienced for the first time. And this was only day one of a seven-day adventure.

The next several days were filled with hiking the scenic trails in Eagle River nature area and in the Kenai Fjords National Park. It was a very strange experience for city dwellers, since most of the time they were completely alone on the trails. In fact, they saw more moose than people during those three days of hiking.

Someone had prepared them for hiking in Alaska by telling them to be sure to wear bells on their waists to ward off the bears. So, they jingled their way through the back country of Alaska happily keeping the bears at a distance. However, someone later told them that the bells only attracted the attention of the animals. So, to this day, Angelo said they still don't know if the bells made the bears afraid or really made him and Gayle "bear bait." All they can say is that the one bear they saw seemed more interested in eating his berries than attacking these two dumb city dwellers jingling on down the trail.

Angelo had planned so carefully that the most exciting part of their trip was saved for their final day in Alaska. Together, he and Gayle drove their rented 4 by 4 to Talkeetna, Alaska, to catch the K2 flight to Mt. McKinley. Pulling into Talkeetna for Gayle and Angelo was like arriving at what they first thought Anchorage would be—a wilderness outpost from some by-gone era they had only seen on television. Log cabins, tiny 6- by 10-foot food stands, and a general store lined the town's dirt road next to the tiny airstrip.

All of a sudden, this was more than a new adventure. Both of them had second thoughts at the same time. But it seemed totally unreasonable to have come so far to let the panic take over now. After regaining their composure and nerve, Angelo and Gayle boarded the tiny six-seater plane and were soon airborne.

Once in the air, they were awestruck with the view of the Alaskan landscape and the expansive mountain range they were heading toward. Circling above a glacier high up on Mt. McKinley, the pilot told them it might be a bit of a rough landing due to the sudden increase in wind gusts. They all prepared. To their delight, it didn't seem all that bad after they had safely landed on the glacier. It was certainly worth overcoming all obstacles to experience the thrill of stepping out of that tiny plane onto the glacier. All of Angelo's work, and of course his luck at winning the trip in the first place, were worth it.

Angelo and Gayle bubbled over as they told us many more of the details of their experiences in Alaska. It was their first vacation adventure to a totally unknown area. They promised themselves that they would be more adventurous from then on because of the richness of their experience in Alaska. Taking the risk to do something so different for them turned out to be fantastic. In their 48 years of marriage, Angelo and Gayle proudly told us, they saved their money and have been able to take six additional adventures to even stranger areas of the world. For them it all started with Angelo's holding the winning ticket. They have definitely gone *Beyond Boring* with their adventures, adding much variety to their marriage.

There are many other stories and anecdotes we could share with you about variety being the spice of life. Just like us, the many successful couples we interviewed have had marriages full of adventure, surprise, and variety. Does your marriage have those moments of surprise and variety? Do you go *Beyond Boring* to spice up your marriage? We sure hope you do. Variety is truly the spice of life. The concept of adding adventure, surprise, and variety simply must be part of any marital relationship if true lasting love is to be achieved.

Another aspect of going *Beyond Boring* is the importance of smiling and laughing at unexpected times. Have you ever gotten angry with someone who is smiling at you? Try it some time. The next time you and your spouse are having a "heated discussion" (sounds better than arguing doesn't it?), smile at her. It will drive her crazy. You know why? It is because you've taken away a large part of her anger. If you shoot several smiles his way, he may even forget what the argument was about. The two of us learned this lesson very early in our marriage.

Right after we got married 43 years ago we learned one of our first lessons about smiling. It was a bright and sunny fall day in mid-Missouri and we were having our first barbecue outdoors for Charley's family on our brand new grill. Everyone was anticipating the meal since they finished the walk around the neighborhood and had worked up quite an appetite.

Liz was busy barbecuing the chicken while Charley was setting the table. As Charley looked over, he saw Liz scurrying for the kitchen. Something seemed to have gone terribly wrong. By the time he made it as far as the grill, Liz burst out of the kitchen door with several utensils in her hands. Then, he saw it. The chickens were lying in the burning coals. Their BBQ dinner was going up in flames. Charley in his infinite wisdom committed the cardinal sin ... he accused Liz of "intentionally" dropping the chickens into the fire to ruin his family's first get-together. Not a very bright statement to make, was it? Well, you know how arguments begin. People lose their rationality and start arguing and accusing and screaming, and, in general, make fools of themselves. We made fools of ourselves quite often when we first got married. At any rate, a rather, shall we say, heated discussion followed the "chicken-on-the-spit" incident. Then it happened. Liz broke out into one of her famous toothy smiles and started laughing. For some reason, that smile made Charley come immediately to his senses. He smiled in return. And you know what ... the next thing we know we're rolling on the bluegrass doubled up in laughter. The argument ended as abruptly as it began. Oh, the power of a smile! We can't for the life of us remember why we started arguing over such a silly incident. But we do remember why the argument stopped … Liz's smile and Charley's counter-smile. Try it some time; try to yell at someone who is smiling at you. Oh, by the way, Kentucky Fried Chicken served great chicken that day, so the first family get-together turned out okay after all.

One word of caution is in order. Not all arguments stop because you smile or make a funny face at your husband or wife. Clearly, that notion is too simplistic, yet it gives you an example of one way to upend expectancies and change a difficult situation into a light-hearted one. Perhaps now is a good time for you to begin examining other ways in which you might upend the expectancies of your spouse by adding variety, adventure, laughter, excitement, and surprises to your marriage.

∽ঔ

— *Advice* —

It can be exhilarating to take a few moments thinking of all the delectable ideas you can imagine to add variety to your marriage. These ideas can bring so much pleasure, without adversely affecting the stability of your marriage. Always remember the benefits of finding ways to enhance the romance and the laughter with a little pizzazz.

Below are seven very simple ideas to add just a little variety to your marriage. These can help you get started until you let your imagination run wild as you create delightful ideas that are just perfect for your marriage. As you try out these new ideas, you and your partner will feel a renewed interest in your relationship. It will enhance your sense of excitement as you look forward to surprise and adventure's becoming a regular part of your lives together.

1. **Understand that variety is necessary for all marriages.** Do not let those deep, well-established ruts get a foothold. If you think variety, then your marriage will be characterized by exciting, adventurous, humorous, and fun-loving experiences that will add to the enjoyment for both of you. Make the sacrifices to go *Beyond Boring* with your experiences.

2. **Periodically—we suggest at least once a month—do something completely different or go someplace together that neither of you has ever gone before.** Find a new place to travel, walk, or sight see. Say something to your spouse that you have never said before. Do something with your spouse that you have never done before. It is a big, wide world out there, with plenty of untried things to still do. Being adventurous can add a spark to the daily routine of everyday life.

3. **Send your spouse a love letter or a romantic email.** Do it when it is least expected, knocking him off his feet with surprise. When you take the time to put into words how much your spouse means to you and how you feel about her, you can only imagine how great it will make your partner feel.

4. **Bring home flowers or have them sent at times other than a birthday or anniversary.** Look for a time when your spouse needs a little picker-upper. Being sensitive to your mate's needs and understanding the message this simple act sends can be quite powerful. Upending expectancies with flowers can break the mundane routine.

5. **Every once in a while, cook something genuinely exciting and different.** Be creative and find ways to serve it with flair. Try a picnic basket dinner in the middle of the winter, served in the den or the bedroom.

6. **Try a new sport together.** Make plans to go white water rafting, mountain biking, skiing, golfing, backpacking, swimming, or ... anything new and different. The planning for this new sports experience can also be great fun!

7. **Occasionally, greet your husband or wife at the door with your sexiest looking outfit on.** Make it so terrific that no matter what happened to your spouse before he walked through that door, he would immediately forget about it. One minor point; make absolutely sure that it is your spouse before you open the door!

We just cannot stress enough that you need to remember that famous old saying that variety is the spice of life. Many marriages get stale because nothing exciting or different ever happens. They just get stuck in that mundane rut of everyday survival, feeling like they never have enough time to catch their breath. Don't let that happen to your marriage. It is so easy to add richness and fullness to your lives with that special ingredient found in successful marriages that requires going *Beyond Boring*.

CHAPTER 14

Seven Secrets to Avoiding
the Seven-Year Itch

*The more basic question is how do you stay faithful
to the one you love and keep your loving relationship
healthy and strong so it survives the ups, the downs,
and the temptations present in all relationships
at one time or another.*

RECENTLY, THE U.S. CENSUS BUREAU issued a press release entitled "Most People Make Only One Trip Down the Aisle, but First Marriages Shorter." Needless to say, the article grabbed our attention immediately since we write about this stuff all the time.

There were a number of interesting highlights reported in the press release but the one that piqued our interest the most was the following: "On average, first marriages that end in divorce last about eight years." This phenomenon has often been referred to as the *Seven-Year Itch.*

First, a little background. Most aficionados of the *Seven-Year Itch* trace it back to a play by the same name written by one George Axelrod. His three-act play was first performed on Broadway in New York City in 1952. Three years later, a movie by the same title starring the late, great Marilyn Monroe was released by 20th Century Fox.

Before we get to the "plot" of this article we also want to remind you that the *Seven-Year Itch* has also been associated with an itchy and irritating skin rash that has been reported to last for up to seven years. Frankly, this notion is very closely related to what happens in a number of marriages, as we explain in the paragraphs to follow.

In the most basic sense, the *Seven-Year Itch* is the inclination of some to become unfaithful to their spouses after seven years of marriage. Most of these marriages end in the eighth year, according the to research statistics.

As an aside, we have written about the importance of honesty, trust, and faithfulness in love and marriage in the chapter called "Character in Love and Marriage" (p. 9). That chapter points out that in our interviews over more than 25 years with couples that had successful marriages we are always struck by their undying trust in each other. They literally trust each other with their lives, their fortune, and their sacred honor. These are the marriages that do not end in the eighth year due to the seven-year itch.

In the play and the movie of the same title, a married man by the name of Richard is currently reading a book about to be published by his company entitled *Seven-Year Itch*. The book offers the notion that a large percentage of men have extra-marital affairs after seven years of marriage; hence, the *Seven-Year Itch*. At the same time he is reading the book, he meets a young, blond television model. As you might imagine, the plot thickens!

As the just-released Census data suggest, there just might be something to the *Seven-Year Itch* when it comes to marriage. The more basic question is how do you stay faithful to the one you love and keep your loving relationship healthy and strong so it survives the ups, the downs, and the temptations present in all relationships at one time or another.

We believe we have learned much from our more than 25 years of research on successful marriage and loving relationships and would like to share some of our findings with you within the context of this conversation about the *Seven-Year Itch*. Here they are in a nutshell.

The first of the seven rules for avoiding the *Seven-Year Itch* is this—understand that infatuation with another person and the temptation to betray the trust of the one you love are perfectly normal feelings when it comes to love and marriage. Getting hitched to another person doesn't make you less human. It does, in many ways, make you more human—more in touch with your feelings and emotions. Accept the feelings.

Rule two is—do not under any circumstances act on those infatuation and temptation impulses until you have taken the time to fully think through the consequences of your making that choice. Cheating on your spouse or loved one can be and often is deadly to your relationship. Rebuilding trust is nearly impossible after committing such an indiscretion.

The third rule to avoid the *Seven-Year Itch* is to recognize that continuing and recurring fantasies and infatuations about another person are strong indicators of something amiss in your relationship with your spouse or lover. These feelings are often associated with a deep-seated problem in your relationship that must be addressed before it is too late.

The fourth rule—the "turn the corner rule" as we like to refer to it—is to address the issue head-on with your loving partner. Failure to do so will doom your relationship to the ash heap of lost love. There is pain to be sure when you address the issues that are destroying your loving relationship, but to not do so will be even more painful, we guarantee it!

Rule five is a tough one. You and your lover may discover in rule four that love is tough. It is sometimes unforgiving. Frankly, sometimes you determine that your loving relationship is lost. But more likely, you discover that you truly love your spouse and that you cannot imagine life without her. You find out what so many before have discovered— you love your mate so much you cannot under any circumstances let him go. You must save this relationship by committing to the hard work it will take to rebuild the love.

Which is why rule six is so critically important. Rule six says, seek help! Find some neutral party to talk to. Sometimes couples turn to a marriage counselor. Others turn to "self-help" websites like www.SelfGrowth.com. Truth is, much of what you need to learn can be self-taught. You can learn to do what you have to do to make your relationship work by reading what others, including us, have discovered. Being educators at heart, we especially like the latter. More often than not, you can learn so much about yourself and your loving relationship by "discovering" what others have already learned!

All of this leads to rule seven. Rule seven is a simple rule, really. At it's essence, it says to us that sometimes we have to "fish or cut bait." The reality is that some marriages and loving relationships cannot be saved. They are doomed. They must end to the mutual benefit of both and to the many that are affected by the relationship. It is time to move on. But in the end, an examination of your relationship will ideally reveal that your relationship is worth saving. More often than not, it can be saved. You should always work toward that end if you are to avoid the *Seven-Year Itch*.

We offer these seven rules to help you avoid the *Seven-Year Itch* so you can be one of those happy and successfully married couples who celebrate their Golden Anniversaries together

CHAPTER 15

The Stress Test

*How is it possible that some marriages make
it through these challenging ordeals while others
do not? The fact is, most successful marriages
experience difficult challenges, yet they survive
and thrive. Our research tells us why.*

EARLY IN OUR MARRIAGE, we lost a child. Charley is still haunted by the image of Dr. Griffin walking down the hall to deliver the bad news, "Your baby has died from a bacterial infection." The word "devastated" does not begin to describe the feeling in your heart and soul about the loss of a child. How could it happen? How is it possible? Who is to blame? Why us?

The feeling of emptiness is crushing and you just want to die on the spot. Yet, you and your spouse somehow manage to survive in spite of the overwhelming sadness you both feel.

All marriages have these types of moments. For some it is the death of a child. For others it is the loss of a parent. For some it is the serious illness of a spouse or child. Sometimes marriages are forced to deal with the trauma of losing a job or an unwanted long-distance move.

The successfully married couples we have interviewed all report events like this. But there is one thing we have learned—those marriages all survive these traumatic events. Why? How is it possible that some marriages make it through these challenging ordeals while others do not? The fact is, most successful marriages experience diffi-cult challenges, yet they survive and thrive. Our research tells us why.

In all marriages over time there will be events and circumstances that test their strength. The stronger the foundation of the relation-ship, the better the chances for surviving the ordeal. And, when the events or circumstances are ended, the process of going through it together builds the bond even stronger.

We have experienced several such events and circumstances over our 43 years of marriage, but one stands out due to its almost three-year length. In the early 1990s several universities were recruiting Charley. Having lived in the same place for nearly three decades, Charley never before seriously entertained the recruiting efforts of outsiders. But this time was different. Something told him it was the right time to take the step. Our daughter was grown and married. We were both highly successful in our careers and needed a challenge. What would Liz think? She was extremely happy with her career, their home, and life in general, so would she even consider a life-altering move to another state?

Two universities contacted Charley within a three-day period with serious intentions for interviews. Both were unsolicited, but intriguing. He got up enough nerve to bring up the subject with Liz. To his amazement, Liz agreed to join him in playing with the idea of taking such a giant step into the unknown. After endless hours of conversation, weighing the pros and cons of a major, life-altering change such as this, they decided together to allow Charley to interview at both universities. Liz was invited to interview with local school districts during Charley's visits. Things went splendidly during the first interviews, until we returned to the hotel in Waco, Texas.

It was the first time in our lives that we fully understood the difficulty celebrities or newsmakers have in dealing with a news media feeding frenzy. The Branch Davidian standoff was in its 51st day and the compound had just started to burn down an hour before we entered one of the major hotels in Waco, Texas, where the university hosts had reserved a room for us. Everyone who was anyone in the news services was camped out in the hotel lobby and front area. It seemed that every major news reporter we admired on television and radio was gathered at the entrance. Since we were both dressed nicely in dark suits for the interviews, the members of the press must have thought we were important. All at once they surged forward, pouncing on us like a pack of wild dogs. Microphones, cameras, and lights were immediately shoved in our faces. It seemed for an instant that we were being smashed against the inner wall of the hotel lobby. The onslaught of reporters and news anchors was overwhelming. We leaned against each other to maintain our upright position, with minimal success. Instantly, a security guard moved forward, opening a slight path to the elevator. We back stepped carefully, but steadily, toward the security guard and the elevator, saying to the reporters, "We're nobody. We don't know anything." We just kept repeating those words as we felt the security guard guiding us into the open elevator. Swiftly the elevator rose to the top floor carrying us to the safety and privacy of our room. What had just happened? We were still in shock as we evaluated what we had just experienced.

First and foremost, both of us were physically all right. Second, we made it to our room in full anticipation that we would be discussing the interviews and all that had happened that day. However, all we could think and talk about were the overwhelming feelings we came away with after the experience we had just had in the hotel lobby. We had turned on the television to learn that the raging fire was nearing its full, sinister outcome. All of the children at the Branch Davidian compound had been lost in the terrible fire. It weighed heavily on our minds as we tried to get a few minutes of much-needed sleep before the interviews continued in the morning. Maybe this should have made us think twice about going ahead with the interviews, but at the time it was a train moving forwards with us along for the ride. The university folks could not have been nicer and seemed to make extraordinary efforts to overcome the tragic circumstances that were occurring just a short distance away.

As we flew out of Waco for the interview with the other university and school district in New York, we had trouble taking it all in. So much had happened in these last three days to us, the community around Waco, and to the entire country. But somehow we needed to continue with the process that had been set in motion when Charley agreed to be interviewed for this university position.

Landing in New York City bought us immediately to the reality that we had embarked on a life-altering path that was probably going to change our lives forever. We were excited about the possibilities of a new challenge and the changes it would bring. Little did we know what that was really to mean and how difficult the challenge would become over the next three years.

The interviews with the university and the school district went splendidly again for both Charley and Liz. Offers were made to Charley and Liz from both Waco and New York City. Now the conversation begins. How to make the decision? In almost 30 years of marriage we had never had to make that kind of decision. Avoidance was probably our saving grace in years past, but now it could not be used. We had to look squarely at the possibilities and talk about them together. Waco, Texas; New York City; and Columbia, Missouri, were the choices. Each brought advantages and disadvantages. Choices of different lifestyles, career opportunities, family issues, finances, and personal preferences all came into the multitude of lists we made of the pros and cons of each location. We were both leaning toward Waco, but Liz still had one reservation. Until she moved to the Midwest, she had serious asthma difficulties as a child in California. The doctors in the 1950s told her that she would probably outgrow the allergies to pollens in the Southwest over time. However, she would be better to move to a different part of the country when she attended college. Due to opportunities and wise advice, Liz attended college in Missouri, the middle of the country. Within a few months, she gained weight, lost all symptoms of her childhood asthma, and lived a healthy life for almost 30 years. So, maybe the doctors were right back in the 1950s. It was mostly a childhood thing and mostly in her head. With that conclusion, the decision became easy. We set off for a new life adventure in Waco, Texas.

We moved into a beautiful home with a spectacular view of the Brazos River Valley. The people of Waco were truly lovely. The welcome could not have been warmer from the school district, the university, our neighborhood, and our church. We had finally come to a point in both our careers that people mostly dream about but never achieve. We had achieved what we both had been striving for. We were at the top of our careers and living in a place close to our daughter and son-in-law. Wonderful people surrounded us in our professional and private lives. How could it be more perfect? We were on the fast track for the first month with new jobs, new lives, new stores, new roads, and a new house. Everything was new, new, new. This obviously was the challenge we had been looking for.

It was the fifth week of our adventure when the first sign of trouble reared its ugly head. Liz experienced her first asthma attack in almost 30 years. It came on quickly and with no warning signs. For the first few seconds, Liz didn't recognize the symptoms and ignored the impending danger. She no longer carried any type of protection, such as an inhaler, with her. Why should she? Remember, she would

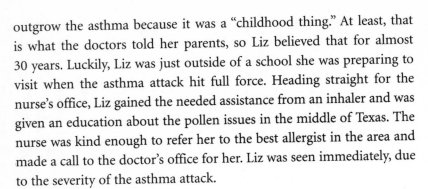

outgrow the asthma because it was a "childhood thing." At least, that is what the doctors told her parents, so Liz believed that for almost 30 years. Luckily, Liz was just outside of a school she was preparing to visit when the asthma attack hit full force. Heading straight for the nurse's office, Liz gained the needed assistance from an inhaler and was given an education about the pollen issues in the middle of Texas. The nurse was kind enough to refer her to the best allergist in the area and made a call to the doctor's office for her. Liz was seen immediately, due to the severity of the asthma attack.

After multiple allergy tests, it was completely clear. Liz was allergic to most of the Southwest pollens that freely roamed the Texas air. Modern medicine had even developed a 5-point scale for each of the pollens. Liz hit the 5+ score on many of the pollens. Since she has always been a high achiever, this would normally have been terrific. However, in this case, it meant that Liz was in serious trouble. After presenting the results carefully to Liz, the doctor talked through the options available. Remember, this was not the 1950s, but rather the 1990s. So, Liz thought there must be an easy medical solution. However, the first option the doctor gave Liz was to relocate to another part of the country, like the Midwest or North. Oh great! Only five weeks into our magnificent adventure and the first option presented was to move out of the area. After the shock of the first option sank in, the doctor proceeded on to the options of shots twice a week, medication, inhalers, breathing treatments, etc. Needless to say, there was no decision to make at this point except try the medication, inhalers, breathing treatments, etc. So, the saga began.

The first few months after learning this, we maintained a blindly optimistic view of the situation. We were both appreciative of the fact that Liz had no serious side effects from the first major asthma attack and had begun the medication and shots. Since modern medicine had come so far since her childhood visits to the emergency room, the faith seemed to be warranted. We moved forward successfully with our everyday lives and our careers. We had met the first challenges in our new positions and our new lives.

When the high mountain cedar pollen blew in from Colorado across the plains into the middle of Texas, our optimism grew suddenly dormant. Liz was on a first-name basis with the emergency room doctors. That was not the way it should be. Her asthma was not under control no matter what the best doctors could do. It was not in her head, it was in her lungs.

After about ten months, we took stock of our circumstances. Liz's health was an ever-increasing concern and our house in Columbia still had not sold. Liz had become so dependent upon the medication, inhalers, and breathing treatments that we could not exercise or go for any extended trips in the countryside. Our savings account was depleted and we were racking up credit card debt because of the two house payments. These were not the challenges we had in mind when we made the decision to change jobs and move. On the other hand, both of us were flourishing in our respective careers and enjoying the work. Being close to our daughter and son-in-law was another benefit of the move. We again hoped that the medical treatments would take hold, making it possible for Liz to breathe easier and go back to enjoying the outdoors if she could just make it through one complete season of pollens and shots.

So, into the second year we went. Instead of the desired improvement, Liz's health continued to deteriorate. No longer could she go outside without enduring an asthma attack. The only solution was to spend her time in an air-conditioned environment, wearing a mask when moving from one air-conditioned environment to the next. In other words, no more riding bicycles, boating, walking, or hiking for us. We were an inside-only couple. What a way to live! Yet, we continued to flourish in our careers, generating creative ideas and making a difference for students from the pre-school to post-doctoral levels. That had to count for something.

We continued to exist, but soon learned that Liz would need to leave the area to regain her strength and her health. So, we began our treks north every six weeks or so to allow Liz the time necessary to gain enough strength to endure the next round of asthma attacks.

Midway through the second year of this existence, Liz was fortunate enough to secure a job that allowed her to travel throughout the United States doing workshops and national presentations. Her health improved every time she left Waco and steadily declined every time she stayed in town for more than a few days. For the next six months, our careers became almost our sole enjoyment. The stress levels due to the health and financial issues were becoming extreme.

At a meeting of deans from the region that Charley was hosting in Waco, a representative from the University of Missouri-St. Louis began inquiring as to Charley's availability for a position with them as dean. While Charley was enjoying unbelievable success at the top of his profession, the life-threatening concerns about Liz's health made the inquiry welcome. However, in Charley's heart, he did not want to interview again so soon or go through the upheaval of another life move.

Later that evening when going to dinner the university representative approached Charley in earnest as they walked down the hotel hallway. Liz was walking a slight distance behind the two to allow their conversation to occur with some level of privacy. All of a sudden Charley realized that Liz was no longer with them. Someone had left the door open to the outside pool area, allowing all of the pollens to rush into the corridor. As he looked a few feet down the hallway, there was Liz lying crumpled on the floor. His heart sunk instantly as he realized she was not able to get her breath. Fear overwhelmed him. What would he do without her? It was unimaginable. Charley fumbled quickly through her purse for the EpiPen. With quick action, he was able to bring her out of the attack. Even though the university representative was horrified with the life threatening disaster he witnessed, he was smiling to himself at the powerful hook he had found to lure Charley back to Missouri to his university. It worked. Charley's love for Liz and the realization that he could lose her to asthma was a powerful incentive to look seriously at moving back home to Missouri where Liz had spent almost 30 very healthy years.

To this day, the university representative teases Charley about how lucky he was to find the hook he needed when Liz collapsed on the floor. We can laugh about it now, but going through it was the most difficult three years of our marriage. There were times that we thought we were permanently trapped and Liz would not make it out alive. She was virtually a prisoner, living only inside from air conditioner to air conditioner. We sometimes think we must have had a guardian angel watching over us to take us out of a place where Liz just couldn't breathe due to the pollens and move us to a place where her health has never been better.

The funniest thing is that after much conversation, we agreed to give up the stellar career moves we had made going to Waco and move back to Missouri—no matter what the professional career consequences—for the sake of Liz's health. Just the opposite happened with the move back to Missouri. The honors and awards for our work have continued coming in and both of us have never been happier. The experience taught us more than we understood at the time and gave us an even stronger bond. Our core values had passed the test.

Sometimes job-related relocations can put tremendous amounts of stress even on a successful marriage for completely different reasons. Josh and Angie had been happily married for 36 years when the opportunity of a lifetime was presented to Angie. If she would relocate with her company to Orlando, Florida, she would be tracked for a vice presidency at the company headquarters. It was everything she had dreamed about and worked for for 34 years with the same company to accomplish. Only trouble was, Josh was 64 and had just recently retired. Finally able to enjoy golfing with his buddies whenever he wished to play and volunteering at the YMCA, he felt his life was as perfect as it could be. He was enjoying the leisure time to tinker around the house while Angie was at work.

Since Angie was the senior member of the company's branch office in Cincinnati, she could come and go pretty much as she wished. That allowed the two of them the flexibility to enjoy special outings together even during the weekdays. One of Angie's assistants covered pretty much all of the evening events, so Angie also had her evenings at home. Josh felt they had arrived at an ideal place in life after all of their years of struggling to get ahead. He could not be happier.

Angie figured she still had at least five years of working before she would turn 62 and be eligible for full retirement benefits with her company. This was the first time in their marriage that their age difference had ever seemed to matter. However, Angie thought maybe it was a blessing because Josh would be free to move now with her job advancement. His work would no longer be an obstacle. Angie never once considered Josh's friends, the golfing, the YMCA, and all of the other connections Josh had to the community. She was just so excited about finally being recognized as vice president material that she couldn't wait to get home and share the good news with Josh.

As soon as Angie entered the house and found Josh she began relating her terrific news. Such excitement filled her thoughts as she continued with her reporting about the advancement that she missed the non-verbal signals Josh was giving off about their potential move. Angie rattled on for about 30 minutes before she paused to get any feedback on Josh's thoughts. By that time, Josh knew it was too late to tell her how he really felt since it just wouldn't be fair. Hadn't Angie moved to Cincinnati with him nine years ago when he had the same kind of opportunity? Didn't she even have to give up a possible advancement with the company to take a lateral move to one of their branch offices in Cincinnati? How could he tell her that he was now retired without his normal business connections and that everything he really enjoyed was here in Cincinnati—his golfing buddies and his volunteer work at the YMCA. He had developed such strong bonds that he couldn't imagine how he could make the change. Besides, he was now 64 years old—hardly the time to start job hunting. What would he do in Orlando? No, he couldn't tell Angie how he felt. That could crush her and be totally unfair. He would just have to work through this.

The company wanted Angie to be there within the next month, so they assisted her with the relocation process. Everything went so smoothly that Josh figured he would just have to find a way to adjust. He couldn't even find anything to complain about. The company had gotten them $15,000 more than they thought their house was worth and assisted them in finding a lovely new house priced almost $20,000 less than their old house with about 500 more square feet. With the $23,000 increase in salary the company gave Angie, they would be able to take an extra vacation or two. What more could they ask for?

With the actual move completed, Angie and Josh dug into the work of unpacking; getting utilities hooked up; and finding new services, such as grocery stores, doctors, and hair salons. Unfortunately, they only had four days in their new home before Angie was called into work because of an important assignment that she needed to be in on from the beginning. So, there sat Josh, a 64-year-old retired gentleman, with the entire household unpacking and relocation woes to deal with on his own. He tried to do some self-talk and find the positive aspects of the situation, but negative thoughts just crept into his head. From the first day Angie left for her new assignment, Josh began a cycle of negative thoughts and quiet despair. What was he going to do with himself? This was not at all what he had imagined retirement would be. How could he wait five more years until Angie could retire to have fun?

Josh found himself moving deeper into depression with each passing day. Angie was so totally committed to her new job that they really didn't see each other much of the time. Even when she was at home Angie had her mind on her job and all of her new responsibilities. She was a quick study, but there were so many new things to learn in such a short time if she was going to be successful and make the promotion to vice president. Josh grew quieter and more despondent, yet he knew if he discussed it with Angie she might take it as a sign that he didn't fully support her achievements. That was the farthest thing from the truth; however, his growing depression was increasing so quickly that for the first time in his life he began to have horrible nightmares and harmful thoughts most of the time. One evening when Angie was out at another one of her required functions, Josh decided to sit down and just have a drink. What the heck, he might as well drink by himself since he now did everything else by himself. In 34 years of marriage, he had never had a drink by himself and he had never kept what he was feeling from Angie. Why was everything now so hard for him? He felt trapped in a no-win situation.

As the weeks turned into months, Josh felt more and more isolated from Angie and the world he knew and loved. He had lost his buddies to play golf with, all of his long-time friends from work, his acquaintances from the YMCA, and his beloved baseball team. His new surroundings still felt uncomfortable and foreign. He did not belong. Josh had no mission, no interests, and no place to go. There he sat day after day turning to alcohol for relief from the pain.

The demands of Angie's new job had her out at least three nights a week and working 12 to 14 hours, six days a week. While she kept saying that things would get better as soon as she adjusted to her new role, it seemed to Josh like things were just spiraling the other direction. They hadn't eaten a meal together in the last two weeks and he couldn't remember the last time they had a meaningful conversation together. Angie was so involved with work that she didn't seem to notice the drastic downward changes in Josh. She thought he just needed a little time to adjust, but never stopped to take stock of just how bad things had really gotten for him.

One Thursday evening about four months after their move, Angie had an extended business meeting that should have long since been over by 8:00 pm. She told Josh she would be home around 8:30 and had tried several times to reach him on the phone to let him know that she was going to be delayed. Josh always answered her calls on the first ring with a warm, reassuring tone saying that it was just fine and he understood fully the demands of a new position. Just come home safely, he would always tell her. When he didn't answer the phone, Angie had her first indication that something might be wrong.

With Josh on her mind, she moved the meeting along as quickly as she could and started home at a little after 10:00 pm. Again she tried to reach Josh unsuccessfully. What in the world was going on? The worry built up as she made her way along the highway leading to their house.

Entering the front door Angie felt a sense of doom hanging in the air. There were no lights on in the house anywhere. Where was Josh? She called his name out loud—no answer. She began going room to room, starting with the kitchen. As she moved through the house she quickly turned on the lights and scanned the area. Then she saw him. Josh was in the recliner just lying there not moving. Was he all right or was there something terribly wrong with him? As she moved closer to him she saw the bottle of alcohol three-quarters empty lying on the floor. An empty glass was sitting on the table next to him. Angie had known that Josh was drinking more and more since they moved to Orlando, but this was so totally unlike anything he had ever done that she didn't know what to think.

Angie tried to rouse Josh by calling his name softly so as not to scare him. That didn't work, so she started to shake him to wake him up and check to be sure that he was okay. When Josh finally woke up, tears filled his eyes as he told Angie just how glad he was that she was finally home. Apparently, he began drinking in the early afternoon and had been there in the chair for the last several hours. There was every indication that he was suffering from full-blown depression that was growing into alcohol dependency. It hit Angie like a ton of bricks. Why hadn't she paid more attention to the warning signs? Why did she let this go on so long before she realized just how bad things were for Josh since the move? She knew the answers to her questions only too well. She wanted things to work out so desperately that she couldn't bring herself to deal with Josh's real issues. She was just hoping that time would make things better.

Hopefully it wasn't too late to put things back together again. Angie was determined to open up the conversation with Josh, who to this point had continued to swear to her that everything was fine with the move. Things weren't fine and he wouldn't tell her again that they were. As Angie began the conversation, Josh continued his same old line about how everything was fine. This time Angie refused to listen. She stopped him dead in his tracks by saying that she knew it wasn't fine and that he had turned to drinking more and more as each day passed. That was not like him and she was worried. Finally, after much coaxing, Josh told Angie the whole story about how he wanted to fully support her, but that he desperately missed his friends, work, volunteering, golf, baseball, etc. Angie's only terse moment was when she verbally scolded Josh for not telling her the truth right from the beginning. Josh said he just could not let Angie think he didn't support her ambitions. He did. This move just came at a time in his life when he wasn't prepared for the changes. He never thought anything like this could affect him so drastically, but it had and there appeared to be no solution in sight.

Angie was determined to keep the conversation going until they found some answers. For 34 years she had always relied on Josh for her support; now he needed her and she would not fail him. Together they talked about what the main issues were for Josh and decided that they would try several things at the same time to see if they could quickly make some improvements in the situation for Josh. First, now that she had been on the job for four months and had already won the accolades of her superiors, she would be in a position to try some creative scheduling to get more time at home, even if it was only to do her paperwork at home instead of at the office. Next, Angie would only attend the critical evening functions by having her assistants attend all of the other evening functions. Next, she would work at least two half days at home on her paperwork and emails to provide Josh with more companionship. And, lastly, they agreed to go to one of the local golf courses together to start playing golf again and get acquainted with some of the local golfers. That was at least a start to changing the atmosphere in the house for Josh right away. Angie anticipated that the drinking would stop as soon as Josh felt better about things. He never had a drinking problem before so she deduced that he was using the drinking only as a way to escape from the loneliness. She would work out her schedule changes at the office in the morning and begin the new plan on Monday.

Over the next several weeks, the changes in Angie's schedule and her attention snapped Josh's downward spiral. He halted the drinking almost immediately as he looked forward to the golf outings and Angie's time at home. As they began to make new friends at the golf course, Josh seemed to regain his interest in golfing and getting out of the house to explore his new community. He found the local YMCA and looked into what programs needed new volunteers. This would give him the direct connection to people that he had been missing so desperately.

Within two months, Josh had made a couple of good friends at the golf course and even set up dates for golf without Angie. His time at the YMCA was also providing him with a great deal of satisfaction and a place to meet new people. It was one of those chance meetings that started Josh in an entirely new direction. A gentleman almost 20 years his junior who came several times a week to exercise struck up a conversation with Josh. Both men it seems thought of themselves as "serial entrepreneurs" but were currently not involved with any projects. However, Eric had an idea he had been playing with that he bounced off Josh for his reaction. Josh instantly grabbed on to the idea, enhancing it with details that Eric never before considered. The two of them found themselves still discussing the idea two hours later.

Over the next week, Eric and Josh met several times to talk about how to get the idea into operation. Josh had 20 years more experience than Eric, but Eric had a unique kind of innovative thinking that brought pure excitement to their conversations. One thing led to another and before Josh realized it, they were setting out together on a marvelous entrepreneurial venture.

Angie and Josh told us that they have never been happier. In the three years since the move to Orlando, Angie received her promotion to vice president and Josh's business with Eric is flourishing. They turned their difficult relocation to Orlando into a wonderful adventure following an extremely stressful transition. Angie and Josh found a way to work together to survive the stress and move their lives in a positive direction.

So why do the successful marriages survive and even flourish under conditions of extreme stress when other couples argue and grow apart under the same circumstances? First, successful marriages survive because the Seven Surprising Secrets characteristics we have described are pervasive throughout. Second, these couples put a strong support system in place, leaning on each other when things are extremely difficult for one or both of them. They seem to gain strength from each other. Third, while successfully married couples all talk about stressful periods in their marriages, they always have a positive attitude about what they had learned from the experiences, never blaming each other for their problems. Fourth, successful couples report that they spend much more time talking together during these stressful periods in order to figure out how to move from stressful times back to normal, happy times. And finally, these couples talk about figuring out long-term solutions together that have even improved their lives together.

Stressful situations are to be anticipated in a long and successful marriage. Working together to make it through the bad times can make the good times even more enjoyable. Don't let the movie or television version of marriage lull you into believing that marriage is only supposed to have happy times. That just isn't reality with the successful couples we studied. All of these couples reported stressful times—some had worse experiences than others—but all had difficult periods in their marriages. The key is to expect stressful times and work together to survive and even grow stronger together from the experiences. That is the only way to pass *The Stress Test* when it appears in your marriage—and it most certainly will.

CHAPTER 16

Marriage as a Torch Red Convertible

All successful couples we have studied over the years
understand that fun, enjoyment, laughter,
and joy are critical to the health and
well-being of their marriages.

"*L*IFE SHOULD BE A CONVERTIBLE!"
This has become Liz's favorite expression since we traded in her
Grandma mini-van for a torch red Mustang convertible. The first ride
in this sensational automobile occurred on a crisp fall day filled with
the glow of gold and scarlet autumn leaves. Nothing could be finer
than touring Missouri's blue highways perched in a torch red
Mustang convertible, particularly on a beautiful fall day. It was so
much fun! It took us back to the days when we tooled around in
our 1964 red Ford Fairlane convertible very early in our marriage.

There is nothing in life like a ride in a convertible. All of the stresses of the day seem to disappear as soon as you sit behind the wheel, put on the safety belt, and push the magic button that lowers the top. Starting up the engine and zipping out of the garage or the parking lot leaves you with a feeling of exhilaration and unadulterated joy. The wind blows through your hair and messes it all up—and you don't care! People whistle at your car and tell you they wish they had one. You smile at the world as it passes by. Riding in a convertible makes you happy and is just plain old fun. It certainly takes the kinks out!

Riding in a convertible is particularly exciting to us as we drive through the canyons of tall buildings downtown, or when we look nearly straight up with an unimpaired view of the glistening Gateway Arch as we drive along the Mississippi River in downtown St. Louis. And just imagine what it is like to see the Mississippi River from the Illinois side as you drive up the Great River Road with the glistening Big River on your left and the bluffs on your right, resplendent and awash with the beautiful colors of fall. And this view is spectacular from the front seat of a torch red Mustang convertible, certainly better than the obstructed view we had sitting in the front seat of our hardtop minivan. So, there you have it, the metaphor for life and for marriage.

The truth of the matter is, many marriages have never imagined life in a convertible. They see the world with the view obstructed. So absorbed in raising the kids, earning money, paying the bills, dealing with the death of a parent, or just getting by, they forget that they must have fun as well. All successful couples we have studied over the years understand that fun, enjoyment, laughter, and joy are critical to the health and well-being of their marriage. They also understand that letting life's myriad challenges obstruct their view surely will diminish their passion for each other and for life. The most happily married couples know that an occasional ride in a torch red Mustang convertible gives them a full view of the world around them—and it gives them joy.

Not long into our first ride, we realized that this new Mustang was a metaphor for our life together in so many ways. Our marriage has always had at its core what we have come to call the "fun factor." While we have worked long hours each day for many, many years, we always manage to have fun together. We love to hike in the woods. Riding our bikes has become an obsession with us. Traveling to distant places delights and inspires us (Argentina and China last year and Chile this year!). Cooking exotic meals together has always been fun, even when indigestion hits us hard later on! Going out to dinner is our favorite pastime. Being with our grandchildren is like being born again. Watching the St. Louis Cardinals together on television and in person is our passion. But the best part of our day is always the walk we take with our Wonder Dog, Jake. Walking in the fresh air, laughing about the events of the day, and watching Jake do all of those things that dogs do (Why do they do that?!). This part of the day doesn't cost a dime, but some of the memories of those walks will last a lifetime. And when we walk, our view is unobstructed. We usually solve all of the problems of the universe. We gain insights that weren't possible earlier in the day.

As you can tell from our fun factor list, we have learned what we both love to do together. We have discovered why *Marriage as a Torch Red Convertible* is the only way to go. Can you rattle off a list of activities, topics, and places you and your spouse include in your personal book of fun? Have you found what clears your mind and gives you an unobstructed view of your world together? How often do you experience fun? What type of priority do you place on making time for fun in your hectic lives? If you are having difficulty answering any of these questions, you can use the *Marriage as a Torch Red Convertible* activity in the Appendix (p. 299) to get started exploring the possibilities with your spouse.

Life for us is a convertible! It is a metaphor for how we try to live our lives. We enjoy each day we are given on earth and try our best to make the most of the time we have together. *Marriage as a Torch Red Convertible* is a metaphor for our marriage. It should be for yours as well.

When we share this concept with others, occasionally some make the mistake of equating *Marriage as a Torch Red Convertible* with having and spending money. Those who think this way miss our point. For example, the majority of successfully married couples we have interviewed claim that their marriage had "humble beginnings." One couple said, "We didn't have a pot to pee in or a window to throw it out of!" Now that's poor! Yet, Raymond and Dorothy told us countless stories about the fun factor in their marriage. They could tell us their humorous stories with great detail and much fondness. Their eyes twinkled as they told their tales.

One of the best stories Dorothy and Raymond told us was about how they learned the importance of having fun together even when they had no way to pay for it because they were just plain dirt poor. They had been married for about two years when the walls of their tiny basement apartment in the city seemed to be closing in on them. Raymond and Dorothy both grew up on farms and longed for the chance to get back to the countryside and around animals. They were both struggling to make ends meet while holding down two jobs and attending the university as full-time students. Between their university studies and their menial jobs they felt like they literally were being crushed in from all sides with no conceivable way out. Their need for some fun in their lives had reached the critical stage. They began to wonder if they were going to make it through school and remain together.

Raymond began scouring the classified adds for additional part-time jobs. He thought maybe a bit of extra spending money would be the solution to their problems. However, as Raymond and Dorothy talked about their situation they reached the conclusion that getting an additional job would only make matters worse. Surely it would only increase the tension and decrease any chance they might have to steal away a few moments of fun together.

About a week after abandoning his idea, Raymond spotted an interesting ad on the student bulletin board: "Student Wanted to Care for Horses." He immediately called the number to inquire about the details. The owner was looking for someone to relieve him on weekends so he could spend more time with his family. However, he didn't have the money to pay much for the help. Raymond was intrigued. Maybe he and Dorothy could take care of the horses in exchange for time to ride a couple of them through the countryside. He arranged to meet the rancher the following Saturday.

Dorothy was just as excited as Raymond about the possibility of being around horses and having an opportunity to enjoy those magnificent horseback rides in the gently rolling hills around Virginia's countryside. When Saturday rolled around, they could hardly wait for their meeting with the rancher. After just 20 minutes of conversation, they had worked out all of the details for their new jobs. Raymond and Dorothy would take care of the rancher's 24 horses every weekend in exchange for unlimited weekend riding time on his 254-acre ranch.

For the next four years Raymond and Dorothy provided a tremendous service for the rancher, allowing him to spend more time with his children and their activities. Even though Dorothy and Raymond could not afford to pay the rental charges for horseback rides while they were in school, the arrangement with the rancher made their dream a reality. Together they spent their weekends caring for the horses and taking long horseback rides through pristine forests, beside cool streams, and along hillside trails. They found a way to have fun in their marriage when they were poor and now, 60 years later, when they are rich by any standard, they are still having fun together. Their recollections of these events made us feel warm all over. And as they recalled those times together, their eyes teared up, they held hands, and stared admiringly into each other's eyes. More important, they believe to this day that those magnificent horses might just have saved their marriage.

Sometimes, finding the fun factor in your marriage can be an enormous challenge due to the hectic pace required just to keep up with myriad responsibilities as a dual career couple or to attend all of your children's many activities or to simply maintain your everyday existence. As we interviewed Tyrell and Jody, who had been successfully married for 33 years, their description of the challenges they overcame to build fun into their marriage intrigued us, to say the least.

During the eighth year of their marriage, Tyrell and Jody found themselves increasingly frustrated with never having time alone with each other to have a little fun. When they first got married, they loved to play touch football in the neighborhood schoolyard. Throwing the football down the field, Tyrell would yell signals to Jody who moved into position for the perfect catch. Running full throttle, Tyrell would attempt to tackle Jody before she ran into the "end zone." Many a fall afternoon was spent with perfect throws, perfect catches, amazing runs, and great tackles. They laughed for hours afterwards, recalling every move on the field. Sadly, it had been at least two years since they entered the school playground, let alone played touch football with each other.

Tyrell and Jody argued more and more frequently about even the most unimportant issues. While they were both working 10 to 12 hours a day to keep up with their careers, they were still in entry-level positions. They didn't seem to be able to make it through to the end of the month without using credit cards to buy the necessities. Their four-year-old son hit a terrible stage, creating messes in every corner of the house, screeching endlessly for attention whenever either of them tried to complete a project for work. Oftentimes their son would exhibit uncontrollable behavior. The weekly visits from Tyrell's mother were always stressful when she went into one of her tirades about Jody not keeping the house clean enough to measure up to her own standards. Why didn't she aim her criticism at Tyrell instead of her, Jody thought.

After one of her mother-in-law's infamous visits, Jody had enough of the criticism. The pressure to get everything done, the noise, the everyday grind, her job, her life—you name it, she was tired of it. She and her husband never had any fun together anymore and she just wanted to run away from everything and everybody. Jody cut loose on Tyrell. He met her explosion of anger and frustration with his own explosion of equal seismic force. All of their pent-up frustrations were exposed, as they held nothing back. Their shouting match lasted for almost an hour until they finally decided to sit down and talk about their situation. It was actually the first time they had faced the reality of how badly things were piling up around them. They had to take back control of their lives together before it was too late.

The first thing they talked about was the time issue. After a few minutes of fruitless discussion about how to get more time, Tyrell and Jody figured out that it should be the last thing they talked about, not the first. They decided to make a list of all of the issues that were causing their overwhelming feelings of stress and negativity.

They began with the condition of the house; then to their jobs; then to the money issues; then to the behavior of their son; then to Tyrell's mother; and finally to the lack of fun in their lives. Their story intrigued us because it was the first time that any of our successful couples had articulated *so many simultaneous issues* related to the lack of fun in their marriage. They not only hadn't searched for their "torch red convertible" early in their marriage, they didn't even know what one looked like at that point in time.

Tyrell started the problem-solving process by suggesting that he ask his mother if she would watch their son one evening a week and on Sunday afternoons so they could do their projects for work in a quiet environment. It would also allow them time to clean the house; do the chores; and have some much-needed, unencumbered time together without attending to the needs of their son. Even though Jody was resistant to the idea because of Tyrell's mother's attitude, Tyrell convinced her that it was far better than her coming over weekly just to complain. At least they agreed to try it!

Next, Jody added her suggestion that they try to live on a strict budget until their finances were back in line. All excess spending would have to be eliminated for a while. They agreed to develop the budget together so it would be realistic and something both could live with.

If their son's behavior did not improve after they made these changes in their lives, they would seek professional help for him. They held out the possibility that his problem might very well be related to all the stress and struggles of their busy lives.

At this point, neither Jody nor Tyrell had a solution for the pressure from their jobs, so they decided to work on the other matters before tackling the job issue. Last, but certainly not least, they discussed their lack of time for anything resembling fun in their marriage. They decided to start by taking at least one hour on Sundays to revisit the school playground for some touch football. While they were desperate for enjoying fun times together, they also were in great need of exercise.

The first few weeks of their plan were admittedly tough, but within six months the pressure on Jody and Tyrell had eased considerably and their son seemed much calmer and happier as a result. They were now ready to search for their fun factor in earnest. Finding time would require them to continue setting their priorities around the fun activities. This was the only way they were going to create more time for the activities they really enjoyed doing together. They had their finances in good shape, their house cleaning down to a quick routine, and Tyrell's mother actively helping instead of criticizing.

Jody and Tyrell put into full gear the search for their personal "torch red convertible." While the touch football was terrific, their son was still too little and his attention span too short to make the experience an enjoyable one for the whole family. They needed to keep touch football just for themselves for a bit longer.

At age five, their son was beginning to develop a real interest in zoo animals. Since their city zoo had an amazing collection of rare animals, it was the perfect family place to go for a weekend of exercise, fun, and education—and they could do it together. And better yet, the zoo was free! The weekend trips to the zoo became, over time, an indispensable part of the family tradition.

The other passion that Jody and Tyrell shared was their love of water sports, including swimming, skiing, and scuba diving. They realized that even though their son was doing well with his swimming lessons, he would have to be a bit older before he would be able to ski and scuba dive. And frankly, their finances at that point were not ready for the expenses associated with either sport. But they both knew that they wanted to keep the possibility part of their fun factor goal, a goal that they not only achieved later in their marriage but one that has also become part of the family tradition. They were successful in their commitment to create the time to have fun with each other and together as a family.

The process Jody and Tyrell went through to get past their many challenges is an excellent example for other couples to follow. It is no wonder Jody and Tyrell have been happily married for 33 years. Oh, and by the way, their son James completed his MBA, got a job as a banker, and married his childhood sweetheart. It seems he "magically" outgrew his uncontrollable behavior and ear-piercing screeches about the same time Jody and Tyrell discovered for themselves how living their *Marriage as a Torch Red Convertible* created a different environment for the entire family.

Finding the fun factor in your marriage sometimes comes unexpectedly when you are relaxed and your view becomes unobstructed. It can alter your lives forever, just as it did for Alan and Jan, who have now been married for 37 years. They found their fun factor during their fifth year of marriage on a trip to New York City. Alan was deep into furthering his education to enhance his career as a high school history teacher and Jan was in her sixth year of a successful nursing career in one of the top ten hospitals in the country. Both were preoccupied with their careers and their own areas of interest. The topic of fun in their lives didn't come up much. They just lived life and forged ahead, trying to keep up with the everyday grind of getting dinner when they both arrived home exhausted, taking care of the household chores, paying bills, and surviving.

Jan had recently lost her mother to cancer and the ordeal had taken its toll on her spirits. Alan planned a weekend trip to get some much-needed relief and to give them some quality time with each other. Little did they know this trip would start them in a direction that would change their lives forever.

The first thing they did after checking into their hotel was to head to the Union Square area to a great restaurant recommended by their best friends. They spent two magnificent hours savoring their delectable meals and sipping a great glass of wine. A new feeling of energy invigorated them as they decided to walk south on Broadway, then cut across the island to Greenwich Village for a cappuccino. Around the 800 block they paused to do a bit of window gazing at one of the many antique shops along the way. Without even a word, they both headed into a shop to browse. For the next 45 minutes each strolled from item to item admiring the delicacy and the preservation of each antique they observed. Alan was staring intently at a gun in the long glass case by the front of the shop. Jan finally asked him what he was looking at, since he seemed to be in a trance. Alan continued to stare at the gun as he explained to Jan that it was a perfectly preserved Aston Muzzle Loader from 1852, adding that it was a U.S. Military issue from the Civil War. He had only read about this type of gun, but had never actually seen one. Jan told Alan that she was amazed, because she didn't even know he liked guns. Alan smiled lovingly at Jan and explained that he didn't care about the gun at all. It was the fact that it was a part of history—the history he loved and shared every day with his students. He was standing in front of the real thing and it was for sale, just like any other item in any other normal store. Yet this was a treasure beyond belief. It was a part of history. Jan could not get over the fact that they had been married for almost five years and she had no idea how deeply Alan would be moved by gazing at an 1852 Aston Muzzle Loader. What else didn't she know?

With this sudden realization about Alan's fascination with this gun, Jan almost forgot her own excitement over finding an armchair just like the one in her mother's home in Maine. She was intrigued by the perfect condition of the caning on the back and seat of the chair. In fact, it was from the same general period as the Aston Muzzle Loader. It was made somewhere between 1820 and 1840. Jan took Alan by the hand and led him over to the chair. She spent the next five minutes telling Alan all about how she and her mother used to go antiquing on school holidays when her father had to work. Her mother's chair was found on one of those trips. It meant a great deal to her because of her memories from that wonderful spring day with her mother touring around Maine to different antiques shops. Alan asked why she hadn't shared that piece of her childhood with him. Jan explained that since her mother had taken ill with cancer, it had been too hard to give up the thought that they would again go antique hunting together. Rather than think about it over the last several years, she had pushed those memories far back in her subconscious. Seeing the chair brought back all of those wonderful memories. Alan and Jan just stood there staring at one another. They both broke out in laughter at the same moment and immediately headed off to Greenwich Village for their cappuccino. Instead of walking they grabbed a cab—they knew it was time to talk.

Alan and Jan spent the next several hours talking about antiques. They both loved them for different reasons, but the fact was that they both loved antiques. What surprised them was the depth of the knowledge that each had about the intricacies of antiques. Yet each had acquired their appreciation from completely different perspectives. Alan found his love and knowledge of antiques from his study and love of history. Jan came to her knowledge of antiques from all of those trips with her mother and the books about antiques they perused together following those trips. Maybe that is why Alan and Jan both seemed so interested in history. Alan's chosen field was obvious, but Jan went in a completely different direction when she chose to enter the nursing profession.

Months afterwards, Jan and Alan found themselves talking more and more about antiques. They planned trips to the local antique shops and ventured further and further from home to seek out new places in which to browse. They didn't have enough money to start collecting, but they made the time to start looking. They had found total enjoyment together in their new antique browsing activities.

One spring day they came across something that was just too good to be true. There it was, an early Flint Lock Musket with the mark of the East India Company on the side. You could still read the 1801 date on the side plate. The shop did not normally deal in antique guns and did not want to keep it in their stock. It was something acquired as part of an estate purchase the owner had recently made. It was priced at about one tenth of its value. Even though they didn't have the money, Alan and Jan made their first antique purchase. They were elated. This was the beginning of many, many purchases to come. In fact, so many purchases that they opened their own antique shop. Their shop has become one of the most successful and respected shops in their region of the country. They had truly found their "torch red convertible." They had discovered fun in their life together and it would be a part of their relationship forever.

Having fun is an integral part of your marriage. It is necessary and essential. Setting aside time for fun, enjoyment, and laughter with your spouse enhances and strengthens all of those characteristics of a successful marriage we have previously described. When you are having fun together you are cleansing your minds and spirits—you are freeing your souls. Laughing and enjoying activities together open your mind to new ideas and to new possibilities. What you discover can literally change the direction of your lives together, now and forever.

Looking for the unobstructed view will allow you and your spouse to find your convertible. It will bring you closer together and strengthen the bonds of your marriage. We enjoy each other and we enjoy life. Life for us is, more often than not, like riding in a convertible. Those in the best marriages we have studied would agree.

We work hard, but more important, we play hard because we learned the underlying importance of the fun factor in enhancing the pervasive characteristics of a successful marriage. It has worked for us. It has worked for those thousands of happily married couples we have interviewed over the years.

When we are tired of writing for the day or just want to enjoy the sights and sounds of our wonderful hometown, you can see us tooling around in our torch red Mustang convertible with the top down. Our personalized St. Louis Cardinals license plate says simply, "2CARDS." We are, without a doubt, a happy twosome—a couple of cards—two fun-loving fools!

CHAPTER 17

A Tribute to Lasting Love

As we concluded our interview with our usual question,
"Can you imagine life without each other?"
we got the answer we expected,
but not a word was spoken.

*L*ASTING LOVE, 'till death do us part. Couples repeat this stanza or some variation of it in most marriage ceremonies. In its essence, two people commit to each other their love, their faithfulness, and their sacred honor for the rest of their lives. Many times, it works out just that way. Other times, the promise falls short. But in the case of Sandy and Pris, love is alive and well and will be sustained for a lifetime.

Over the past 25 years we have interviewed couples who have been successfully married for as few as 30 and as many as 77 years. We have shared 43 wonderful years together ourselves. But of all the interviews we have conducted, no love seemed greater than the love between Sandy and Pris.

We interviewed them in their home about a year and a half ago. Sandy has retired as CEO of a large American corporation. He is now investing his time and money in philanthropic causes across the United States, particularly in character education. Pris has always been interested in the arts and is a big supporter of opera theater, in particular. Their passion for their philanthropic causes was amazing and their commitment to their work was heartwarming. If you ever wanted to spend an evening with two of the most generous, endearing, enchanting, and wonderful people you could meet, these are the two that you wanted to be with.

Before we interviewed Sandy and Pris, we thought we knew a lot about love and relationships. That evening, however, we got an education for which we will be eternally grateful.

Sandy loves Pris absolutely and completely. He loves her without conditions. He has loved her since the first time he saw her on the ski slopes near Santa Fe, New Mexico. During our interview, he looked at his bride of nearly 60 years and said, "She is still the same beautiful woman I married 60 years ago!" He had tears in his eyes. Pris choked back the tears, as she looked deep into his eyes. These were the faces of love.

Pris responded that she fell in love with this handsome, dashing man with his white skis as soon as she saw him glide effortlessly down the snow-covered mountain.

Sandy and Pris love each other from the bottom of their respective hearts and both say this today, "We have been married for more than 60 years and are more in love now than ever." Everything they said to us during the interview reinforced their unqualified love for each other.

There are many lessons to be learned from Sandy and Pris. We want to share with you what they believe to be the most important.

First, they share a mutual admiration society. They always support and encourage each other.

Second, they love each other very much and say so many times during each day of their lives.

Third, they are totally honest with each other. They show integrity in their interactions, have undying trust in each other, and demonstrate their characters by their words and by their actions.

And finally, their most important lesson of all—"Never go to bed mad at each other."

Sandy and Pris have great admiration and respect for each other. It shows in their words; their actions; their expressions; and in Sandy's case, in his voice as he sings love songs to her every morning—off key sometimes, but always full of love and emotion.

As we concluded our interview with our usual question, "Can you imagine life without each other?" we got the answer we expected, but not a word was spoken. Their eyes welled up with tears, they gazed lovingly at each other for an extended period of time, and then they looked at us and smiled. No words were necessary. We knew their answer as well as we knew our own—lasting love until death do us part.

We know you will agree—Sandy and Pris are an inspiration to everyone. Their wonderful 61 years of marriage attest to the power of their relationship and the depth of their love. There is much to learn from these two lovebirds who have found *Lasting Love.*

Just like with Sandy and Pris, the most powerful question that we ask with every successfully married couple is always, "Can you imagine life without your spouse?" The question always draws tears to the eyes of the couple we are interviewing. We have asked them a question they have repressed. It is a question no loving couple wants to think about. The answer is, however, nearly always the same—"No!"

When we take our marriage vows—"until death do us part"—we never imagine that some day it will all come to an end. But all marriages and relationships do end, of that you can be sure. So, how do we prepare for it?

Our advice is, never dwell on or contemplate the question. It does not matter. What is important is that we love our spouses, that we enjoy our spouses, and that we live our lives with them to the fullest. If you think about the inevitable, your relationship will end in a different way. Yes, a different way.

Here is how it works. If you spend your time imagining the end you will never do all of the things required to deal with the beginning and the middle. You will lose the richness and beauty of each moment. You will, in the end, misplace the essence of your relationship with each other. Your relationship will be based on the end instead of the possibilities.

When you cannot imagine life without the one you love, you have reached the "nirvana" of your loving and committed relationship. But to dwell on the inevitable end of your life together diminishes the here and now and spoils all the joy that lies ahead.

ॐ

Failure Is an Option

*Maybe even with all of the benefits of marriage you have
still concluded that your marriage isn't worth
the hard work it will take to celebrate your
Golden Anniversary together. If that's the case,
then we offer you some surefire advice about
how to make your marriage fail.*

THE NOTION IS SIMPLE. If you want
your marriage to succeed, learn about the Seven Surprising Secrets
pervasive characteristics of a successful marriage and practice them
until they become part of the fabric of your relationship.
However, perhaps some of you don't really want your marriages to
succeed! Maybe even after realizing all of the benefits of marriage you
still have concluded that your marriage isn't worth the hard work it
will take to celebrate your Golden Anniversary together. If that's the

case, then we offer you some surefire advice about how to make your marriage fail. If you pay close and particular attention to what follows, you can virtually ensure the destruction of your marriage.

Tip #1: Compromise is only for the weak. You know when you are right, so stick to it. Never give in, even a little! Compromise is an idea created by people who don't know how to fight it out with their spouses. If it comes to an all-out war, then so be it. When you got married you didn't give up your right to argue, even about unimportant and trivial matters. You didn't get married to learn anything about your spouse's interests, talents, or areas of expertise. When your spouse finally figures out that she doesn't really understand much of anything and needs to have you around to provide all of the correct answers, you will be a happy camper. If you work this one just right, your divorce can be just around the corner. Just think of the possibilities.

Tip #2: Go it alone—help is only for the feeble. Never, we repeat, never share life's burdens with your spouse! Go it alone! "You do your thing and I will do mine. God forbid if we should find a way to help each other!" Pay no heed whatsoever to those who talk about four arms, four legs, and two heads in describing a good marriage. You can't walk with four legs. All you will do is trip all over yourself. And four arms … forget it! Shirts only come with two armholes anyway! The message here should be clear. Do not share life's burdens with your spouse if you want your marriage to fail. Go it alone.

Tip #3: Tune Out! Since your spouse rarely has anything important to say anyway, just don't listen. No matter what is said, just keep nodding your head and saying yes like you were really listening even when you aren't.

Or better yet, just pretend you've lost your hearing. Sooner or later your spouse will get the idea that you really could care less what he is saying. Besides, it is already a well-established fact in your household that your spouse doesn't know anything anyway, so why not make sure that your spouse understands fully that you are not even going to attempt to listen to what is being said. You trust your perceptions, don't you? So why should you understand what your spouse is saying? And think of all the glorious misunderstandings this approach can create. Once you establish those misunderstandings, your job is to be argumentative, critical, and judgmental about everything you thought your spouse really meant. Divorce can be expedited if you fully implement this approach as soon as possible.

Tip #4: Take silence or arguments to new heights. Continue where you left off after dinner. Even while your spouse is still cleaning the kitchen turn on the television as loud as possible. Then, when your spouse is finally ready to sit down to talk after cleaning everything, remind her that the best part of the show is now on and you would really rather not be interrupted. If possible, make a concerted effort to fall asleep in your favorite chair. If you are lucky, you will miss your after-dinner walk by waking up just in time to go to bed. Be certain that you go to sleep before your spouse gets in bed. Ah, you will sleep so well tonight knowing that you did not have to communicate with your spouse at all this evening. Hopefully, you can do the same thing tomorrow and the next day, and the next day, and the next day. If you follow this scenario for several months, you may even discover that you and your spouse have absolutely nothing to talk about.

However, this particular tip is a bit tricky and silence may not be the thing that works best with your spouse. In fact, you may need to try yelling at him instead of giving him the silent treatment. Getting into a heated argument—where there are no winners—may be the best approach. If you select this method, you will need to perfect your skills to the point that you and your spouse can go to bed angry at each other. It may even take some pre-planning on your part, but your job is to make sure you get into an outrageous and pointless argument. Be sure to pout for a few hours. And whatever you do, do not make any attempt to talk or make eye contact with your spouse following the argument. When you crawl into bed, be sure that you both sleep back to back. In this way, you will find it easier to not converse. In addition, make absolutely certain that you seethe all night long. It is important that you convince yourself of your rightness and your marriage partner's essential wrongness. Sleeping on it is the best way we can think of to ensure that this will occur. We offer this suggestion because we know you want to wake up in the morning even more convinced that your spouse is wrong again.

Tip #5: Always treat your spouse as if he or she were your own personal slave. You have the brains in the family and make all the decisions, don't you? Doesn't that entitle you to have a personal slave? After all, your spouse did promise to obey when you both took your marriage vows, right? Hold your partner to that agreement. It is extremely important that you be consistent. If you give in just once, your spouse will come back wanting exceptions to the nuptial agreement. It would not be fair to confuse your spouse, would it? When you want or need something, order him to go get it for you.

After all, why should you have to get your own coffee? Any lawyer in America will tell you, obey means obey! One other thing, make sure you tell others publicly about who really runs things around your house. It would be a real shame to confuse your friends into thinking your spouse had any rights in this marriage. Tell it like it is. Make it clear that your spouse really is your own personal slave.

Tip #6: Never let your spouse have a moment of peace. You are absolutely going to love this tip! It is a surefire winner. Make positively certain that you never give your spouse one tiny little moment by herself without interruption. The next time your mate is engrossed in a good book (preferably this one) bug him. You know, ask him a series of pointless and irrelevant questions. After all, he was busy all day. What would a little more bother do to him? When she goes outside tonight for a few minutes of mindless thought and stargazing, follow her. It's easy. Every time she moves, practice walking in step with her. It may even take two or three times before your spouse's view of your antics changes from being cute to being totally annoying. Besides, when the two of you got married, it was understood that the need for privacy and aloneness was something non-married people expected, not married folks like the two of you. Whatever you do, do not let your spouse have any time to putter in the garden. If you leave him out there by himself, he will think you do not love him. This is for his sake anyway, isn't it? There are tons of ways to make a marriage fail. Never giving your spouse time to be alone is one of the best. Try it. Your mate will just hate you for it and may even ask for a divorce.

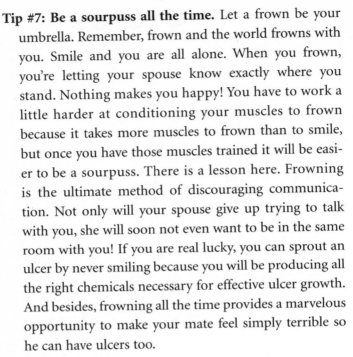

Tip #7: Be a sourpuss all the time. Let a frown be your umbrella. Remember, frown and the world frowns with you. Smile and you are all alone. When you frown, you're letting your spouse know exactly where you stand. Nothing makes you happy! You have to work a little harder at conditioning your muscles to frown because it takes more muscles to frown than to smile, but once you have those muscles trained it will be easier to be a sourpuss. There is a lesson here. Frowning is the ultimate method of discouraging communication. Not only will your spouse give up trying to talk with you, she will soon not even want to be in the same room with you! If you are real lucky, you can sprout an ulcer by never smiling because you will be producing all the right chemicals necessary for effective ulcer growth. And besides, frowning all the time provides a marvelous opportunity to make your mate feel simply terrible so he can have ulcers too.

Tip #8: Take over the menu planning and meal preparation to ensure that your spouse has only foods high in fat, sugar, preservatives, and calories. We would guess by now you are sitting on the edge of your chair waiting for tip number eight. Instead of giving it to you straight out, we would like to describe a little mealtime scenario. And please, rest assured that attention to the details that follow is absolutely critical to mastering this tip about the destruction of your marriage. First of all, remember one important point as you prepare the menu and meals … it is not the quality of the food you serve that counts, only the quantity. Begin with breakfast on the run—doughnuts topped with lots of sugar coating and at least six cups of caffeinated coffee will start the day off with a bang. If you pack a lunch for your spouse, by all means, send along a nice brown paper bag full of all the good stuff—gooey pastries, soda pop, and potato chips to accompany a nice bacon sandwich topped with lots of mayonnaise. And please, no fruits or vegetables. Later on, you will be ready for your favorite meal—dinner. By all means, cook up a mess of fatty foods (over-processed junk food preferred), high in caloric content, filled with lots of salt. We would suggest such things as deep-fried cheese strips, fried hamburgers, deep-fried potatoes, and deep-fried onion rings. Clogged arteries are fun! And for desert—chocolate cake with chocolate icing topped with heavy whipped cream. Go ahead and have two pieces. Whatever you do, do not buy or serve any fresh fruits and vegetables. When you sit down to eat, make sure you each have a newspaper to read. For special effect, have the television blaring. You would not want to hear anything that was said at the dinner table. Then race to eat the meal as fast as possible to enhance your indigestion. Finish off the occasion with a nice loud belch, then immediately leave the room so it is clear that cleaning up the kitchen is not your responsibility. If you can, get as far away from the kitchen as possible, so as not to let the sound of running water and clanking dishes inter-rupt your favorite television program. Adhering to this regime every meal is a sure way to kill your marriage and your spouse!

Tip #9: Don't hold anything back—buy everything on credit. You deserve it! This is one of the easiest ways we know to promote a failed marriage. Starting today, when you have an urge to buy a new car, don't give it a second thought, just go right out and buy it! Why ask your mate? You do not need her permission. You're not a wimp, are you? After you have purchased everything you have always wanted, you should have your marriage in critical financial trouble. This will place your relationship exactly where you want it. You can now blame each other for your financial plight! But you are the one who can walk tall knowing that after all is said and done, it is your spouse's fault, not yours. Your spouse should have earned more money or been more careful so you could buy everything you always wanted for yourself. What was he thinking?

Tip #10: Don't talk about your finances at all with your spouse. Remember that the rule "Silence is Golden" applies to all aspects of your financial decisions if you want your marriage to fail. Since your spouse has no sense for finances anyway, just go ahead and make all the financial decisions without talking to your spouse about any of the issues involved. Lack of effective communication about the financial aspects of your marriage is the most effective way we know to ensure the destruction of a marriage. This is, after all, the failed marriage you wanted, right?

Tip #11: Pretend your spouse doesn't exist. Remember, being ignored does even more damage to the ego than criticism. For example, make sure that you never mention how nice your spouse looks, even when she does. Surely it doesn't bother you when your spouse forgets to tell you how nice you look or when he fails to compliment you when you do something well. Remember, if you want your marriage to fail quickly, ignore everything about your spouse. The promise to cherish your spouse was only said at the wedding to appease your mother-in-law anyway, right?

Tip #12: Pretend your spouse has the plague. In other words, avoid touching her. You never know, she might have a communicable disease. You must try hard to avoid touching your mate at all times. Do not hold hands. Your children will be embarrassed anyway if they see their parents holding hands. You are too old to hold hands anyway! And please, please, please, do not kiss in public view! Somebody watching the two of you might get the impression you actually do love each other. Do not hug your partner. They might bruise. Do not forget to sleep on opposite sides of the bed. What is the sense of buying a king-size bed if you are going to sleep on the same side? Do not pat your lover on the fanny when he does something great, only jocks do that. The marriage vows you took did not mention anything about touching as a way to show love and affection for your spouse.

Tip #13: Dull, boring, and predictable are the attributes you should strive for in your relationship. Spend each day with your spouse trying to make sure everything remains exactly the same. Just say "NO" to any attempt by your spouse to try a new restaurant, see a different kind of movie, make a change in her wardrobe, or engage in a new hobby. Make sure you work hard to keep the conversation centered on the routine, the annoying, and the mundane topics that are of no interest to your spouse or for that matter to anyone else. Keep your daily rituals predictable and boring. Keeping everything perfectly predictable will make your life easier and cause your spouse to be completely bored and lack interest in the entire relationship. Never spark your spouse's interest with new or scintillating ideas because it might stir his enthusiasm and excitement about your marriage, decreasing the chances for a quick divorce.

Tip #14: Never bring your spouse flowers, write a love note, or send a romantic email. It takes far too much of your valuable time to do romantic things for your spouse. And besides, why would your spouse ever agree to a divorce if you took time to put a spark in her life with surprises like flowers and love notes? No—that's not the way to make your marriage fail!

The tips for failing at your relationship and your marriage that have been offered in this chapter are clearly tongue-in-cheek. If you did not get our message in the preceding chapters, perhaps you get it now. Sometimes, taking a look at the ridiculous side of things that go on in many marriages can draw our attention to the seriousness of the mistakes we often make in our day-to-day interactions with our partners. Recognizing these mistakes is the first step toward correcting them.

CHAPTER 19

Reflections on Love and Marriage

May your love be as strong as ours and your commitment to make your love work even stronger.

*T*HIS PAST AUGUST, WE CELEBRATED our 43rd Wedding Anniversary. Just imagine, being successfully married for 43 years! And as a friend of ours used to say, "And to the same person!" Having a successful marriage is certainly a life goal. We are well on our way to being one of those fortunate couples who celebrate Golden Anniversaries.

While we spend a lot of time studying and writing about the successful, long-term relationships of others, we decided to spend some time today thinking about our own wonderful marriage that has spanned more than four decades of our lives.

One of our favorite lines from a song says it all—"Still crazy after all these years." That's the way we feel about each other—still crazy in love after all these years.

Forty-four years ago, a small, town Missouri boy met a California girl at college. His friends were the sons and daughters of Missouri farmers and other good folks who worked on the railroad. Her friends were California surfers and swimmers. She was bronze colored, tall, and had that look of a long-distance swimmer. It was fun for Charley to see her walking down the sidewalk grooving to the sounds of the Beach Boys as her hair blew in the wind. He still marvels today at how much he loved her then and how much more he loves her today. Think Golden Anniversaries!

Liz used to listen for hours while Charley sang Elvis songs to her. She once said, "Gosh, you really do sound like him!" Charley turned red, but he was proud. Elvis was his hero. And now Liz was!

Liz tells Charley every day how much she loves him and how she couldn't imagine life without him. Charley smiles, then cries. It feels so good to be loved so much. He reflects on his life with Liz and wonders how he got so lucky. He loves to tell everyone within earshot how he "married up"! He swears that most men do. Liz says she feels the same way about him. Hmmmm … maybe we both married up!

It's always fun for us to reflect on life together. We have so, so many common interests. We are alike in many, many ways. But through it all we have maintained our individuality and our respective identities—with enormous respect for our differences as well as our similarities.

As we think back to the measures we articulated in Chapter One of this book, "How Will I Know I Am in Love," it is clear that we are still crazy in love after all these years.

Helping build loving relationships that last a lifetime has become one of our greatest goals in life. Being in love and being loved is a great way to spend your life. And while we truly and sincerely believe that successful loving relationships are not all that difficult to understand and make work, we continue to be surprised by the fact that so many "people in love" will not do the simple things required to make their love last.

On the occasion of our 43rd Wedding Anniversary we are renewing our commitment to help others learn the important lessons about love and relationships so that they can practice the simple truths about love every day of their lives together.

May your love be as strong as ours and your commitment to make your love work even stronger.

Go be happy and in love.

There is nothing like it.

Let's celebrate our Golden Anniversaries together!

Appendix

_____

THE BENEFITS OF MARRIAGE

A SEVEN-WEEK PROGRAM FOR DEVELOPING ONGOING
SHARING IN YOUR MARRIAGE

SALAD RECIPES FROM "AMERICA'S #1 LOVE AND
MARRIAGE EXPERTS"

FILING A JOINT RETURN ACTIVITY

MARRIAGE AS A TORCH RED CONVERTIBLE ACTIVITY

THE BENEFITS OF MARRIAGE

WHEN YOU CONSIDER WHAT SOCIAL SCIENCE
RESEARCH TELLS us about the benefits of being married and what our
research reveals about the seven characteristics of successful marriages, you have many powerful reasons to work hard to celebrate
your Golden Anniversary with your spouse.

Now that you know the recipe for a successful marriage takes a lot
of hard work, this chapter should convince you that it is absolutely
worth whatever it takes for you to achieve a long-term successful
marriage. After a lengthy review of the current research on the benefits of marriage, we have selected what we think are the top ten
reasons why you should work hard to achieve a happy, successful
marriage. It has been proven time and time again that your life can be
improved in a great number of ways by staying in a successful,
long-term marriage!

Top Ten Benefits of Marriage

Reason #1: You will live longer. The preponderance of evidence
from research shows a relationship between longer life and being
married. In fact, one study found that married men live an average of
ten years longer and married women live an average of four years
longer than those who are unmarried.

Reason #2: You will be healthier. There have been a great
number of research studies throughout the world since 1987 demonstrating a positive relationship between being married and better
physical health. The links between marriage and good physical health
are overwhelming. Married individuals have lower rates of serious
illness and are less likely to die in hospitals.

Reason #3: You will be happier. Married people report being happier than unmarried people. They are hopeful, happy, and feel good about themselves. A multitude of studies demonstrate the same results. In fact, in a ten-year survey involving 14,000 adults, James Davis found that 40% of married individuals were happy with their lives compared to only 15 to 20% of any of the unmarried groups.

Reason #4: You will experience higher levels of psychological health. Married people have lower rates of depression and schizophrenia than unmarried people. They are better balanced and less likely to experience mental illness.

Reason #5: You will have a built-in support system. Research indicates that individuals in a marriage feel supported, saying that they have someone to share their feelings and thoughts with. They always have someone they trust to confide in and to lean on in times of need.

Reason #6: You will be less likely to abuse drugs or alcohol. Numerous studies indicate that married individuals are less likely than unmarried persons to engage in risky behaviors, including the use of drugs or alcohol, because of their feelings of responsibility.

Reason #7: Your earnings will be greater. Numerous studies found that married men's earnings are significantly greater than unmarried men's earnings. The most recent studies of women's earning power demonstrate that married women earn more than unmarried women even when their husband's income is not considered as part of their earnings. The vast majority of the studies take all of the various possible factors into consideration and the results still demonstrate greater earnings for married individuals than for unmarried ones.

Reason #8: You will save more money. Couples with enduring marriages tend to be more financially responsible. In the United States, married individuals in their 50s and 60s have a net worth per person roughly twice that of other unmarried individuals.

Reason #9: You will have sex more often and enjoy it more. Married couples report greater physical and emotional satisfaction with sex then their unmarried counterparts. Married couples also have sexual intimacy more often than unmarried couples.

Reason #10: Your children will be healthier, do better academically, and have fewer emotional problems. Children living in families with married parents are more likely to have proper health care, better nutrition, and less stress to deal with at home. These children have fewer serious illnesses and grew up healthier than children not raised in households with married parents.

On average, children who are raised in households with stable marriages enjoy better developmental outcomes than children raised in households with unmarried individuals. These children have significantly better grades, test scores, and overall success in school than their counterparts raised in households with unmarried individuals.

The research indicates that children living with married parents have fewer reported behavioral problems at school or at home than children who do not. They experience better psychological health than children raised in households with unmarried parents or guardians. Your children are less likely to engage in risky behaviors if you remain in a stable marriage. For example, sexual activity and drug, alcohol, and weapons use are less likely to occur with children raised in married households. Children have a better opportunity to grow to fully functional adults if married parents raise them.

Linda Gallagher and Maggie Waite, after analyzing the results of their comprehensive study on the benefits of marriage in 1990, suggested that there should be a similar warning about not being married as the Surgeon General's warning on cigarette packages. They want divorce decrees to carry the warning label, "Not being married can be hazardous to your health." They could not have said it better.

Our research among couples who have been happily and successfully married for more than 30 years demonstrated the presence of the seven pervasive characteristics in successful marriages. When you consider what social science research tells us about the benefits of being married and what our research reveals about the importance of the seven characteristics of successful marriages, you have many powerful reasons to work hard to celebrate your Golden Anniversary with your spouse.

A SEVEN-WEEK PROGRAM FOR DEVELOPING ONGOING SHARING IN YOUR MARRIAGE

The series of open-ended statements in this program are intended to help you examine the relationship you have with your spouse and practice new methods of interacting in conversation. One of the underlying assumptions of this exercise is that periodic sharing of information with your spouse is good for your marriage and serves as a sort of periodic renewal of your relationship. It is also a way to take time out from everyday living to look at yourself, your relationship with your spouse, where your relationship is, and where it is going.

We suggest that you and your spouse set aside at least 30 minutes per week for sharing your responses to each group of open-ended statements. After the seven weeks, you can begin the process over again or you may wish to generate a list of topics of your own, responding to those that interest you the most (careers, money, family, sex, etc.). Remember, the most important thing is that you develop the habit of routinely sharing with each other. The topics do not really matter.

Sharing Starters

INSTRUCTIONS: For each sharing starter, think about how you would like to complete the sentence and what additional information is needed to help your spouse understand your thinking about the issue. Alternate turns completing each statement so each one of you will have the opportunity to begin with a fresh idea. Add as much as you can think of about each of the sharing starters. Remember, real sharing can only occur in a non-judgmental atmosphere of acceptance.

WEEK *1*

1. The first time we met was …

2. The amount of time we have known each other is …

3. The kind of relationship we have is …

4. One adjective to describe our relationship would be …

5. One way that we are alike is …

6. One way that we are different is …

7. A place I would like to share with you is …

8. I find your friends to be …

9. When we meet new people, I …

10. When I am with you in a social situation, I feel …

11. One of the most "fun" things we ever did was …

12. The needs you satisfy in me are …

WEEK *2*

13. I am proud of you when …

14. Right now I feel …

15. The amount of time I spend alone is …

16. One of your greatest assets is …

17. Some of my needs that are not being completely satisfied are …

18. Something you have helped me to learn about myself is …

19. One of the feelings that gives me the most trouble is …

20. The way I deal with troublesome feelings now is ...

21. I feel indecisive when ...

22. I assume you know that ...

23. If I could make you over, I would never change ...

24. You are most helpful when ...

WEEK *3*

25. I am afraid ...

26. I like it when you ...

27. You annoy me when you ...

28. One thing I regret having done is ...

29. A habit of mine that bothers me most is...

30. Your greatest strength is ...

31. I do not like it when you ...

32. Something I would like to talk about
    but we seldom do is ...

33. I have the most fun with you when ...

34. If I had all the money in the world, I would ...

35. A frequent fantasy I have about you is ...

36. When we have an intellectual discussion ...

WEEK *4*

37. You tend to talk a lot about ...

38. When I don't want to answer questions, I ...

39.   When I cannot express something to you, I …

40.   A thing that is helping us to grow closer is …

41.   The things I most like to do with you are …

42.   I tend not to tell you about …

43.   Something I am usually reluctant to discuss is …

44.   Something I have always wondered about is …

45.   I think you avoid me when …

46.   An area in which I would like to feel more equal to you is …

47.   I am most proud of you when …

48.   I need you most when …

WEEK *5*

49.   To keep from being hurt, I …

50.   It hurts me when …

51.   When I hurt you, I …

52.   I get discouraged or frustrated when …

53.   I think you are unfair when you …

54.   When you are pouting, I feel …

55.   The things that hold us together are …

56.   Right now I am feeling …

57.   I become most defensive when you …

58.   I am most happy with you when …

59. When we fight …

60. When I feel as if I have lost, I …

WEEK 6

61. If I wanted to make you laugh, I would …

62. I think that you do not give me a chance to …

63. An important thing or issue between us right now is …

64. I find that being open with you is …

65. One thing I have always wanted to talk more about is …

66. I wish you would let me know when I …

67. I think it would be fun to …

68. A pattern I see in our relationship is …

69. The part of my body that I like most is …

70. The part of my body that I like least is …

71. What I like most about your body is …

72. The ways I like you to touch me are …

WEEK 7

73. What makes you most attractive to me is …

74. Right now I am feeling …

75. I feel jealous when …

76. I feel most tender toward you when …

77. One of the times that bothered me most in our relationship was ...

78. What I like best about our relationship is ...

79. In the future, I would like our relationship to become more ...

80. The most exciting thing about our future is ...

81. The thing I value most in life is ...

82. I believe in and am committed to ...

83. In five years, I see us ...

84. The main reason I love you is ...

SALAD RECIPES FROM
"America's #1 Love and Marriage Experts"

Just as the ingredients in the Seven Surprising Secrets of Successful Marriage are balanced and blended together uniquely for successful couples, so are the ingredients in delightful salads. Too much of one ingredient or not enough of another can spoil the balance and flavor of a salad.

So, here are 14 uniquely balanced salads for you to try out. As you can tell, we had fun with the recipes by naming them after the important concepts from this book. Including generous portions of fruit and vegetables in your diet each day will enhance your communications and also improve the overall health of you and your spouse.

From these 14 recipes, discover your favorite recipe or use variations of them to start your own set of uniquely balanced salad recipes. Each of these recipes is made with fresh ingredients and sized generously just for the two of you. Bon Appetit!

Learning to Dance

DATE AND PECAN SALAD ~ APPETIZER

Make a bed of bib lettuce ~ torn into 2-inch pieces

6 dates ~ pitted and quartered

1/4 cup pecans ~ quartered

Recommended Dressing:
Gorgonzola & White Balsamic Vinaigrette

It Takes Two to Tango

TANGERINE AND BEET SALAD ~ APPETIZER

Make a bed of baby spinach

1/8 cup shallots ~ thinly sliced and chopped

1/4 cup cooked and chilled beets ~
cut thin julienne style 1 inch long

1 seedless tangerine ~ peeled, divided into wedges, and placed on top

Sprinkle with pine nuts and grated Parmesan cheese

Recommended Dressing Choices:
Citrus Vinaigrette
Ranch

Two into One

TOMATO AND CUCUMBER SALAD ~
APPETIZER OR SIDE DISH

1 1/2 cups ripe tomatoes ~ cut into 1/2-inch cubes

1 1/2 cups small seedless cucumbers ~
peeled and cut into 1/2-inch cubes

1/2 cup red onions ~ diced

1/4 cup pitted Kalamata olives ~ sliced or halved

1/2 teaspoon chopped garlic

1/3 cup crumbled feta cheese

Recommended Dressing Choices:
Balsamic Vinaigrette
Greek

No Sacred Cows

FRUIT SALAD ~ APPETIZER OR LUNCH ENTRÉE

1 banana ~ sliced

1 orange ~ sliced

4 strawberries ~ quartered

1/3 cup blueberries

1/3 cup seedless grapes

2 cups orange juice ~ toss fruit and pour juice
over to keep color fresh

Tuned In

WELL-BALANCED SALAD ~
APPETIZER OR MAIN ENTRÉE

Make a bed of Boston, radicchio,
and romaine lettuce torn into 1- to 2-inch pieces

1/8 cup red bell peppers ~ diced

1/8 cup carrots ~ thin julienne cut into 1-inch pieces

3 radishes ~ thinly sliced

1/8 cup baby cucumbers ~ sliced

1/4 cup jicama ~ thin julienne cut into 1-inch pieces

1/8 cup snow peas ~ sliced into 1/4-inch pieces

2 stalks celery ~ sliced

Top with toasted almonds and dried cranberries

As entrée double ingredient amounts and
add grilled chicken breast ~ thinly sliced

Recommended Dressing:
Balsamic Vinaigrette

Observing and Remembering

BERRY SALAD ~ APPETIZER

Make a bed of bib lettuce ~ torn into 2-inch pieces

1/2 cup sweet red onions ~ thinly sliced then chopped

1/3 cup baby cucumbers ~ peeled and sliced

1/3 cup blueberries

2 large strawberries ~ sliced

Top with almond slivers

Recommended Dressing:
Raspberry Vinaigrette

The Golden Rule

GRANNY APPLE SALAD ~ APPETIZER OR MAIN ENTRÉE

Make a bed of field greens

1/4 cup granny apples ~ thinly sliced julienne style
with skins left on

1 stalk of celery ~ thinly sliced

8 to 10 red seedless grapes ~ cut into halves

1/4 cup walnuts ~ quartered (use candied walnuts if available)

Top lightly with crumbled feta cheese

As entrée double ingredient amounts and
add grilled chicken breast ~ thinly sliced

Recommended Dressing Choices:
Gorgonzola & White Balsamic Vinaigrette
Balsamic Vinaigrette

Do Not Disturb

VEGETABLE SALAD WITH SHRIMP ~
APPETIZER OR MAIN ENTRÉE

Make a bed of baby spinach, field greens,
and romaine ~ torn into 2-inch pieces

1/4 cup zucchini ~ diced

6 snow peas ~ cut into 1/4-inch slices

3 white or red radishes ~ diced

1/4 cup carrots ~ diced

1/4 cup cooked and chilled beets ~ diced

1/4 cup boiled and chilled small white potatoes ~ diced

Top with grated cheddar cheese

As entrée double ingredient amounts
and add boiled or grilled shrimp ~ chilled

Recommended Dressing:
Any of your favorite dressings will work with this salad

Your Body Is Your Castle

BABY SPINACH SALAD ~ APPETIZER

5-ounce bed of baby spinach ~ divide between
the two salad bowls or plates

1/3 cup dried cranberries

1/4 cup honey roasted almonds

1/2 cup white mushrooms ~ thinly sliced

1/3 cup crumbled feta cheese

Recommended Dressing:
Drizzle over salad to taste
Balsamic Vinaigrette

Filing a Joint Return

ROMAINE AND CRAB SALAD ~ MAIN ENTRÉE

Make a bed of romaine lettuce of
meal-size portions ~ cut into 2-inch pieces

1/2 cup white mushrooms ~ sliced

1/2 cup carrots ~ shredded

6 snow peas ~ cut into 1/4-inch slices

1/3 cup jicama ~ shredded or cut into small julienne pieces

1/2 cup tomatoes ~ cut into 1/2-inch pieces

1 hard-boiled egg ~ chopped

2 tablespoons red cabbage ~ thinly sliced
and cut into 1-inch long pieces

Top with cheddar cheese ~ grated

Add cooked crab leg pieces to taste
(artificial crab can also be used)

Recommended Dressing Choices:
Thousand Island
Creamy Parmesan

The Loving Touch

RED CABBAGE AND CARROT SALAD ~
APPETIZER OR SIDE DISH

1 cup red cabbage ~ thinly sliced and cut into 1-inch strips

1 cup carrots ~ thin julienne cut

3/4 cup jicama ~ peeled and thin julienne cut

1 tablespoon shallots ~ chopped

1 teaspoon medium hot fresh chili ~ finely chopped

1 teaspoon fresh lime juice

1 1/2 teaspoons white balsamic vinegar

1/8 cup safflower oil

1/4 teaspoon sugar

Sprinkle of Kosher salt

*Toss and let stand 10 minutes before serving

Beyond Boring

WATERMELON AND GREENS SALAD ~ APPETIZER

Make a bed of field greens and bib lettuce ~ torn into 2-inch pieces

1/4 cup baby cucumbers ~ peeled and thinly sliced

1/3 cup watermelon ~ cut into 1/4-inch cubes

1 stalk of celery ~ chopped

Recommended Dressing Choices:
Raspberry Vinaigrette
Balsamic Vinaigrette

Stress Test

EASY STRESS-FREE SALAD

1 bag of already washed salad lettuce
from the grocery vegetable department

1 tomato ~ vine ripened and cut into 1-inch pieces

1 large cucumber ~ peeled and sliced

1 red onion slice ~ place rings on top of salad

Top with garlic croutons

Recommended Dressing:
Any of your favorite dressings
will work with this salad

Torch Red Convertible

THE JUST FOR FUN RED SALAD

Make a bed of romaine lettuce ~
cut up into 2-inch pieces

3 red radishes ~ sliced

1/4 cup cooked and chilled beets ~
cut thin julienne style 1 inch long

1/4 cup red bell peppers ~ chopped

1/4 cup boiled and chilled small red potatoes ~
thinly sliced

1/8 cup sweet red onions ~
thinly sliced and chopped

1/8 cup red cabbage ~ thinly sliced
and cut into 1-inch pieces

Recommended Dressing:
Any of your favorite dressings
will work with this salad

FILING A JOINT RETURN ACTIVITY

Since difficult unresolved financial issues can destroy a marriage, it is very important to invest the time to review together your entire financial status and future goals. In this activity, you will be able to begin that process.

Short Financial Quiz

Do you regularly discuss the status of your finances?

Do you have a single checking account that you both share?

Do you pay your bills together in the sense that you both understand fully where the money you make is being spent?

Do you own all major assets jointly? In other words, are both of your names listed on the car titles and all other major assets?

Do you have a monthly conversation about your expenses and financial status?

Have you determined what constitutes a major purchase?

Do you have a process for deciding whether to make a major purchase or not?

Do you discuss fully, come to an agreement, and then sleep on the decision before making any major purchases?

Have you discussed your financial goals for one year, five years, and ten years in the future?

Are your credit cards in both of your names?

Can you reasonably manage your outstanding credit card debt?

Have you made a realistic budget, taking into account your monthly income, regular bills, and an amount for unexpected financial obligations?

If you answered "no" to any of the dozen questions in this short financial quiz, please take the time to fully discuss them with your spouse. Gaining consensus on these questions will facilitate financial stability in your marriage.

———

MARRIAGE AS A TORCH
RED CONVERTIBLE ACTIVITY

Do you and your spouse make fun a regular part of your lives together? Do you know what you and your spouse both enjoy? When is the last time you did something spontaneous to surprise your spouse? This activity is designed for you and your spouse to openly think about and discuss what you enjoy doing together and how you can "spice up" your marriage.

Fun Factor Inventory

Please rank your favorite activities in the following list from 1 to 12 with your highest interest being ranked as 1:

☐ Antiquing   ☐ Attending Sporting Events

☐ Bike Riding   ☐ Boating

☐ Camping   ☐ Cooking

☐ Craft Activities   ☐ Eating Out

☐ Fishing   ☐ Gardening

☐ Hiking   ☐ Hunting

☐ Listening to Music   ☐ Movie Watching

☐ Running   ☐ Shopping

☐ Skiing   ☐ Traveling

☐ Volunteering Activities ☐ Walking

☐ Other: ☐ Other:

After you have ranked the items above, spend some time talking about the similarities between your rankings and your spouse's rankings. How much fun do you have in your marriage?

Fun Factor Discovery Starters

INSTRUCTIONS: For each fun factor discovery starter, think about how you would like to complete the sentence and what additional information is needed to help your spouse understand your thinking about the activity. Alternate turns completing each statement so each one of you will have the opportunity to begin with a fresh idea. Add as much as you can think of about each of the fun factor starters. Remember, the purpose of this exercise is for the two of you to discover what activities you really can enjoy doing together.

The most fun we have had together is when we ...

If I could do anything I wanted for fun, I would ...

I would love it if you would join me doing ...

If there were one thing that I take the greatest
pleasure in doing that I wish you knew more about,
it would be ...

I have always been interested in learning more about ...

I really like it when you surprise me with ...

If I could do anything in the world it would be ...

The activity we do for fun that I enjoy the most
is when we ...

If we could make more time, I would like to ...

The biggest obstacle stopping us from having
fun together is ...

Maybe we could get more time for fun together if we ...

If we find more time to have fun together, I believe we will ...

About the Authors

D RS. CHARLES AND ELIZABETH SCHMITZ are renowned love and marriage experts and multiple award–winning authors. As the "Official Guides to Marriage" for www.SelfGrowth.com, the top self-help website on the Internet, they provide inspiration and guidance to readers around the globe.

Affectionately dubbed "America's #1 Love and Marriage Experts" by their clients, fans, and workshop participants, Drs. Charles and Elizabeth Schmitz know that simple things matter in relationships. They understand what makes relationships work because they have conducted nearly three decades of research on successful marriages, as well as sharing personal experience drawn from their own 43-year marriage. The doctors are popular speakers and talk show guests.

Dr. Charles D. Schmitz is a highly successful faculty member and administrator in higher education. He is currently the dean of the College of Education at the University of Missouri-St. Louis and a long-time professor of counseling and family therapy at three major universities, where he has focused on counseling psychology and leadership. During his distinguished career, Charles has received more than 40 local, state, and national awards; published 200 articles, manuscripts, books, and scholarly papers; delivered 600 speeches and professional presentations throughout the world; and has frequently appeared on radio, on television, and in print. He received his Ph.D. from the University of Missouri-Columbia.

Dr. Elizabeth A. Schmitz is a full-time writer and lecturer. She has served as an award-winning administrator and educator for 36 years. She received her Ed.D. from the University of Missouri-Columbia and has lectured at numerous colleges in the areas of counseling and leadership. As the former chief operating officer of a large organization, she also specializes in human relations issues that span the workforce. Elizabeth has received 25 local, state, and national awards; published over 150 articles, manuscripts, and books; delivered over 400 speeches and presentations; made numerous radio and television appearances; and has been quoted extensively in the media. She is president of Successful Marriage Reflections, LLC in St. Louis, Missouri, where she and Charles reside with their Wonder Dog, Jake.

Index